"Joe Wheeler's latest book hits a lot of my hot buttons—immersive experiences, customization at scale, flywheels of learning, and of course digital technology. Get your highlighter out before you open it up and let Joe's principles and case studies lead you in developing your own playbook for thriving in today's Experience Economy."
B. Joseph Pine II, coauthor, *The Experience Economy: Competing for Customer Time, Attention, and Money*

"A timely treasure for those who wonder whether why, and how, "digital" fundamentally changes the customer experience, with an added bonus playbook for designing business models up to the task."
Susan Fournier, Allen Questrom Professor and Dean, Boston University Questrom School of Business

"A must-read for managers looking to stay current on this rapidly changing topic. The book could not be more timely or useful!"
Leonard A. Schlesinger, Baker Foundation Professor, Harvard Business School

"Joe's book reminds us that in a digital-first world, our people have never been more important—and that the brands customers love understand how to design experiences that create enduring value for employees, customers, and shareholders. I highly recommend it."
Maxine Clark, Founder, Build-A-Bear Workshop, and CEO, Clark-Fox Family Foundation

"Creating a best-in-class digital experience requires a design that resonates with your consumers. This book focuses on the role of design and the importance it plays in creating the deepest relationship with your consumer and the impact that is possible for your business."
Chris McCann, Chief Executive Officer, 1-800-FLOWERS.Com

"Joe Wheeler is my 'go to' for anything related to customer insights and customer experience. There is no one better. This new book shares the wisdom of a true master."
Robert C. Wolcott, Co-Founder and Chair, TWIN Global

"A focused manifesto for companies looking to leverage digital technologies to deliver a highly valued customer experience. Joe's ability to boil this down to seven intuitive strategies with carefully chosen examples to bring these to life with actionable playbooks make this a must read for multiple departments."
Abhi Ingle, Chief Operating Officer, Revenue Operations, Qualtrics

"A hallmark of Joe Wheeler's work has always been his clear-eyed understanding that it's not enough merely to design a great product or service. You also have to be able to deliver it consistently, at reasonable cost, and in a sustainable manner. This practical perspective permeates *The Digital-First Customer Experience*. Joe outlines an approach that is both simple and sophisticated, both immediately impactful and enduring. And he does it through a series of engaging and enjoyable stories, making it as accessible as it is essential."
Rob Markey, Partner, Bain & Company, and co-author of *The Ultimate Question 2.0*

"What Joe's book *Managing the Customer Experience* did for the experience economy, so his latest book will do for the digital economy. If you want to understand how to create leading edge CX, this book is for you."
Shaun Smith, Founder, Smith+Co

"I deeply admire Joe's passion for creating enduring customer experiences. He is relentless in seeking to understand how human centered design can improve the digital experience to create shared value for the customer, employee, and enterprise."
Brad Warner, Board Member, Capital One

"I've seen firsthand the perils and promise of digital-first strategies. Wheeler's playbook ensures the former is avoided and latter is achieved. I highly recommend it."
Dana Stalder, Partner, Matrix

"Joe Wheeler's book is a gift to those who work to take up the cause which I love and have made my own life's work – and that is to improve lives. I know you will find his book an outstanding arrow in your quiver of resources to elevate your company to one that is admired and loved."
Jeanne Bliss, author of *Chief Customer Officer 2.0* and *Would You Do that to Your Mother?*

"Joe Wheeler continues to innovate as the global market leader in customer experience strategy. Through Digital-First, Joe has created the digital road map that customer-centric leaders can execute to grow their business."
Michael Crosby, Chief Executive Officer, AquOm Incorporated

"I love this book. If you are operating a business 2023+, it's critical you understand and master the CX Digital space. *The Digital-First Customer Experience* by Joe Wheeler tells you how you do it."
Brad Smith, Founder, President of Vector Business Navigation, Inc, and CXPA Board member alumnus

"Joe Wheeler's new book succinctly describes the 'digital tsunami' that is changing the way all companies will deliver customer experiences in the future. His advice? Instead of just adapting to it, put it to your advantage. I couldn't agree more, and this book shows you how."
Diane Hessan, Founder and Chairman, C Space

"*The Digital-First Customer Experience* provides actionable strategies to design next generation experiences, move AI from the back office to the customer, and to help you make the right choices in a digital first world."
Geoffrey Parker, Charles E. Hutchinson '68A Professor of Engineering Innovation, Dartmouth College, coauthor of *Platform Revolution*

"*The Digital-First Customer Experience* provides peek into how successful companies across different industries deliver a personalized path to engage customers throughout their journey. Key AI/ML tech enablers serve as a backdrop while the design principles framework provides structure to innovate an engaging CX driven solution."
Sherri Dorfman, Chief Executive Officer, Stepping Stone Partners

"Joe Wheeler is a long-time friend and colleague who I respect and admire. I highly recommend reading his new book, *The Digital-First Customer Experience*. The fusion of digital and its impact on looking at holistic experiences vs. fragmentation is essential for the success of CX and employee experiences in the future. The time has come if not long past for CX and EX professionals to be well versed in the essential shift from the Industrial Age perspectives to the Age of Transformative Experience value creation has been with us for a while yet CX perspectives seem siloed and fragmented, a recipe for ineffectiveness."
Lou Carbone, Chief Executive Officer, Experience Engineering, Inc.

The Digital-First Customer Experience

Seven Design Strategies from the World's Leading Brands

Joe Wheeler

KoganPage

Publisher's note

Every possible effort has been made to ensure that the information contained in this book is accurate at the time of going to press, and the publishers and authors cannot accept responsibility for any errors or omissions, however caused. No responsibility for loss or damage occasioned to any person acting, or refraining from action, as a result of the material in this publication can be accepted by the editor, the publisher or the author.

All content presented and any views or opinions represented in this book are personal and belong either to the author or to the person they are directly attributed to. Any case studies presented do not constitute an endorsement of any material unless explicitly stated.

First published in Great Britain and the United States in 2023 by Kogan Page Limited

2nd Floor, 45 Gee Street
London
EC1V 3RS
United Kingdom
www.koganpage.com

8 W 38th Street, Suite 902
New York, NY 10018
USA

4737/23 Ansari Road
Daryaganj
New Delhi 110002
India

Kogan Page books are printed on paper from sustainable forests.

ISBNs

Hardback   978 1 3986 1266 2
Paperback   978 1 3986 1263 1
Ebook   978 1 3986 1265 5

British Library Cataloguing-in-Publication Data

A CIP record for this book is available from the British Library.

Library of Congress Control Number

2023937865

Typeset by Integra Software Services, Pondicherry
Print production managed by Jellyfish
Printed and bound by CPI Group (UK) Ltd, Croydon, CR0 4YY

To James (Jim) Heskett, Professor Emeritus at Harvard Business School, business partner, co-author, and mentor to scores of students and colleagues. Jim's contribution to the science of management is immeasurable as he continues to challenge conventional thinking on how organizations can succeed in serving their employees, customers, and shareholders.
With heartfelt thanks for all your wisdom and guidance over the years, Jim.

CONTENTS

Epilogue 256

LIST OF FIGURES AND TABLES

TABLES

Design Strategy 1: Achieve emotional peaks
across channels, finishing strong

A truly omni-channel world requires us to think beyond "staging" experiences to "structuring" emotional peaks across channels that finish with a strong, memorable ending. Few companies exemplify this better than the insurance industry disrupter Lemonade. We make a long, thirst-quenching examination of how they are delivering a powerful digital-first experience.

Design Strategy 2: Create a personalization flywheel
to grow customer engagement

Personalization can drive loyalty or invite disaster. Putting personalization to work to create a differentiated experience requires machine learning capabilities generating a customer flywheel that drives an extraordinary level of customer engagement. Put on your headphones as we listen to the sounds of Spotify, and in doing so, reveal the details behind the "Spotify Machine."

Design Strategy 3: Strengthen customer
commitment by providing choice and control

When customers are given control, real or perceived, good things happen, especially if they are able to make choices that are relevant to them and engage them in the experience. As organizations embrace digital-first technologies, getting the *choice architecture* that works for your brand promise can be tricky. Not so if you are a customer of CEMEX Go. We go behind the scenes to learn how this award-winning touchless customer experience from CEMEX is laying a new foundation in the construction industry.

Design Strategy 4: Foster ownership through customer community and co-creation

We know growing customer communities effectively can generate strong brand advocacy. But the details of what is required to turn a user group into an indispensable source of competitive advantage are worthy of further investigation. Here is where you will learn how VMware broke tact with their industry to take their user group, VMUG, and empower it with a life of its own that has returned dividends that are as significant as they are measurable.

Design Strategy 5: Inspire rituals that create shared meaning

Recent research reports that if you ritualize the customer experience, you have a customer for life, yet few organizations are intentional about designing rituals into their experience. Time to change that. We go right to the source: Starbucks, the company that taught us that coffee is a ritual, not just a beverage, and have pioneered a path that brings their Third Place into the digital age with the recent return of their founder, and the beginning of a new CEO who will guide them into the next leg of their journey.

Design Strategy 6: Empower customers through immersive experiences

Digital technology provides new ways to scale immersive experiences, though this section is about more than augmented or virtual reality. Engineered with some precision, both physical and digital mediated immersive experience can create significant differentiation through customer empowerment. There are several best practice examples of this, but few come close to the experience Nike have created through their digital transformation agenda. Lace up those sneakers as we are planning an extended stay at the Nike House of Innovation.

Design Strategy 7: Link digital assets to leverage value over cost

Applying the 7 Design Strategies provides the opportunity to connect reinforcing digital assets that together amplify their combined value, forming the hub of a digital ecosystem. Once these start to scale, it can be hard for competitors to compete without a major change to their business model. In this chapter we venture down the Amazon (the company, that is) to understand how Amazon Retail is building an ecosystem that creates both a powerful value proposition and a value network that change everything you knew about competing in retail.

Start by Solving the *Right* Problems

Avoid designing experiences that customers don't value by applying proven qualitative and quantitative methods to separate the "signals from the noise" and identify moments of truth for exceeding expectations that will earn you long-lasting loyalty and advocacy.

Build your business case

No mystery. Just the facts of how to construct a business case that your CFO will find compelling and will guide your implementation going forward.

The design process

Time to get down to how you will bring your business case to life. In this section you will learn a seven-step process for improving or redesigning a whole new digital-first experience that will exceed the promise you make in your business case. Quickly.

Execute to scale

How do you take your well-researched, ideal customer storyboard and turn it into an operational blueprint that all departments can align around? We get into the details through an illustration that brings together all seven design strategies for you to start applying tomorrow.

Appendix: CX/Digital maturity assessment

Visit cxdigital.ai and discover where you stand on delivering a digital-first experience, starting from a baseline of where you are to guide you toward where you want to be. Other tools and resources not included in the book can be found here as well.

ABOUT THE AUTHOR

Joe Wheeler is a best-selling author, speaker, and consultant. He is the CEO of CX/Digital, a subsidiary of the Service Profit Chain Institute (SPCI), a Boston-based consulting firm he co-founded with Professors Len Schlesinger, James Heskett, and W. Earl Sasser of the Harvard Business School. He is the co-author of two books on the topic of employee and customer experience: *The Ownership Quotient* (2008) and *Managing the Customer Experience* (2002).

Prior to launching The Service Profit Chain Institute, Mr. Wheeler was the Quality and Productivity Executive for Bank of America. Prior to this, he was an Executive Vice President with The Forum Corporation where he managed the firm's customer experience consulting practice.

He earned his MBA from the Edinburgh Business School and lives in Massachusetts and Nova Scotia.

FOREWORD

I've known Joe Wheeler for over 30 years. During that time, I've hired Joe to consult with me, we've worked side by side on multi-billion-dollar client engagements, and I've watched him lead both inside and outside of organizations through every incarnation of this work that we bear responsibility for in business—which is to improve lives.

I have observed that Joe always leads with gusto and joy. Conversations with Joe are filled with the same high level of optimism we had when, as a very young executive, I called upon him for help many moons ago. If you've never spoken with Joe, and I hope someday you will, the zeal of his voice carries you away. That wrapped with his deep wisdom and humility is an uncommon blend of human. And that is who you will meet in this book as your guide.

There is no one whose foreword I'd be more honored to write than Joe's.

All of our lives are lived digitally. We cannot live in this world now without this component of commerce impacting our lives. But our lives are also lived emotionally. They are impacted by our families, our goals, our hopes for what we will become and what we can achieve. The most admirable company embraces and enables this in blending a whole experience—so that they have a positive impact on what's important to customers' lives—for the time they are in their lives.

Joe's book connects all those dots for you. For example, he shows you the inside of the clock of Lemonade Insurance, which dared to make emotional and value-based needs of customers the foundation for earning profit and enduring admiration. Joe explains in detail how Lemonade did the hard work of starting with customers' frailties, concerns, and worries about insurance—and used that knowledge to build an entire system of operational integrity in how they price, deliver, create community, and establish long-lived trust.

He addresses how every company must keep its eye on understanding the customer and employee landscape, and bravely change to continue to earn admiration and its place in the marketplace. Joe walks us through how even the great stalwart and beacon of customer experience Starbucks recommitted to its core values to ensure that what catapulted Starbucks into hearts and minds and lives can continue to earn that place in today's marketplace.

Joe addresses the inner working of organizations, exposing the struggles that get in the way. More than a roadmap, Joe offers you the elusive decoder ring to gain the mindset, leadership, and practical operational behavior for how to go about shifting and elevating how you do work inside your organization. For example, he explains how CEMEX gained a seismic shift in how to achieve customer-driven growth by departing from the traditional Agile method of developing "minimal viable products" as this approach did not support customers' goals. Eventually they landed on the concept of testing a "minimal lovable experience." Homero Resendez of CEMEX explains why:

> We eventually started calling protypes of CEMEX Go "minimum lovable experiences" because we wanted them to give us feedback about both the digital and analog experience since what we were delivering was truly omni-channel and we needed to ensure that our customers were really satisfied with the changes we were testing. We were working to exceed their expectations, not just meet them.

Joe's book doesn't leave you just yearning to have the ability to do what these companies do—he then delivers you his proven tools that he has used in his consulting practice with clients all over the world. And he gives these tools to you generously.

First, he gives you the approach so you can engage your organization in focusing on what customers care about—their goals, so that you can earn yours. For example, many companies' customer "journey map" is their sales cycle. Joe helps you avoid that trap of silo-based customer journey maps so you can unite to focus on the few things versus the many individual silo-based to-do lists that make up our annual planning and priorities.

He helps you build your business case—elevating "experience" to be about the growth imperative of the business, including all operational dimensions of the business. In doing so, Joe helps to banish the most misunderstood part of this work, which is that it is not about the year of the customer or a program, but rather a fundamental shift in the way leaders lead to earn growth that is sustainable through customer and employee love and admiration.

Joe guides you on how exactly to design across and with the entire organization so that high tech can improve high touch. This means what is worked on and prioritized will be the priorities that customers crave from you—and those are what will propel you to higher growth. Uniting and designing to improve lives is a skill set so elusive—but one that Joe shares for you here.

Finally, Joe addresses the threat of all of this work—which is that when the champion leaves the building, or when the moment of focus on the customer is over, the work tumbles. Everyone (sometimes with relief) goes back to their own silo corners, doing their own thing. Executing for scale and sustainability is the great Achilles' heel of this work, and Joe guides you in this book to find the solution that is right for your company, its maturity, and its culture.

Customer experience is not one thing. It is all things that an organization can do and should do to earn their customers' and employees' love and admiration. It is everything all at once. And sorting through that can feel like a minefield and cause companies to push the work into separate "work streams" and silos. Some even pass on the great burden to improve lives to vendors to execute as actions and tactics separate from one another. But without an essential purpose and the leadership glue to hold it all together… it will not stand out. You will not stand out.

Joe Wheeler's book is a gift to those who work to take up the cause which I love and have made my own life's work—and that is to improve lives. I know you will find his book an outstanding arrow in your quiver of resources to elevate your company to one that is admired and loved.

Jeanne Bliss
Author of *Chief Customer Officer 2.0* and *Would You Do That to Your Mother?*

ACKNOWLEDGMENTS

Had I been more organized at the beginning of this journey, I would probably have kept better notes. That is a somewhat half-hearted disclaimer to suggest if you are reading this and I forgot to recognize you, then my only defense is one of oversight, not intent.

As anyone who has taken on such a task knows, there are so many people to thank, it is hard to know where to start.

Let me begin by recognizing the team at Kogan Page: Chris Cudmore, Jeylan Ramis, and Vanessa Rueda. Thanks for agreeing to take on this project and shepherding it forward with your deep expertise and shrewd eye for an idea whose time had come, and for being willing to get behind it with the full force of your firm. Here is to our continued partnership and future success.

I can go no further without recognizing my "beta readers." One of the things I decided to do early on was to take the advice of author Rob Fitzpatrick who wrote a book entitled *Write Useful Books*. In it, he suggests inviting lots of feedback over several rounds prior to publishing. It was like Agile development came to publishing. What a concept. I heeded his advice, and to all of you who took the time to suffer through the early drafts, I offer you my most sincere thanks and appreciation. You include Sherrie Austin, Parrish Arturi, Jelane Casper, Mike Crosby, Brian Lillie, Alyson Kline, Daniel Hong, Patricia Hambrick, Susan Fournier, Craig Harper, Garnette Weber, Dan Weber, Meghan Moore, Tabitha Dunn, Natalie Wong, Kenneth Peterson, Marc Mandell, Vivek Bhaskaran, Barbie Fink, Jeanne Glass, Dana Stalder, Derek Wang, and Chris Zulinov. Your feedback and advice were instrumental to getting what began as a wide-ranging set of ideas into a well-formed manuscript, fit for publishing between two covers. So, thank you.

Of course, what have filled many of the pages between these two covers are the insights and best practices of some incredible companies. To everyone inside those organizations that believed in what I was trying to do and put their faith me, well, it isn't that there aren't any words to describe my appreciation, it is that there are just too many. You include Jordan Deagle, Dilip Kumar, Utpala Menon, Chanda Stevick Herinckx, John Donahoe, Yael Wissner-Levy, Nicole Braman, Jean Williams, Ann Johnson, Steve Athanas,

Lindy Herring, Teresa Streit, Edson Santos Freitas, Homero Reséndez, Jesus Caviedes Mondragon, and Jonathan Holden Hernández. And a special thank you to Emmy Giarrusso (Capital Records recording artist Evan Giia) for spending some time with me to better understand how the music industry is changing from an artist's point of view.

On that note, I have to give a special shout-out to Howard Behar, leadership expert and former Starbucks executive. Howard, your wisdom and advice on how to tell the Starbucks story, to go beyond the *details* and understand the *heart of the matter*, made all the difference. Thank you.

To colleagues of mine who served as just-in-time subject-matter experts on a variety of topics. You were all instrumental in advising on specific elements that shaped my thinking. My sincere thanks to Stuart Patterson, the co-founder of LifePod, Eloise Cook from Pearson Publishing, David L. Rogers from Columbia Business School, Abhi Ingle from Qualtrics, Andrew McInnes who is with Genesys, Rob Markey of Bain & Company, Joana de Quintanilha with Forrester Research, and Scott Mair, formerly with AT&T.

Of course, to my colleagues at The Service Profit Chain Institute and CX/Digital who helped with so many aspects of the project from research to development, especially in the playbook section that walks the reader through our approach to helping clients deliver a digital-first customer experience, my sincere thanks to all of you—Wendy Kelly, Cate Rafferty, Brian Goodman, Ann Remy, and Ken Ramaley.

2022 marked the passing of a longtime mentor of mine, John Humphrey, who co-founded The Forum Corporation, a place where I and so many others honed our skills and knowledge on how to deliver a world-class customer experience. John once told me, "People of action don't write books." Having spent the past 12 months doing just that, I can appreciate what he meant. John didn't get the chance to read the manuscript, but what he taught me about what was important, how to "separate the signals from the noise," lives in every chapter. He was a legend in our industry, and it was my greatest privilege to have worked with him.

Twenty years ago, Shaun Smith invited me to collaborate with him to co-author *Managing the Customer Experience*. I don't think either of us had any idea of the degree to which that book would help propel both of us forward in our respective careers. These many years later, it is one of my most treasured aspects of this work, to have invited Shaun to help me bring this book to life with his extraordinary experience on the topic of customer experience. Thank you, Shaun.

To my co-founders of The Service Profit Chain Institute, Len Schlesinger, Earl Sasser, and Jim Heskett. In this case, there may very well be no words. If there are, they have eluded me as it is hard to know how to thank three people who have had such an impact. I will always be in your debt for your support and collaboration over the years and for your keen eye in finding ways to make this book better, more readable, and more relevant to the reader.

And now to my friend and customer co-conspirator Jeanne Bliss. For all who have spent their careers advancing the cause of the customer, we know what the highest standard of our craft looks like, and no one practices it with more purpose and integrity than Jeanne Bliss. I so appreciate you agreeing to write the foreword. I hope the pages that follow live up to the promise you so articulately described. With deep gratitude for your collaboration and partnership over these many years.

I'd better wrap this up. As you might expect, you don't get a book like this out the door without the people you live with covering for you. So, to my partner on the journey of life, Laura Gallant, thank you for your constant support and faith in this effort. To our two daughters Amelia and Ciara, thanks for your encouragement and willingness to share the views of your digital-first generation. And finally, to our two dogs, Guinness and Pepper, thanks for getting me up at all hours of the night to work on this. It appears to have paid off.

Introduction

Back in 2018, a company named Zume was making headlines for its robotic pizza-making operation in California. Not only did the company use mostly robots to make and deliver pizza, but they also created software to forecast what kinds of pizzas would be ordered when, and where the majority of those orders would most likely be placed. The software guided their drivers to those areas so that the pizza you received would have come out of one of the 28 ovens on board the truck, just as they arrived at your home. In a 2018 *Forbes* article, CEO Alex Garden was quoted as saying, "I am up to my eyeballs in discussions with a number of companies about this technology who are starting to understand the applicability better. I wildly underestimated the market demand for this."[1]

Others clearly agreed with him and Zume raised $375 million from SoftBank in late 2018.

However, just one year later there appeared to be some bumps in the strategy. Alex Garden, commenting to a CNBC reporter, shared that "one of the problems that we encountered was, our beautiful pizza—with no stabilizers in it—in a traditional box declined in quality from the time you cooked it until the time it was delivered, to the point that we didn't think it was good enough."[2]

By late 2019 the road had got even bumpier and by early 2020 the company had laid off most of their staff.

But it started with a powerful idea to deliver an experience customers would love, create safer, more creative roles for employees, and reduce labor costs as a percent of revenue. To be honest, I was more than a little skeptical when I first read about Zume. Clearly, they had reduced the labor required to make a fresh pizza, but their product quality issue aside, exactly how long would it take to make back the capital cost of all that robotic and AI technology? Perhaps more relevant, though I wasn't completely in love with Domino's, they did manage to improve the quality of their pizza and deliver what seemed like an extremely freshly made pie in about 30 minutes or less and their Pizza Tracker sort of had me hooked (for reasons we will discuss later).

Digital first—promise or peril?

The good news is that in a digital-first world, your organization has a lot of choices. The bad news is that making the wrong one can have serious consequences.

I don't share this example to scare you or to try to sow fear, uncertainty, and doubt into your dream of delivering a more digitally enabled customer experience. In fact, one of the world's leading experts on digital transformation, Mohan Sawhney of the Kellogg School of Management, has said: "A zero-touch customer experience should be an aspirational goal for all companies."[3] Given the impact of COVID-19 on the world, being able to deliver a touchless experience clearly isn't bad advice.

Though let us also remember the words of Charlotte Beers, Chairman Emeritus, Ogilvy & Mather, when she said, "The truth is, what makes a brand powerful is the emotional involvement of customers."

But how do you reconcile these two statements? Can a zero-touch customer experience actually create emotional involvement? Has digital transformation advanced enough that the level of empathy and emotional connection, typically delivered by frontline staff, achieves similar levels of loyalty and advocacy?

Over the next several chapters, we will explore the answer to this question in depth by drawing on our own client experience and research, as well as examining the way some of the world's leading brands are tackling this question themselves and are delivering experiences their customers love.

The goal is to help you land on the right assembly of human and digital elements to create an experience that not only exceeds your customers' expectations but turns them into advocates that won't be stopped in promoting your brand.

This book will help you design the next-generation customer experience in a world where you can order a pizza from a pair of sneakers. (Totally true by the way—look it up. They are called "Pie Tops II" from Pizza Hut. One shoe orders the pizza and the other pauses the TV while you answer the door.)

Your takeaways

Here is what you will learn from this book.

In Part 1, we dive right into the heart of the matter and discuss the 3Cs of *convergence, competition* and *culture* as the key drivers forcing brands to rethink the experience they deliver.

In Part 2, we introduce you to the 7 Design Strategies that have proven invaluable in guiding customer experience solutions that achieve measurable results. The next seven chapters will go more deeply into each and highlight a leading-brand case study to make it even more tangible. In each example we describe the design strategy through the experience it delivers, then break it down in terms of the operating details, the "heart of the matter," and the results they have achieved. Each chapter is summarized with key insights before previewing the next chapter.

Part 3 begins with a definition of what delivering a digital-first experience is all about and clarifies some common terms needed to get the most out of the playbook.

The four playbook chapters will:

- help you separate the "signals from the noise" to uncover and validate those things in the experience that if you exceed expectations, will lead to customers rewarding you with their loyalty and their spending;

- take those insights and turn them into a business case your CFO will be delighted to fund because of the incremental revenue and operating margin it will generate;

- apply a proven design process to turn that business case into a digital-first experience that sets the standard for your industry;

- finally, review an example of the 7 Design Strategies brought to life from several client projects to demonstrate how you go from your new customer storyboard to a blueprint for successful implementation that can scale across your organization.

During a recent CNBC interview commenting on their performance through the pandemic, Nike president and CEO John Donahoe stated, "We know that digital is the new normal. The consumer today is digitally grounded and simply will not revert back."[4] In the frenetic pace of a post-pandemic world, it is easy to lose sight of what creates real value for customers. It just isn't as simple as saying "technology is an enabler" to the value you seek to deliver. That may be true for many experiences, but in other cases, as you will read here, the technology is more than an enabler, it actually is the experience. (As I wrote this, I just received a notification from Duolingo, the language learning app, that I have new "daily quests" available to me. Très bien.)

In a *Harvard Business Review* article entitled "How smart, connected products are transforming companies," Professor Michael Porter and co-author James Heppelmann conclude: "Smart, connected products are dramatically changing opportunities for value creation in the economy. A revolution is under way in manufacturing. The effects are not confined to manufacturing, however, but are spreading to other industries that use—or could use—smart, connected products, including services."[5]

If these authors are right, and the revolution in manufacturing is spreading to other industries, including yours, it might be time to consider how your company is adapting to this new reality.

That is when this book will come in handy.

"Technology" is more than the enabler, it is the experience"

01

Part 1: The new 3CS

"For the past four years, I've been living alone. I don't feel alone anymore. LifePod is a great companion."[1]

JULIETTE, COMMONWEALTH CARE ALLIANCE (CCA) CARE RECIPIENT

Boston-based Commonwealth Care Alliance® (CCA) is a not-for-profit, integrated care system providing in-home care services while also managing several senior care centers. In 2018, CCA decided to launch a beta test of the LifePod virtual care services platform with an overarching goal to improve health and wellness outcomes by providing a proactive, voice-first platform. The aim was to increase CCA care partner-member engagement, promote improved care plan adherence, and achieve patient-defined health and quality-of-life goals.[2]

When CCA member Juliette agreed to participate in the beta test, she didn't quite know what to expect. "CCA came to set up my LifePod so there was nothing for me to worry about."[3] During the program, LifePod greeted her each morning and Juliette asked LifePod about the weather forecast. At a pre-scheduled time of day, LifePod would suggest: "Hello Juliette, this is LifePod, now would be a good time to get up and stretch."

Juliette remarked, laughing, "I like to have fun with LifePod."[4]

What is exceptional about this story is that it isn't exceptional at all. It is one of dozens of similar experiences that came out of CCA's pilot test of this technology. LifePod is a proactive voice remote monitoring and caregiving platform that identifies and manages social, behavioral, and medical needs of its users. It increases engagement and reduces isolation for seniors living alone or in care facilities. Unlike reactive voice assistants like Google

Assistant or Alexa, LifePod is configured by a caregiver to be proactive, triggered either by an event (for example, an alert generated by a change in a continuous glucose monitor connected to the device) or through scheduled reminders ("Did you remember to take your medication, Juliette?").

LifePod provides the caregiver with a portal that includes preconfigured voice templates for different versions of three types of dialogs or routines: check-ins, reminders, and prompted access to streaming content. For example:

- Check-in: "Good morning, Juliette, how did you sleep last night?" When Juliette responds, LifePod captures it in her patient records.

- Reminder: "Hello Juliette, today is your grandson's birthday, would you like me to call him for you?" or "Hello Juliette, just a reminder that you have a doctor's appointment today at 2 pm."

- Access to streaming content: "Good evening, Juliette, it's six o'clock and time for dinner. Would you like to listen to some Frank Sinatra music while you eat?"

As a 24/7 personalized voice-based service, daily status reports are sent to the caregiving team (doctors, family members) and the assigned caregiver can configure all of the above to personalize the experience for the care recipient.

The quantitative outcomes from the beta test were impressive. Among them, CCA saw inbound calls for LifePod Members reduce 12.5 percent from the control group and care partner encounters decreased 27 percent for total cost savings of $63.52 per member per month. Outstanding results, only exceeded by their qualitative outcomes which included "100% satisfaction with LifePod support throughout the day" from their members.

Stuart Patterson, a LifePod co-founder, believes the biggest breakthrough of voice will be "the advent of a truly proactive user interface to online services that can be configured and controlled by a third party."[5]

For Juliette, all she knows is she doesn't feel alone anymore.

The new 3Cs: convergence, competition, and culture

Management expert Kenichi Ohmae coined the classic industry model of the 3Cs when considering a business strategy: the Company, the Customer, and the Competition. By integrating these three elements, a sustained competitive advantage could be achieved. He referred to this as a "strategic triangle."[6]

Today, a new 3Cs model has emerged that must be considered when formulating a business strategy that suggests a different "strategic triangle":

- Convergence: as demonstrated by the opening example, the convergence of technologies that are leveling the playing field and fueling a new movement of industry disruption and with it, opportunity.
- Competition: though not in the traditional sense of incumbents and new entrants, technology-enabled competition is blurring the lines between industries and sectors.
- Culture: beyond the human tragedy, the impact COVID-19 has had socio-economically, on supply chain disruption and the employer/employee social contract, has been significant. Add to this a new climate change awareness brought on by new reports of the seriousness of the crisis as well as first-hand experience of climate disasters, and the culture shift around the world toward businesses and governments committing to more aggressive greenhouse gas (GHG) emission-reduction standards is rapidly reaching a consensus.

Convergence

The way voice technology is reinventing healthcare is compelling but not unique. When you consider convergence, five specific technologies are rewriting the rules around customer experience design, making the whole greater than the sum of its parts and evolving the *Internet of Things* (IoT) toward the *Internet of Everything* (IoE).

1 Ambient, proactive, conversational AI-based user interfaces

Ken Washington, Amazon's Vice President of Consumer Robotics, describes ambient technology as the next revolution of conversational artificial intelligence (AI): "In the first revolution humans were typing on keyboards and touching devices to make things happen for them. The second revolution was you talk to the computer like our smart speakers. With ambient it's gone to the next level, where it kind of knows what you need."[7]

When digital interfaces progress from being a "channel" to a "conversation," they become a trusted, convenient, and natural part of day-to-day behaviors. Further, when AI "learns" to calibrate to our individual idiosyncrasies, this technology becomes more than frictionless; one could argue it becomes a member of the family. As characterized in a widely read blog post, Microsoft product manager Darren Austin attributed Alexa's broader success to "its ability to alleviate the stresses of an over-booked life. It's the companion that is always ready to engage."[8] Juliette would wholeheartedly agree.

Fast forward to a future when generative AI and proactive conversational AI intersect. Generative AI is a type of machine learning that can create new content, including audio, code, images, text, simulations, and videos.[9] An example of this is OpenAI's ChatGPT. I decided to ask it if proactive conversational AI and generative AI would merge in the future. Here is how it responded:

Merge
GenAI
+ Conversational
AI

It's possible that generative AI and proactive conversational AI will merge in the future. As technology advances, the capabilities of both generative AI and proactive conversational AI are likely to improve, and it's possible that these improvements will bring the two fields closer together. One way in which generative AI and proactive conversational AI could potentially merge is through the use of generative models to create more natural and contextually appropriate responses in proactive conversational AI systems. Additionally, generative AI models can be used to create new data, such as images or text, that can be used to train and improve proactive conversational AI systems.[10]

It doesn't take much to imagine the elevated level of engagement with the user that this sort of innovation could produce. Not only could it remind Juliette of her grandson's birthday, it might also help her design a personalized digital birthday card and send it to him with her best wishes.

2 Edge-based computing

Gartner defines edge computing as "a part of a distributed computing topology in which information processing is located close to the edge—where things and people produce or consume that information."[11] Edge computing brings computation and data storage closer to the devices where it's being gathered, rather than sending it to the cloud, which may exist in an entirely different geography. As a result, data processing does not suffer latency issues that can affect an application's performance. In addition, companies can save money by having the processing done locally, reducing the amount of data that needs to be processed in a centralized or cloud-based location.[12]

3 Blockchain, Web3 and the metaverse

Put simply, blockchain is a distributed accounting ledger, more fully defined as a ledger that is spread among all peers across the network, with each peer holding a copy of the complete ledger. What makes blockchain far more secure and scalable than traditional systems is the fact that there is no central authority to hold, control, or tamper with the information. All parties talk to each other directly, and the use of cryptography makes the ledger tamper-proof. Further, data can be added into the blockchain in time-sequential order only. The fact that it is basically impossible to change data once it's been added to the blockchain means it can be considered, for the most part, incontrovertible. When needed, blockchain updates are validated against defined blockchain protocol criteria, taking effect only after a consensus has been reached among all those participating on the node network.

Web3 is the next, semantic version of the internet. As Harvard's Thomas Stackpole explains: "Put very simply, Web3 is an extension of cryptocurrency, using blockchain in new ways to new ends."[13] The key features of Web3 include:

- Open and trustless: data in a Web3 world is accessible from anywhere and from any device. Web3 extends the scale of interaction, ranging from payments to trusted data transfers. Web3 will enable the user to interact with any machine and offers the freedom to interact publicly and privately without an intermediary exposing them to risks referred to as "trustless" data.[14]

- Permissionless and decentralized: anyone, including users and providers, can engage without the need for permission from a controlling organiza-tion.[15] Web3 creates the promise of the decentralized autonomous organ-ization (DAO). This is an entity "based on transparent rules written in code and defined by a smart contract. It is governed by its members and independent of a central authority. A DAO is considered decentralized if unaffiliated with any specific nation-state or central bank. Developers designed it to provide an automated and decentralized form of govern-ance without the traditional bureaucracy and hierarchy limitations."[16]

- Distributed ownership: multiple customers can share ownership for a product or digital asset through the blockchain. For example, "Otis is a distributed ownership platform where users buy, sell, and trade SEC-securitized shares of collectibles like artworks, comics, jewelry, or fashion clothing items."[17]

Web3 has its drawbacks. Stephen Diehl, a technologist and prominent critic of Web3, dismissed blockchain as "a one-trick pony whose only application is creating censorship-resistant crypto investment schemes, an invention whose negative externalities and capacity for harm vastly outweigh any possible uses."[18] Web3 also presents significant environmental challenges despite the carbon offsets the major players are purchasing as it requires enormous data center processing power and storage.

In the coming pages you will read about companies including Nike and Starbucks that are committing resources and dollars to increase their presence in the metaverse, the platform-based virtual world, in which users explore and interact as avatars of themselves. Some analysts predict the market size of the metaverse will reach $800 billion[19] by 2024. With trading volumes of NFTs rising by 704 percent between Q2 2021 and Q3 2021,[20] they may not be far off the mark. (NFTs are non-fungible tokens which allow customers to digitally own art, music, and real estate within the metaverse.)

There is much more to understand about the implications of blockchain, NFTs (a topic we will take on when we go into Starbucks' "digital third place"), Bitcoin, and the other Web3 features that lay ahead. Like any new technology innovation, some elements will be embraced, others adapted, and still others ignored. But the internet is changing as the Internet of Everything begins to blossom and demands more real-time, ubiquitous access.

4 Application networks

In Stephen Orban's book *Ahead in the Cloud*, Andy Jassy suggests that one of the key factors responsible for Amazon Web Services' (AWS) staggering growth was decoupling their technology components to make them accessible via application programming interfaces (APIs).[21]

The impact of this across industries is game changing. Financial services firms that had traditionally invested in on-premise applications with hard-to-penetrate firewalls can open up their APIs for third parties to develop new apps and services. Now banks can partner with fintech companies rather than try to compete with them, and make data available to other apps that customers use every day to increase convenience and access. For example, Spanish multinational financial services giant BBVA launched its BaaS open platform in the US by opening its APIs to third parties in order to provide customers with financial products without needing to provide a full suite of banking services that BBVA already offers elsewhere. The next stage of this is something called an application network—essentially a way to connect applications to each other and to devices through APIs that share some of their assets and data on a network. This allows for other permission-based consumers of this data to access and reuse these assets in their applications as required.

5 LTE-M and 6G

LTE-M (Machine Type Communication) is the industry term for the low-power, wide-area technology standard that is specifically suitable for IoT applications while reusing features of the current LTE network. It derives benefits from all the security and privacy features of mobile networks, including support for user identity confidentiality, entity authentication, data integrity, and mobile equipment identification.[22] It also allows for device battery life as long as 10 years and a reduction in costs of 20–25 percent. But its real value lies in the fact that everything just works—automatically. For example, one of our clients has piloted a "smart socks" product for a connected healthcare application. To start using it, a patient needs to do only one thing: put on the socks.

And although it is still on the drawing board, coming right behind our current 5G network are the plans for 6G, the sixth generation of wireless technology. A 6G network builds on the current infrastructure but uses higher-frequency radio bands, giving networks much faster speeds and lower latency, and providing support to sophisticated mobile devices and technologies like autonomous vehicles (AVs).

Kaniz Mahdi, Vice President of Advanced Technologies at VMware, a best-practice example we will study later, commented on the implications of 6G by saying, "The connectivity becomes like air. Just imagine if you have that level of connectivity—what is the impact to society? What is the impact to our daily lives?"[23]

The performance enhancement 6G will bring will be significant. Current 5G speeds range between 40 and 1,100 Mbps (1.1 Gbps), depending on the type of 5G network you're on. Today, the IoT primarily connects smartphones and smart home devices like those "smart socks" mentioned above. Much like edge computing and some aspects of decentralization from Web3, the Internet of Everything becomes a far greater reality with 6G as some experts believe that these networks could allow you to reach maximum speeds of one terabit per second (Tbps) on an internet device. That's 1,000 times faster than 1 Gbps, the fastest speed available on most home internet networks today, and 100 times faster than 10 Gbps, the hypothetical top speed of 5G.[24]

This convergence represents the underpinning of "digital first." Why?

One: conversational AI not only reacts to us but when well designed, "proactive" conversational AI (when the device asks *you* a question as it does with Juliette) can, over time, "learn" to predict and adapt to our behavior by making its training set more domain specific and with it, more personalized to the customer. Extend generative AI to this in future years and the level of engagement increases significantly.

Two: edge-based computing will complement future 6G broadband speed and throughput breakthroughs to deliver extremely low latency at the customer interface, enabling immersive experiences even more engaging than the ones we will share later in this book.

Three: blockchain and Web3 apply forensic-level accounting to the transfer of goods and services between platforms and create the opportunity for direct interactions between people (or their avatars) and machines, enabling wholesale changes to security, privacy, and data ownership.

Four: application networks connect everything to everything else securely, and when burned into hardware accelerators, real-time transactions between even large-scale applications become a reality.

Five: last but not least, the icing on the cake (or the stack): a low-power, broad-range LTE-M network provides pathways for all of these devices to connect with embedded security and authentication today, followed in the coming years by a 6G broadband network that will make the internet "like air."

A 2019 Google/Ipsos research study reported that 83 percent of US shoppers who had visited a store in the past week said they used online search before going into a store.[25] Digital first accentuates the point that our initial interactions with a brand, now and in the future, will most likely begin with some form of silicon. With technologies like these five and others to follow, the digital pathways those customer journeys will follow are heralding a digital revolution, the likes of which none of us could have imagined.

Said more simply, as technologies allowing us to "just put them on" or "just walk out" (Amazon Go) become more widely adopted, the line where digital starts and stops doesn't blur, it disappears.

> ❝ With "just put them on" or "just walk out," the line where digital starts and stops doesn't blur, it disappears.

Competition

Consider the following passage, reproduced from the Blockbuster 2010 Annual Report under the section "Risks Related to Business Operations":

> Although we are pursuing, and may pursue in the future, initiatives related to alternative methods of content availability and delivery and believe that certain of these initiatives may be successfully integrated into our business model, we have limited experience with certain of these initiatives and cannot assure that they will be successful or profitable.[26]

Hindsight being a perfect science, reading these words is nothing short of *harrowing*. Here is what happened over the next three years.

The writing on the wall should have been impossible to misread. The damage to come was more than just the clever moves of a savvy competitor but a fundamental disruption of Blockbuster's business model. However, the Netflix threat did not fit the classic textbook model of disruption described in *The Innovator's Dilemma*[27] by the late Clayton Christensen, formulated before the internet era.

FIGURE 1.1 Revenue performance. Reproduced with kind permission of David L. Rogers

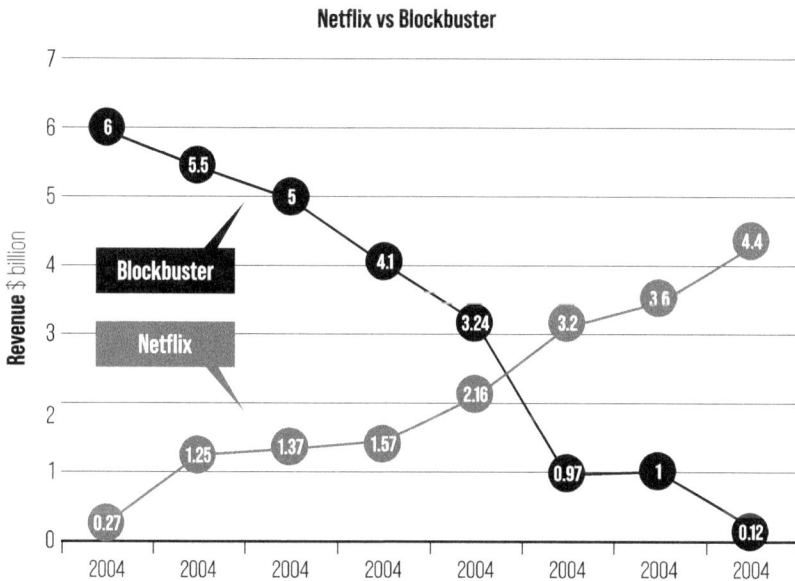

In my colleague David L. Rogers' best-seller, *The Digital Transformation Playbook*, he presents an updated "business model theory of disruption" to precisely explain this new kind of competitive threat. A digital-age disruptor like Netflix enters the market with a well-delivered, one-two punch:

- a value proposition that dramatically displaces the value provided by the incumbent; and
- a value network that creates a barrier to imitation by the incumbent.[28]

Professor Rogers goes on to show how his model explains the competitive threat that Netflix posed to Blockbuster.[29]

Value proposition

Blockbuster was the clear market leader in the video rental market, so Netflix had to compete by doing something different. They began by abolishing late fees—a Blockbuster practice that infuriated customers. Instead, customers were simply charged a flat monthly fee that allowed them to rent three movies at a time and exchange them when convenient. They also ensured that their product was easier to access. Customers could browse the Netflix website, select their three movies, and receive them in the mail a few days later, complete with a return envelope. As the final blow, Netflix also beat Blockbuster on selection, offering a library of 100,000 movies from a centralized warehouse supported by a recommendation engine on their website.

The impact on Blockbuster was devastating. Customers loved Netflix's superior value proposition and never looked back once they'd tried it. Which provokes an obvious question: why didn't Blockbuster respond with a similar service?

Value network

You might be surprised to learn that they actually did try to launch their own mail-order service. But for Blockbuster to succeed with a mail-order service of their own, they would have had to address some significant challenges, easily identified in hindsight by examining each firm's respective value networks.

The first and perhaps most obvious one was the pricing model (subscription pricing vs. per product fees), but that was easily copied from Netflix.

The second was Blockbuster's attempt to reproduce Netflix's website experience. Blockbuster did not have a way to replicate Netflix's large data sets or its proprietary recommendation engine. Although Blockbuster did try to replicate Netflix's warehouse and distribution system, it was simply too little too late as Netflix had spent years perfecting the efficiency of its system. It would take Blockbuster at least that much time to match Netflix's unit cost levels and, burdened as they were with the additional capital cost of their network of 9,000 retail stores, it wasn't long before management experienced the full force of the implications of their position.

Blockbuster's foreboding about the future in 2010 proved to be justified, and although it was able to offer a roughly comparable value proposition to customers for a while, it could not manage to do so profitably at the same price. After years of rapid decline, Blockbuster closed its final 300 stores in the US and sold off all its popcorn machines in 2014.

Business model disruption that leverages digital technologies is not the same animal as a traditional competitor trying to outpace you with features or pricing campaigns. Those wars you can win by staying on your toes and making smart choices. But don't risk falling short of the competitor who tips the scale in their favor, both in terms of the value they provide and the connected digital assets that enable it.

Now, as Disney+ recently announced, they have surpassed Netflix in streaming service subscriptions[30] with a very competitive value proposition. We will be watching to see if they can do what Netflix did to Blockbuster and create a significant competitive moat by shaping a defensible value network.

Culture

The economic and social challenges posed by the COVID-19 pandemic have found their way into every corner of the planet. Beyond the direct human tragedy and the ripple effect felt across supply chains, industries, and labor markets, the pandemic revealed deep divides in social and racial injustices that have existed for decades. Record unemployment rates improved as the pandemic was brought more under control, but industries such as hospitality appear permanently impacted as their labor supply failed to return to work. LinkedIn's chief economist, Karin Kimbrough, appeared on *60 Minutes* and reported that "at the nationwide level, the number of Americans quitting their job is higher than ever."[31] Further, the number of LinkedIn job postings including remote work as an option went up by a factor of 10 (from 1 in 67 to 1 in 6) as a result of the pandemic. A new employee/employer social contract has emerged as remote work has become the norm rather than the exception.[32]

Any organization that did not have its digital act together before the pandemic became a fast learner as industry after industry found their analog or rudimentary digital channels cracking under the pressure of new lockdown restrictions. Blaine Hurst, Vice Chair of Panera Bread, a company that led their industry in digital experience prior to the outbreak, told us during a webinar that managers needed to start asking different questions, such as, "How do I increase the flexibility of my team, my organization, my processes etc. to actually deal with the unknown because to survive we have to innovate on the fly?"

And innovate on the fly we did. Plexiglass went up, PPE became a common term, and new sanitation and masking rules were adopted. Shopping delivery services skyrocketed, DoorDash and SkipTheDishes skipped right through to unprecedented growth, and Amazon's profit soared 220 percent[33] as consumers turned to online ordering.

The digital revolution that was coming, came, crippling global supply chains in its wake, prompting Prof. Willy Shih of Harvard Business School to suggest:

> The economic turmoil caused by the pandemic has exposed many vulnerabilities in supply chains and raised doubts about globalization. Managers everywhere should use this crisis to take a fresh look at their supply networks, take steps to understand their vulnerabilities, and then take actions to improve robustness.[34]

Add to these tectonic-level shifts to our socio-economic condition, the findings from a recent Intergovernmental Panel on Climate Change (IPCC) report have confirmed that "the rise in weather and climate extremes has led to some irreversible impacts as natural and human systems are pushed beyond their ability to adapt."[35]

John Ruffolo, one of Canada's foremost tech investors, put it quite simply in a LinkedIn post: "There is a climate emergency. Let's not make this political. If we do not collectively fix this trend, nothing else really matters."

Many companies from Amazon[36] to Xerox[37] have committed to achieving net zero GHG emissions across their operations by as early as 2040. Nike, a best practice company featured later, introduced its "Move to Zero" program, an action plan to reduce and eliminate emissions and waste, use renewable energy and recycled materials, and complete the transition to becoming a 100 percent sustainable company.[38]

Now, as the Task Force on Climate-related Financial Disclosures (TCFD) recommendations turn into policy (83 of the world's largest 100 companies now support or report in line with the TCFD's recommendations), the metrics and targets proposed in this committee's recommendations will have a far-reaching impact.

BlackRock chief Laurence D. Fink wrote a letter to the world's CEOs with an urgent message about this:

> Climate change will be a defining factor in companies' long-term prospects…
> We are on the edge of a fundamental reshaping of finance… I urge companies to move quickly to issue them rather than waiting for regulators to impose them…
> If we want these disclosures to be truly effective—if we want to see true societal change—they should be embraced by large private companies as well.[39]

Even if the company you are leading or work for will not be required to report on these metrics and targets, I would suggest you understand them for three reasons:

1 Though you may not be required to meet these standards, a competitor may choose to, and with it create some important differentiation aimed at your most profitable customer segment.

2 Although the data is still mixed[40] on whether consumers will follow through on their stated willingness to pay more for green or climate-friendly products, there is an argument that with the accelerating awareness of climate change, that behavior may change—and change in a hurry.

3 Finally, if the product managers in your company have not started formal efforts to rethink packaging, product energy use and end-of-life treatment, then they will soon and you want to be ahead of those conversations, not trying to catch up.

A stark example of the impact of ignoring environmental, social, and governance (ESG) guidelines was felt by the Chinese fast-fashion e-commerce company Shein, which grew like wildfire through the pandemic and in 2022 was valued at $100 billion.[41] It became a favorite of Gen-Z buyers who

> " We are on the edge of a fundamental reshaping of finance.

would share "haul videos" on TikTok and YouTube in which they would open their boxes and could be seen pulling out the many clothing items they received, each individually wrapped in Shein-branded plastic bags. A fashion student named Ava Grand created a runway collection out of the bags crowdsourced from strangers. It did not take long for an outcry to reverberate around the social media world and among college newspapers, speaking out against fast fashion and its lack of respect for environmentally responsible packaging. This was acutely felt in France where a Shein pop-up store in Toulouse was mobbed by protesters, blocking traffic.[42]

Shein tried to respond by announcing a $50 million Extended Producer Responsibility (EPR) fund, which was poised to address textile waste. In fact, the company hired American Adam Whinston as their global head of ESG. In a recent interview he remarked on Shein's target demographic of 18- to 25-year-olds, "We see that sustainability is very important... We see this on TikTok and other social media. We are developing programs to address customer concerns more and more."[43]

Summary

Technology convergence, new forms of competition, and the impact of the global pandemic have ushered in unprecedented cultural changes. The new 3Cs combine to form a "perfect storm" of turbulence in which organizations are competing.

Key insights

- Five technologies are converging with the effect of accelerating the adoption of digital technologies that deliver on the promise of "digital-first."
- Companies that compete by providing a superior value proposition and value network represent a significant threat to incumbent firms.
- The socio-economic impact of the COVID-19 pandemic has revealed social and racial injustices that have existed for decades.
- The impact of the pandemic on some industries has been severe and has signaled a change in the employee/employer social contract as remote work has become the norm over the exception.

- New ESG requirements are forcing companies to understand how mandatory disclosures will impact the design of their products and services as well as the experiences they deliver.

What's next?

Creating a sustainable competitive advantage has never been harder or more tenuous. To imagine how to succeed going forward, let's consider seven design strategies that some of the world's leading brands apply to compete and win in a digital-first world.

02

Part 2: The 7 Design Strategies

"I am EXCITED to have insurance!! (Like, who can say that?!?!) Every once in a while, I encounter something that exemplifies just how GOOD a quality product can make a user FEEL. @Lemonade_Inc is just one such product."[1]

LEMONADE CUSTOMER

"What sets CEMEX apart is they've always been responsive to our needs and it's a complete solution because it will cover all the issues that I have: ordering, tracking. Wherever we go, CEMEX Go is with us."[2]

CEMEX CUSTOMER

"As a card-carrying introvert—who takes the stairs at work to avoid elevator small talk, who wants to beeline to what he needs and be done with the whole affair, who always chooses the wrong Safeway glacial line, knowing that "there has got to be a better way than this 'Precambrian checkout method'—it simply doesn't get better than this."[3]

AMAZON GO CUSTOMER

"It simply doesn't get better than this." These are experiences customers *love*. These testimonials, from three of our best practice examples, set the stage for this section. We can all think of brands that delivered an experience that was so exceptional, so memorable that we can close our eyes and quickly remember the feelings it generated. Exceeding customer expectations creates "emotional involvement"—so wonderfully described by these verbatims. As Timothy Keiningham and Terry Vavra say in *The Customer Delight Principle*, "exceeding expectations corresponds with Delight,"[4] and these companies exceed their customers' expectations in spades.

Staying ahead of competitors in a digital-first world requires some new thinking, new tools, and new design strategies. It has been our experience that each of these 7 Design Strategies applies to both B2C and B2B companies quite powerfully, though perhaps through different forms.

Achieve emotional peaks across channels, finishing strong

This design strategy is the "bookend" to the rest to provide an overarching frame to all of them. This requires designing experiences with the customer's holistic experience in mind, not just around what you deliver to them. Whether digital, human, or operational (like assembling an Ikea bed), design emotional peaks across channels at key moments of truth, especially at the end of the experience. We will examine insurance industry disrupter Lemonade to take a refreshing look into how this company has structured powerful emotional peaks to change the game in one of the world's oldest industries.

Create a personalization flywheel that grows customer engagement

At some point in the future, the drive-thru menu displayed to you at your favorite quick-service restaurant will reflect your past orders, present your personal preferences, and invite a simple voice response to reorder any of these items while suggesting a dessert that an algorithm working in the background predicts with a greater than 93 percent chance you will add to your order. Privacy issues aside, personalization, and in some cases hyper-personalization, is in full swing and there are algorithms and rules-based engines out there just waiting to detect your online behavior to deliver that cappuccino just the way you like it. To get beneath what is required to win with personalization, we will consider the way Spotify applies machine learning to deliver personalization that grows customer engagement by focusing on the transition from the attention economy to the value economy.

Strengthen customer commitment by providing choice and control

This design strategy was introduced to us by management experts Richard B. Chase and Sriram Dasu[5] and it is central to designing experiences that create customer engagement and advocacy. Behavioral scientists refer to this as choice architecture, which is defined as the practice of influencing choice by "organizing the context in which people make decisions."[6] When we are given choices, or control, even if it is just cognitive control (such as Domino's Pizza Tracker), we are co-creating the journey, not just experiencing it. Digital first is creating a new level of consumer empowerment that new research has revealed leads to greater customer retention and brand trust. We will take a look at how industry leader CEMEX applied an almost touchless digital experience they call CEMEX Go to the delight of their customers and as a result became a recognized digital transformation leader.

Foster ownership through customer community and co-creation

Customer communities or user groups are not a new idea, but companies that take them seriously and treat them as a strategic asset achieve significant levels of brand retention, spending, and advocacy. Few strategies will create greater brand trust and affiliation than being part of a customer community that shares a common set of values and that is invited to help the organization drive continuous improvement to their products and services. We will look at how VMware has fostered its VMUG user group into such a community, boasting over 150,000 members that engage with the company in everything from new feature development to onboarding new customers.

Inspire rituals that create shared meaning

Marketers have become enamored with the repeat business opportunity that institutionalizing consumer rituals can have for sales performance. But it isn't as simple as you might think. "Apply, rinse and repeat" may appear like a ritual but it isn't—it's a habit. There is a difference. We go deeper than most of the marketing hype on the subject to discover the underlying factors that produce consumer ritual and how you can put it to work to drive greater customer loyalty by considering how Starbucks enables both habits and rituals as Howard Schultz returns to launch the company's reinvention plan and to mentor a new CEO who will lead them into the next chapter in their global journey.

Empower customers through immersive experiences

Immersive experience is not limited to just augmented or virtual reality, it can include physical experiences like those you would find at a Disney theme park. Again, this matters only if it matters to your customers, but this is one of the things that if you don't experiment with it, they probably won't tell you they are looking for it. That is, until after they experience it, and then they won't want to live without it and will be more than willing to pay for it. We will consider how Nike connects personalization with immersive digital and physical experiences that create a whole new level of customer engagement and empowerment.

Link digital assets to leverage value over cost

Our second bookend in some ways represents the culmination of a well-thought-out digital-first design—but pushes it even further. As an example, consider from what we discussed in the previous chapter around how Blockbuster eventually had to surrender to Netflix's dominance in the movie rental business. It wasn't just that Blockbuster struggled with matching Netflix's value proposition. What eventually led to their undoing was Netflix's value network that included their pricing model, their massive data sets, their proprietary recommendation engine, and the years they spent driving inefficiencies out of their innovative distribution system. It was the power of the convergence of all of these digital assets into a formidable value network that Blockbuster could not compete against without a wholesale change to their capital structure, and by the time they did, it would have been too little, too late. We will examine how Amazon Retail has combined a powerful set of digital assets to deliver a new vision for the retail experience and the competitive advantage that Amazon's digital ecosystem has produced.

There you have it. The 7 Design Strategies to consider as you reflect on the experience your company delivers today. The next seven chapters will take you into each a little deeper and then we will regroup to consider how you get started to understand what data you will need to apply these 7 Design Strategies, build the business case to fund your effort, apply a set of proven steps for putting them into action, and then lay out how you go from customer storyboard to a blueprint for successful execution across your organization.

Summary

The impact of the digital revolution predicted by Porter and Heppelmann has been well entrenched for some time. And although how we are designing solutions to delight customers through digital channels may have changed, some things remain the same. There are still a few key moments in the customer experience that make it memorable, that create that overwhelming feeling that you can't wait to "do this again." The 7 Design Strategies provide a set of guideposts for you to consider as you imagine how you will adapt the experience you currently deliver to respond to the new 3Cs described previously.

What's next?

There is no time to waste. Let's dig into our first design strategy: achieving emotional peaks across channels, finishing strong, with our best practice example, Lemonade. You are about to go on a journey that I think you will agree is a refreshing take on one of the world's oldest industries.

Unwrap a new highlighter (be it physical or digital). We are going to give it a good workout.

03

Design Strategy 1: Achieve emotional peaks across channels, finishing strong

"If you design a system that assumes trust, you get trust back. If you create a system that assumes distrust, you get distrust back."[1]

DAN ARIELY, JAMES B. DUKE PROFESSOR OF PSYCHOLOGY AND
BEHAVIORAL ECONOMICS, DUKE UNIVERSITY

A friend recently shared the experience they had with a continuous glucose-monitoring product distributor that offered refill notifications for reordering, allowing customers to order their replenishments through multiple channels. However, the company's back-end system apparently never captured these order updates from all channels and as a result, critical health-related deliveries were often late. It's one thing when a bookseller delivers your "Travel Guide to Tuscany" a few days late on Friday instead of Wednesday, but missing a glucose refill delivery?

It speaks to the first of two things that must exist as foundational elements to everything that follows this paragraph. The first is brand trust.

In the words of our colleagues at the Chicago-based consulting firm Brandtrust: "Brands don't build trust, they are born of trust." In a recent paper, they explain: If a brand can be seen as "the promise of a future performance," trust is the assurance of "the accomplishment of that promise... [resulting in] future satisfaction." Trust develops when a brand demonstrates the qualities of a committed partner, including the following:

- a positive orientation toward the consumer/customer (i.e., making the consumer/customer feel cared for);

- consistent delivery of what is desired;
- accountability for its actions.

Interestingly, the opposite of trust isn't mistrust, it's disgust.[2]

Which is exactly the emotion embodied by our colleague as they described their continuous glucose-monitoring (or lack of it) experience and what led them to change providers as soon as their insurance company permitted it.

The second foundational element is *brand authenticity* (BA). A 2019 study by Stackla that surveyed 1,590 consumers in the US, UK, and Australia reported that 90 percent of consumers say authenticity is important when deciding which brands they like and support.[3] HawkPartners reported in their 2021 Brand Authenticity Index that "57% of respondents felt that it was more important that a brand is authentic after the pandemic."[4]

What exactly is brand authenticity? Research published in the *European Journal of Management and Business Economics* found that three factors positively influence consumer perceptions of BA: individuality, consistency, and continuity. These in turn drive higher perceived brand value (BV) and brand trust (BT).[5]

These researchers go on to make an important point worth pausing for when we consider what we are trying to achieve in strategy 1:

> Positioning a brand based on product superiority, quality and great service is all too common in the competitive market, whereas authenticity allows a brand to be true without being perfect.[6]

"True without being perfect." Other research by our associates at C Space, the online customer community firm, reports that "customers prefer companies that value openness, relevance, empathy, experience, and emotion. These are all qualities that signify honesty in a brand."[7]

Now coming back to design strategy 1: Achieve emotional peaks across channels, finishing strong—within the context of brand trust and brand authenticity, we may want to approach this differently. Taken at face value, you might be tempted to default to tactics that drive faster conversions, or design in an incentive to upgrade a new customer seconds after they sign up for the free version. Perhaps if your only goal is to crush a conversion metric, that may work with some good A/B testing. But if your goal is to exceed customer expectations and engender brand trust, you might think of how

66 *Interestingly, the opposite of trust isn't mistrust, it's disgust.*

you operationalize Design Strategy 1 by adding the lens of brand authenticity. Depending on the goals and needs of the customer at that particular stage of the journey, you might ask:

- How might we apply technology to help anticipate customer needs and design a sequence of interactions that makes it easy and convenient for them to achieve their goals?
- How might we apply cognitive analytics to detect a customer's emotional state to trigger the appropriate digital or human response?
- What interactions could we design that would demonstrate to our customers how much we care about them?
- What sort of cues or interactions would demonstrate our brand authenticity? Also, what interactions exist today that erode brand authenticity, and with it brand trust, and how do we eliminate them?

The COVID-19 pandemic was an effective way of revealing brands with strong authenticity and those without. My colleague in the United Kingdom, Shaun Smith, the founder of Smith+Co, shared a story with me about a client of theirs who is one of the largest private healthcare providers in the UK. They quickly assessed the impact of the pandemic on their customers and their business, which led them to take a hard look at their company's purpose, which is to be there for their patients and have a positive impact on their lives. As a result, they contacted the National Health Service to make all of their facilities and resources available and accelerated their investments in digital technology to help customers (patients) achieve faster access to telemedicine and diagnostic tools when clinical visits were discouraged due to the massive demand COVID-19 had put on all hospitals.

There is an old saying about leadership that during a crisis, "character isn't tested, it is revealed." The same might be said about brand authenticity.

But let's come back to brand trust and consider the insight that brands earn their customers' trust, in part, through the "consistent delivery of what is desired." Some might argue, in referencing how this chapter opened, that digital transformation has made it worse. But if we are trying to structure "emotional peaks" across channels, being consistent is a basic standard of performance. Given most customers tend to start an experience with a digital interaction, on a website, a voice-response device, or a mobile app, what does this mean for how you might structure multiple emotional peaks? Perhaps even more important, how do you ensure you remember the customer's previous interaction when they start a transaction on your mobile app, get interrupted, and so have to stop, but then expect to pick up the same transaction on the website, or with a call center agent, or when using a store kiosk or navigating your IVR? This functionality is called "pause and resume" and having this in place is where you must begin to even consider how to structure multiple emotional peaks.

With pause and resume functionality, customers can start an interaction in one channel, pause it, and then automatically resume in another channel. Pause and resume literally "freezes the journey state" and when the user reengages, it simply resumes, eliminating the need for call center teams to have to read CRM notations or frustrating customers by putting the burden of effort on them to repeat the same information over again. Customers can seamlessly move from one channel to another with ease.

Luckily, today there are many software platforms that can provide not just effective pause and resume functionality but also low-code development tools to create, integrate, and publish cross-channel customer journeys without the need to re-code legacy systems.[8] "Drag and drop" API tools provide predefined connectors to endpoints between applications, meaning that the back end can be integrated with the front end without a complete rewrite of legacy systems.

With this sort of technology, both consistency and channel persistence are possible, meaning responses to customers could be triggered based on any number of customer behaviors or transaction events, regardless of where your customer is in the journey. Start your order or inquiry on the web, finish it on the app, and pick it up on arrival at the store, and still receive bonus points from the cashier based on your order history across channels.

Let's spend a moment on "finishing strong." It doesn't have to be expensive or even cost a penny in some cases to provide your customer with an emotional peak at the end of the experience. Think of the hug that a guest receives from a Bear Builder at the end of a Build-a-Bear Workshop visit after they have made their new "best friend" or when a retail salesperson walks you to the door at the end of your store visit. And what is not to like about digital notifications you receive once you have launched Domino's Pizza Tracker and your taste buds are put on notice as you learn that Thomas should be arriving in 22 minutes with your pepperoni pizza, and 22 minutes later, there he is!

B2B companies excel here as well. Think of the attention paid to new customer onboarding processes and the certificate generated after an end user has completed training on a Microsoft or Oracle product. Or the annual customer awards presented near the finale at client conferences.

Since we were just talking about brand authenticity and brand trust, perhaps we should consider the issue of trust that exists in the insurance industry prior to examining our best practice example, Lemonade, Inc.

An industry synonymous with distrust

A 2017 survey by Statista of 1,151 US consumers reported the percentage of people that said they "don't trust insurance companies very much" or "at all" ranged from 29 percent to 54 percent.[9] In New Zealand, survey research revealed that only 13 percent of customers reported having confidence they could trust insurers with covering their claims, and only 18 percent felt they fully understood the terms of their policies because of the difficult wording. As many as one in four people had experienced a problem with their insurer, with the top complaint being about having a claim unreasonably, unexpectedly declined.[10] The other reason for distrust is selling practices that incentivize brokers to put their commission ahead of what is the best solution for their customer, "fearing and expecting that people tend to act first against the insurance companies, whom they see as possible enemies: phrases such as 'crash for cash' or 'insurance fraud' aren't uncommon."[11]

Enter Lemonade

Renowned behavioral economist and Lemonade's former chief behavioral officer Dan Ariely is one of Bloomberg's "most influential thinkers" and has written three *New York Times* bestsellers, including *The Honest Truth About Dishonesty: How We Lie to Everyone—Especially Ourselves.*

In an article published in *Judicature*, Ariely describes how he and his colleagues rethought the insurance industry through a completely different lens and set about removing the inherent conflict of interest that has existed for decades:

> If you think about the regular insurance company, they take money from consumers … At some point, something bad happens to the consumer, and then the insurance company has to pay. But of course, the insurance company doesn't want to pay; they would be better off not paying than paying. And consumers, of course, know that the insurance company prefers not to pay, so they cheat. So, we said, "Let's fix it." How? We decided to build a system with three parts: we

have consumers, an insurance company, and a charity … We take a fixed income, so our amount of profit doesn't change depending on whether we accept or deny claims. And at the end of the year, all the money that is left over in the pool of those consumers that picked the World Wildlife Fund goes to the World Wildlife Fund.[12]

Let's now take a look at how Lemonade eliminates the conflict of interest, endemic across the industry, and delivers several emotional peaks while finishing strong as experts Chase and Dasu instruct—through a seamless digital experience—all in about 90 seconds.

The experience

Entrepreneurs Daniel Schreiber and Shai Wininger decided to shake up the industry by launching Lemonade, Inc. in the US in 2016, a totally digital insurance company with absolutely no physical agencies or written policies that embeds digital technology into the core operating model.

Making Lemonade

The Lemonade experience includes three ingredients. The mobile app uses an intuitive design to make the entire process of buying insurance more appealing and less frustrating. The second ingredient is chatbots: AI Jim to handle claims and AI Maya, a chatbot capable of creating personalized insurance policies and quotes for customers, serving them with customized responses for their queries, complaints, and reimbursements. It also can make changes to existing policies. Finally, eye-catching, colorful, and short ad videos with minimal words deliver their message as concisely as possible. Mobile app, chatbots, and ads. Simplicity personified. However, for emergencies related to the customer's car, home, or property, there is a Lemonade 800 number for those who don't have access to the app or the website. As Jeanne Bliss, one of the world's leading customer experience experts, often says, "Everybody wants self-service until they don't."

Big data gets granular

"At twenty data points much of humanity looks alike so you price and underwrite large numbers of people as if they are a uniform, monolithic group, but we found that the data we were gathering … showed us that groups our competitors seemed to consider to be monolithic were actually made up of predictable subgroups with over 600 percent variation in their likelihood to file a claim."[13] Thus, Daniel Schreiber's explanation of how Lemonade's AI is able to price policies by classifying insurance risk using the "volume, variety, and velocity" of big data resounded across the oak-paneled executive board rooms of his competitors. The company uses big data analytics to quantify losses and predict risks by categorizing the customer into a risk segment and quoting an appropriate premium based on their risk behaviors. Each segment is created using algorithms that warehouse extensive customer data, such as health conditions and other factors. This real-time, back-end pricing engine is integrated with AI Maya's natural language processing engine, engaging customers as she presents choices and options. This becomes a powerful digital design that marries the "best of both worlds:" elegant, simple, engaging, mobile-first, empathic design with powerful, real-time, sophisticated machine learning.

It's all about training

But it is harder than it looks. Lemonade uses natural action synthesis and natural language processing to ensure that AI Maya gets smarter daily. In 2017, Forbes reported a story of a customer wearing a disguise who uploaded a video on how his camera and other items were stolen and in two days received a claim deposit of $677. Later that year, he changed his disguise and account information and submitted an even bigger claim, but this time the AI caught the fraudster and escalated the information to the authorities. "Fool me once …" as the saying goes.[14]

> 66 *At twenty data points much of humanity looks alike.*

FIGURE 3.1 Lemonade screenshots

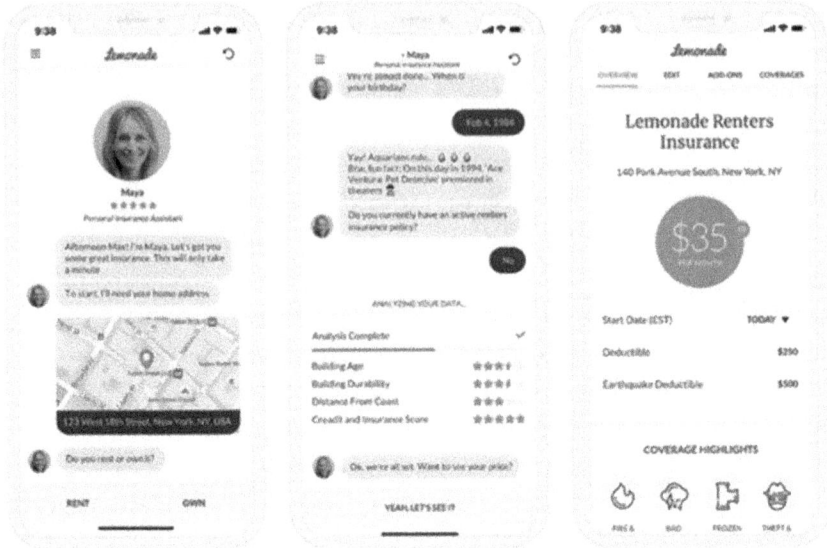

Lemonade takes a stand

The company's mission is simple:

> Harness technology and social impact to be the world's most loved insurance company.

Perhaps the most important thing about Lemonade, however, isn't how AI and machine learning drive the customer experience, it is the company's business model itself. When a customer interacts with AI Maya, buys insurance (often in just 90 seconds), and starts paying their premiums, Lemonade takes 25 percent as a flat fee in order to cover its operating expenses, while the remaining 75 percent is used to pay claims (including reinsurance) submitted by users.[15] (By way of comparison, a typical for-profit insurance company would take 35 percent of premium fees.) At year-end, after paying off operating expenses (though no need to pay broker fees as they don't have any) and paying claims that are approved (quickly and painlessly), what's left over is donated to a charity of the user's choice. Lemonade calls this the "Giveback" concept. As discussed, regular insurance companies apply those dollars to their income line. But Lemonade addresses the obvious conflict of interest that a traditional insurance company makes more money by denying claims. Lemonade takes that off the table because they allow their customers to guide what charitable organization those would-be profits should go to. So, no conflict in paying your claim (which is all done about one third of the time through AI Jim, and paid really quickly).

GIVEBACK AND THE LEMONADE FOUNDATION'S CRYPTO CLIMATE COALITION

Giveback

In 2022, the Lemonade community gave back $1,873,588 to support aid for global poverty, the environment, LGBTQ+, animal rights, among other causes. Highlights included:[16]

- environmental causes grew 72 percent as compared to the previous year with $492,461 in donations in 2022 amid worsening climate change;

- civil rights organizations saw a 52 percent increase in donations from 2021, totaling $272,331 in 2022;

- healthcare-related nonprofits saw an 18 percent increase from 2021 with $379,320 in donations;

- LGBTQ+ organizations saw an 11 percent increase with $154,649 donated to support projects including 1,100 LGBTQ youth given lifesaving mental health services.

The Lemonade Crypto Climate Coalition

Separate from their Giveback program, the Lemonade Foundation has funded the Lemonade Crypto Climate Coalition to provide crop insurance in low-income countries where a lack of meteorological infrastructure and other factors deter traditional insurers from operating.[17] The coalition will tackle this problem by solving three main challenges: accurately quantifying weather risks, automating claim assessment, and providing adequate funding and reinsurance. Avalanche, Chainlink, and DAOstack will contribute their knowledge of blockchain technology while Lemonade, Etherisc, Hannover Re, and Pula will build highly accurate, fully automated weather insurance models.

Lemonade co-founder Shai Wininger commented: "We're excited by this rare opportunity to bring together some of the most innovative companies on the planet to solve a pressing problem. While all coalition members have their own everyday businesses, this is a unique opportunity to join forces and make a collective impact."[18]

Multiple emotional peaks and a big finish

If you have ever spent time on hold trying to confirm that your insurance company received your claim and has even agreed to process it, well, you can appreciate the series of emotional peaks Lemonade generates, all without human intervention. This is the most searing pain point in the insurance industry—a real moment of truth—and one that Lemonade completely reimagined to the benefit of their customers by aligning interest with incentives and stripping out the friction, complexity, and delays that currently exist with most of their competitors. Claims are usually paid in seconds and submitted via the app with no paperwork. The money is deposited back into your account minutes later.

> I was shocked by how easy the process has been with Lemonade. I signed up for Lemonade because it was no frills, the most affordable option, and took no more than two minutes on my couch ... I already assumed there was no way that I'd recover my losses: other insurers either pile paperwork or deduct tons of charges that I don't understand. But this time was different. I signed an honesty pledge, answered a few questions, and Lemonade reimbursed me in a matter of seconds! The service is amazing, and I am so happy that I signed up![19]

And rising to my challenge of asking *How might we demonstrate to customers that we care about them?*, Lemonade's Giveback program allows the customer to choose which charitable organization should receive the pool left over from unpaid claims. Talk about finishing strong. Customer comments reproduced below are from the Lemonade website:[20]

> This company made INSURANCE of all things fun and exciting. And then backed it up with a fantastic biz. I'm in awe of @Lemonade_Inc. 👏

> I had just joined the "Lemonade" family and can't tell you all how elated as well as fortunate I am to be part of the wonderful experience! What a truly caring and amazing team, too! #SanDiegoCitySendingLove

> Love Lemonade as a thing in the world. Glad it's here.

> Just bought a new 20-year term life insurance policy from @Lemonade_Inc. The process in the app was seamless (dare I say kinda fun!), & their quote was slightly more than half the cost of another I received (and turned down) from a competing insurer. Well done.

> @Lemonade_Inc has one of the best new user onboarding flows. They've streamlined the hell out of it and it was so easy to sign up.

Not going to lie … @Lemonade_Inc is a model example of how easy every insurance company should make it to buy their products.

My mind is blown every time I use @Lemonade_Inc.

When your customers start telling you that you have "blown their mind" every time they interact with you, you can stop buying books like this one. This company has more peaks than a train ride through the Swiss Alps. But let's come back to the question I posed back in the introduction: Can a zero-touch customer experience actually create emotional involvement? Has digital transformation advanced enough that the level of empathy and emotional connection, typically delivered by frontline staff, achieves similar levels of loyalty and advocacy?

The customer testimonials above seem to provide a pretty categorical answer. When asked a similar question by Banking Transformed podcast host Jim Marous, Lemonade CEO Daniel Schreiber replied just as emphatically:

> We have seen by so many measures how consumers who do use digital interfaces disdain this idea that humans can always do a better job than a bot. Humans are slow. Humans aren't available all the time. Humans are forgetful and there are things that bots already do today, and that list of things is growing and growing, that they can do cheaper, better, faster, and without less empathy than humans, at least not from the experience point of view. If you go on to our app and you're chatting to AI Jim and AI Jim is asking a bunch of questions patiently (about a claim), never irritated because he's a bot … And then you press "I'm Done" and three seconds later, he says, "Your claim has been approved. The money is in your bank account." Are you begrudging the system for not being more empathic? I don't think so. You're feeling thrilled that the level of service was what you needed in your hour of need.[21]

On that note, let's have a look behind the curtain to see how Mr. Schreiber and his fellow Lemonade Makers (the name for employees) quench the thirst of those many first-time insurance buyers.

> *There are things that bots already do today, and that list of things is growing and growing, that they can do cheaper, better, faster, and without less empathy than humans.*

The details

There is quite a bit to unpack in terms of the elements that underpin the experience described. Let's dig into Lemonade's strategy and operations to see if we can't thread the needle on how they deliver so robustly on our first design strategy.

Flywheel strategy

In reading through Lemonade's 2020 Securities and Exchange Commission S-1 filing document, one statement stands out:

> "In insurance, data science is not helpful to the business, it is the business."[22]

Although the industry has been mining data for decades to define pricing and other decisions, Lemonade, without the constraints of legacy thinking and systems, has built a vertically integrated platform that gets better over time as it ingests more data. In effect a "flywheel" that delivers greater value over costs for their customers the faster it turns. They summarize their strategy as including three elements:[23]

1 Harnessing our delightful experience, aligned values, and advantaged cost structure to appeal to more consumers broadly, and particularly to the next generation of consumers, whom incumbents struggle to serve.

2 Then growing with those customers as their insurance needs increase naturally and substantially.

3 All the while leveraging our closed-loop system, by which the copious amounts of data we generate make our business ever faster, cheaper, and more precise, to further delight consumers and extend our competitive advantage.

Target customer

While much of the insurance industry focused on the "I switched and saved" formula, Lemonade targeted younger, mobile-first, first-time buyers of insurance. Approximately 90 percent of Lemonade's customers were not leaving another carrier to join them and about 70 percent are under the age of 35, a demographic that has grown up digitally native, with a general distrust of institutions and the feeling that Lemonade's Giveback feature aligns to their

FIGURE 3.2 Lemonade's flywheel—Form 10-K Lemonade, Inc. Annual Report 2021

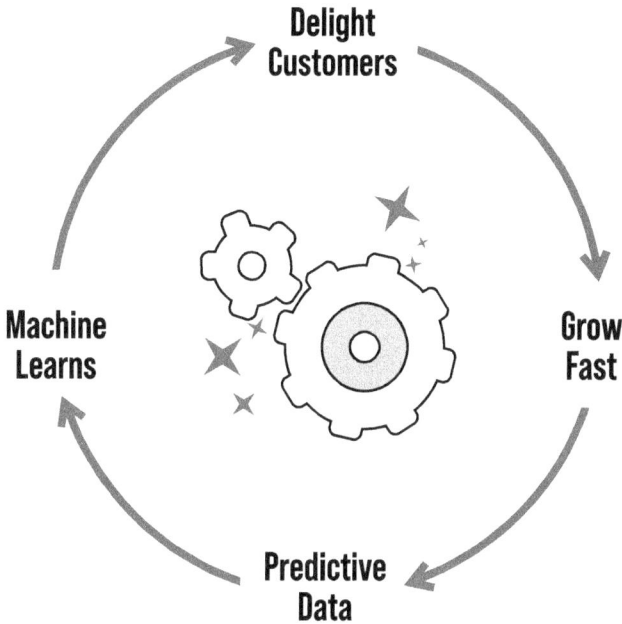

own values. Most importantly, as they age, their needs for insurance grow. Case in point, three years after signing up, Lemonade's customers on average increase their spending with the company by 56 percent. In fact, the company's data reflects that of the economy in terms of the curvilinear increase in net worth of Americans from the ages of 35 to 75. This has two implications: 1) in terms of coverage, Lemonade identified a theme they call "graduation," which is when an original renter upgrades to a condo and their average annual premium goes up $150 to $900 per year; 2) the diversity of their needs increases from property and causality to auto, pet, life, etc.

As Lemonade add more products to their portfolio, they are seeing the confluence of their customer life cycle approach with product bundling. In one quarter alone, bundle rates in Illinois increased 40 percent versus the national average. Customers with two Lemonade products outspent the average single-product customer 3:1. For customers with three Lemonade products, the ratio was 7:1 and for customers with all four products in the two markets where they are available, that ratio jumped to 9:1.[24]

But one salient point, unique to the insurance industry, cannot be overlooked. Because of Lemonade's structural cost advantages (no brokers, no branches, no paperwork, faster processes, etc.), the pricing they can offer to these target customers is typically 50 percent cheaper than the minimum premiums offered by their competitors. But here is the sweetener that makes Lemonade: the industry regulators must approve pricing to ensure policies aren't offered below cost, and as a result, no subsidies can be offered to "buy" market share. Now *that* is a tall cool glass of competitive advantage served with plenty of ice.

Business model

A second advantage not to be missed is the operating leverage that comes from what they describe as their "closed-loop system." At its highest level, Lemonade's digital experience creates delighted customers that are retained and grow their spending as their needs expand, which itself generates a lot of data, which provides greater granularity to feed the firm's predictive analytics and machine learning algorithms to improve their ability to price and evaluate risk more precisely, further delighting customers, who share their experiences with their friends and family through social channels and this virtuous cycle continues. A run-on sentence, I grant you, but I didn't want to break the flow. But as one of my colleagues asked me while I was writing this: "Don't other insurance company use data science and machine learning to compete in the marketplace? What makes Lemonade that different?"

A fair question and one that deserves a thoughtful response. There are three parts to the answer.

Every insurance company hires data scientists. They all have machine learning capabilities. The challenge is that the data they are working from is generated from their legacy processes. For example, when signing up a new customer, a human-based broker model might capture 20–50 data points on a specific customer (birthday, address, etc.) and the variation generated from each individual broker's notes about that customer will vary dramatically. When AI Maya onboards a new customer, in just 13 questions prior to providing a quote, she generates 1,700 data points. Machine learning that produces insight is only as powerful as the quality, quantity, recency, and corollary attribution of the data it is based on. Here, Lemonade wins hands down since AI Maya doesn't decide to call it a day at 4 pm and expedite a customer through the forms that need to be completed, ticking a box here and forgetting to fill in an answer there.

In many insurance companies today, data is still pretty siloed and desperate. Call center logs are retained by some CRM system. Claims data resides on a mainframe. Field data is often sparse and fraught with human bias and error. Lemonade, however, was developed on a "digital substrate" with integration designed from the beginning to share both data and feedback loops between customer data, quotes, pricing, customer support, claims, marketing, vendors, etc. And this all happens in real time. For example, while Lemonade's competitors might release updates to their software systems a few times a year, Lemonade generates an average of nearly 16 daily releases updating the entire platform.

Because part of their business model asks customers to pick the charitable organization they wish to see their "Giveback" dollars go to, Lemonade is able to segment those customers into cohorts based on the charity they choose. This generates significant insights about those customers, including the probability that people that choose a charity like the World Wildlife Fund might be open to an offer of pet insurance at some point.

A flywheel strategy of this magnitude has to be turned by some powerful technology. Let us take a brief tour of the elements of Lemonade's technology stack.

> **"** When AI Maya onboards a new customer, in just 13 questions prior to providing a quote, she generates 1,700 data points.

DIGITAL-FIRST CUSTOMER LIFETIME VALUE

Digital-first companies like Lemonade calculate customer lifetime value (LTV) differently because of the massive data sets they accumulate over time. They use it as a leading indicator of performance and to guide myriad decisions, from marketing spend to pricing and customer segmentation targeting (or avoidance.) Lemonade recently released the sixth generation of their LTV model, LTV6, which for every individual customer predicts their likelihood to file a claim, churn, or be cross-sold another product.

"LTV1 through LTV3 were humdrum in comparison," Lemonade reported in a recent news release. "For instance, they allowed us to estimate claim frequency, but not claim severity. We were able to differentiate high-risk users, but overall, the models weren't as granular or accurate as we'd like."[25]

LTV6, trained on Lemonade's proprietary and highly textured data, comprises machine learning and deep learning models using state-of-the-art natural catastrophe models. Hindsight may be a perfect science, but at Lemonade, so is foresight. For example, thanks to LTV6, the analysis was able to flag certain homeowner policies in California that proved riskier than originally expected and would prove to be loss-making over time. With six years of data to pull from, LTV6 revealed the mix of profitable pockets within California, reducing the likelihood of worsening loss ratios and aligning pricing accordingly.

In fact, by using big data and machine learning to predict lifetime loss ratios, Lemonade can time shift a "lifetime" of future data into the present, allowing for optimization of the current business for the long term.[26] Now as they continue to grow their customer base and observe data points from longer retention levels, claims, and cross-sell behavior, their machine learning becomes even more precise, as the next releases of LTV7, LTV8, etc. will inform critical decisions from pricing to marketing spend and more.

Technology—Lemonade's customer cortex

At the center of Lemonade's flywheel strategy is something they call the customer cortex. It's a fitting analogy as it combines artificial intelligence, natural language processing, and machine learning across both customer-facing and back-office platforms.

On the customer-facing front, we already talked about AI Maya's role to onboard new customers, personalize their coverage options, and facilitate secure payments. Two other bots are important to mention:

- AI Jim, Lemonade's claims bot, takes the first notice of loss from a customer over 95 percent of the time and can handle the entire claim from submission to payment about a third of the time. When he can't, he assigns it to a human claims expert based on their qualification and capacity, and forwards on to them much of the data they will need to approve or deny the claim.

- CX.AI is a support bot designed to instantly resolve customer requests, handling about a third of all inquiries. Like AI Maya and AI Jim, it uses Natural Language Processing (NLP) to handle requests and machine learning to improve its impact. On one specific request—questions around when a customer moves from one location to another, perhaps going from renting an apartment to buying a condo—CX.AI improved its training and "learned" how to handle these requests. The support organization saw an 87 percent drop in these types of requests handled by a Lemonade Maker and this learning cycle has increased fivefold across a variety of other support topics.

The back office includes "behind-the-scenes" technologies:

- Forensic Graph is Lemonade's fraud detection system that looks at relationships between different data points that would be invisible to a human, but through the application of AI, big data and behavioral economics, saves the company millions in potential losses.

- Blender is just that: a proprietary, in-house built insurance management system to power the customer's experience, underwriting, claims, growth, marketing, finance, and risk management.

FIGURE 3.3 Lemonade's customer cortex

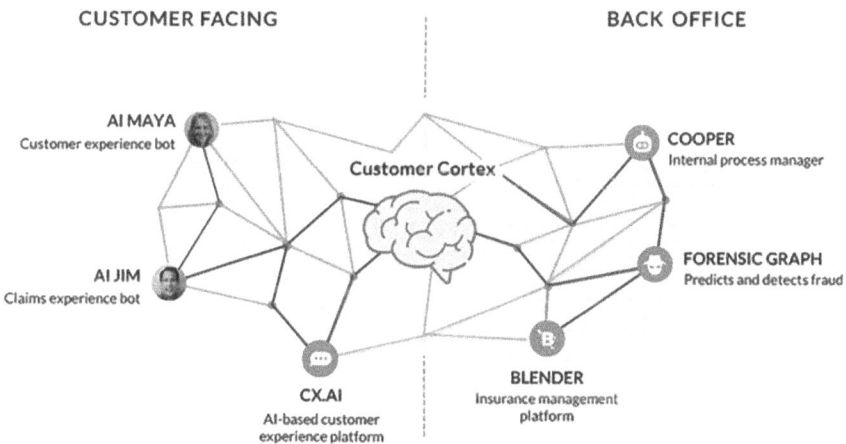

CUSTOMER FACING   BACK OFFICE

AI MAYA
Customer experience bot

Customer Cortex

COOPER
Internal process manager

AI JIM
Claims experience bot

FORENSIC GRAPH
Predicts and detects fraud

CX.AI
AI-based customer
experience platform

BLENDER
Insurance management
platform

- Cooper is Lemonade's internal bot that streamlines processes like check processing and QA testing. It leverages data from NASA satellites to identify wildfires in real time to block ads and sales in the impacted areas. Like AI Maya and AI Jim, Cooper gets better as its training grows with additional feedback, driving even more internal productivity for every Lemonade Maker that uses it.

Culture

Lemonade has developed a culture based on clear values of inclusivity, respecting differences, and seamless teamwork. Pivoting off of the company model made popular by Spotify, Lemonade has designed an organizational structure providing Makers with high degrees of agency and ownership. Each product group represents a "company" with specific objectives and key results (OKRs). Makers are grouped together into squads—multifunctional, autonomous teams with a clear scope and set of objectives. Tribes include a cluster of squads running under a company leadership team, and to ensure duplication is minimized, there are support functions (finance, office ops, etc.) that serve all lines of business. As Adina Eckstein, Lemonade's chief operating officer, has said, "At the end of the day, though, it's important to keep one key fact in mind: your customers don't care about your organizational structure—they care about having a streamlined, delightful, unified experience."[27] That seems to be working.

Growth opportunities

We could keep writing about this company for another 10 pages but central to making this valuable to you is knowing when to stop. Lemonade has expanded to include pet insurance and life insurance in some markets. On November 8, 2021, Lemonade announced their acquisition of Metromile, a leading AI-based auto insurer. Their press release stated:

> While Lemonade has been at the forefront of using big data and AI in home and pet insurance, Metromile has been trailblazing a parallel path for car insurance. Metromile's car-mounted precision sensors took over 400 million road trips in recent years, covering billions of miles and sending real-time streams to the Metromile cloud. These were cross referenced with actual claims data, yielding precise predictions for losses per mile driven. These algorithms hold the promise of propelling Lemonade Car from a newcomer in the car insurance space to its vanguard.[28]

The heart of the matter

There are many elements of behavioral science at work in the Lemonade experience, a few of which are worth noting.

Trust and reciprocity

We opened this section talking about how brand trust and brand authenticity are "table stakes" in designing an experience that achieves emotional peaks and finishes strong. Lemonade entered an industry with structural norms that erode trust between insurers and policy holders, removed the conflict of interest and, with it, all of the billions of dollars of costs associated with the friction it creates. In terms of human behavior, trust is a mental construct with implications for economic behavior—one that Lemonade has tapped into with undeniable success. Once a new customer takes the Lemonade "honesty pledge," a psychological contract has been struck, laden with reciprocity between the policy holder and the company. "In fact, reciprocity exists as a basic element of human relationships and behavior, and this is accounted for in the trust extended to an anonymous counterpart."[29]

Number roundness

Buying insurance can be complex and the greater the complexity, the greater the chance for what behavioral scientists describe as "choice overload" and "cognitive load." As a result, providing customers with rounded numbers like $35 per month rather than $35.17 per month decreases the customers' cognitive load, making decision-making easier and simpler.

Automation bias and chunking

There is a human tendency to take the road of least cognitive effort while completing a task which can generate an "automation bias." When combined with "chunking" (as a set of information or items that are treated collectively as a single unit[30]) as it is with the Lemonade app, the flow of the experience reduces stress and anxiety, especially given most new customers are onboarded in two minutes or less.

Peak-end rule

This is at the heart of our first design strategy. Behavioral science teaches us that "our memory of past experience (pleasant or unpleasant) does not correspond to an average level of positive or negative feelings, but to the most extreme point and the end of the episode."[31] Lemonade is a classic example of designing an experience, from new customer onboarding to support and filing a claim, that delivers multiple positive emotional peaks that finish strong.

Results

How are they doing? As of Q3, 2022, YOY in-force premiums grew 76 percent to $609 million, while gross earned premiums increased 71 percent compared with the prior year to $136 million. Their customer count grew 30 percent to 1,775,824 from Q3 of 2021. At the time of writing, Lemonade had yet to turn a profit, since their goal is to grow quickly and reap the rewards from the long tail generated by their closed loop virtuous cycle. This delay in profitability is driven in part by the dynamics of both the industry and Lemonade's strategy. Customer acquisition costs (CAC), which are front-end loaded, coexist alongside year 1 loss ratios, which tend to be the highest. As CEO Daniel Schreiber explains, "Even though they (customers) will be profitable over their lifetime, they're not profitable in the same accounting period and that is the predominant dynamic that's driving losses."[32]

A fact worth noting is that unlike other insurance companies that would typically see loss ratios get worse as premiums increase, Lemonade has seen simultaneous improvements in all three: lower risk, greater premiums, and increased conversions, which is evidence that their flywheel strategy is working. Finally, Lemonade's net promoter score (NPS) is over 70, in an industry which often reports single-digit or negative NPS results. (Net Promoter®, Net Promoter System®, Net Promoter Score®, NPS®, and the NPS-related emoticons are registered trademarks of Bain & Company, Inc., Fred Reichheld, and Satmetrix Systems, Inc., and are used under license.)

> " *Our memory of past experience (pleasant or unpleasant) does not correspond to an average level of positive or negative feelings, but to the most extreme point and the end of the episode.*

Summary

This level of innovation, as we will see in our next section as well, is often pioneered by managers outside of the industry, so in some ways perhaps what we have shared isn't a completely new idea in terms of its individual technology components. What is new is how the playing field becomes leveled pretty quicky with the availability of big data and the machine learning/AI platforms which can turn an industry on its ear, leaving the incumbents with nothing more than—shall we say it?—lemons.

Key insights

- Brand trust and brand authenticity are "table stakes" to delivering a Branded Customer Experience.®
- Pause and resume functionality ensures a "digital-first" experience delivers a consistent, intentional, differentiated, and valuable experience.
- Digital interactions that are developed based on empathic, human-centered design principles provide some advantages over human interactions.
- Apply behavioral science strategies to your core business model to have maximum impact.
- Design an organizational structure that drives resources and ownership guided by clear objectives to ensure employees fully understand the impact of their contributions.
- Implement digital technology and data science to enable a flywheel effect that drives both customer growth and greater operating leverage.

What's next?

Now, since we are on the topic of data, let's get into what is perhaps the biggest trend in experience design: the application of data to create more relevant, personalized experiences that build loyalty. Turn up the volume, we are about to learn how Spotify generates a personalization flywheel that drives extraordinary levels of customer engagement.

04

Design Strategy 2: Create a personalization flywheel to grow customer engagement

"We are accelerating our move from a one-size-fits-all, to a much more dynamic and open platform. A platform that will entertain, and inspire, and educate more than one billion users around the world."[1]

DANIEL EK, CEO, SPOTIFY

In 350 B.C., Aristotle wrote, "Music possesses the power of producing an effect on the character of the soul."[2] Clearly Aristotle was onto something as over 2,300 years later, Spotify has found a way to harness this power to the benefit of its many stakeholders. Just in case you thought this chapter was going to serve up your standard menu of insights around the value of tapping into consumer stated and derived preferences for the purposes of predictive analytics, well, rest assured we are about to raise the bar. Spotify takes the idea of personalization much further, creating a personalization "flywheel" fueling their ambitious growth strategy, which we will visit a bit later.

Let's talk about personalization before we dive in too deep. When we think about personalization in a digital-first world, it is defined as a "process of using individuals' own information to tailor the service and the transactional environment to improve the benefits accruing to them."[3] And of course, in the same breath as we mention personalization, we have to mention privacy. Because pursuing such a strategy is not without its risks. In fact, research suggests that "personalized ads can lead consumers to feel manipulated or threatened in their freedom of choice when perceiving a personalized ad inappropriately close to their preferences,"[4] eroding trust that can be difficult if not impossible to recover later.

Amplifying these experiences, revelations like the Cambridge Analytica scandal and a multitude of worrisome data breaches have created urgency in consumers to protect and secure their personal information.[5] As a result, regulatory bodies have defined clear consequences through policy making like the General Data Protection Regulation (GDPR), put in place by the EU on May 25, 2018 to introduce enforceable privacy and security laws.[6]

Not surprisingly given this new reality, a recent Edelman Trust Barometer Special Report found that 81 percent of consumers said they needed to trust a brand to buy from them.[7]

Now assuming I haven't scared you enough to skip ahead to the next chapter, personalization is here to stay, and in fact "90% of leading marketers say personalization significantly contributes to business profitability,"[8] and "61% of people expect brands to tailor experiences based on their preferences."[9] Because the fact of the matter is that we as consumers tend to speak out of both sides of our mouth when it comes to privacy.

The acceptability gap

A large research study reported in a *Humanities and Social Sciences Communications* article looked into the public's attitudes toward algorithmic personalization and the use of personal data in Germany, Great Britain, and the United States. Among the findings was the identification of something called "the acceptability gap." It exists because a large majority of respondents on average rated personalized services as more acceptable than the collection of personal information or data on themselves for the purposes of personalization. Said more simply: "I like receiving personalized services just as long as I don't have to share too much personal data about me." The study also found that "Despite this widespread concern, respondents reported taking few steps to protect their privacy online—although those who were more concerned about privacy were more likely to change privacy settings and use privacy tools."[10]

Personalization drives engagement

Regardless of this backdrop, pursuing a precise, value-based customer personalization strategy that uses data, including big data, can have a significant pay-off, as evidenced by a multitude of companies from Amazon to Netflix. Why? Because research has shown that done well, personalization can generate a significant amount of customer engagement, defined as:[11]

- Enthusiasm: an individual's strong level of excitement or zeal and interest in a brand;
- Attention: a customer's level of focus, consciously or sub-consciously;
- Absorption: a customer's level of concentration and inclination toward a brand;
- Interaction: customers exchanging the ideas, thoughts, and feelings about their experiences with the brand;
- Identification: customers tend to relate with some brands over others. This happens because they tend to relate themselves with brands, by matching their self-image with the brands.

Personalization that drives engagement goes far past standard recommendation engines, entering a world where the symbiotic flow of interactions and learning between the customer and the brand are deeply intertwined. Although privacy never ceases to matter, the idea of an acceptability gap does not even enter the consideration set. It gets trumped by something far more valuable.

But we are getting ahead of ourselves. Let us consider the music industry that spawned companies like Apple Music and Spotify and how streaming has become so dominant around the world in a relatively short timeframe.

The transition from "owning music" to "renting music" is what streaming music is all about. Today, 524 million listeners are streaming music worldwide at a growth rate of 24 percent, and now streaming accounts for 24 percent of total global recorded music revenue. This has clearly had a massive impact on an industry that in 1999 produced global revenues of $38 billion from the sale of physical products like CDs that were more convenient and provided better sound quality than cassettes or vinyl.[12] However, it was in June of that very year that the company Napster decided it was time to put the internet to use and launched their now famous song-sharing service that ripped tracks from CDs, sending the recording industry into a frenzy. Of course, the industry sued Napster and shut them down, but a new era in music delivery was born and the proverbial "genie was out of the bottle."

> **" Personalization that drives engagement goes far past standard recommendation engines.**

Spotify

Spotify was founded in Sweden in 2006 by Daniel Ek and Martin Lorentzon and at the time of writing boasts over 500 million monthly active users, including 205 million paying subscribers. The company operates in 183 countries, offers a catalogue of over 82 million songs, and employs a staff of approximately 8,300 across 15 offices.[13] Besides their phenomenal growth rate against some formidable competitors that include Apple, Amazon, and Google (could it get more formidable?), the company gained some notoriety among tech firms a few years ago for their Agile-based organization design that has been the inspiration for a host of companies, including our first best practice example from the previous chapter.

The experience

When you think about Spotify, consider that this is really a multi-sided platform business that is always ensuring it is balancing the needs of both users and artists, the creative talent that provides content in the way of music and other audio products such as podcasts. As Spotify personalization executive Oskar Stål said recently, "We're focused both on creators and listeners at the same time. So, we view this as a symbiotic relationship. One can't really succeed without the other."[14]

The company serves a wide demographic, but music streaming became a second reality for millennials from the very beginning. In fact, in 2017, Spotify collaborated with YPulse, a marketing research group that specializes in youth, to publish *Understanding People Through Music: Millennial Edition*. As Spotify noted on their landing page prior to downloading a copy of the most recent version of the study, "Millennials are literally soundtracking every moment of their lives. They actively stream music to help them get through the less desirable moments in their day, improve the more positive ones and even discover new things about their personality. 46% even stream audio as they go in and out of other social media apps."[15]

This is important to understand because, to their "heavy user," the service they deliver is not just a more convenient way to listen to music. As Spotify themselves promote, they provide the "soundtrack to your life." These customers do not just listen to music when the spirit moves them; music is embedded into their daily living as a "default setting" for perceiving the world around them.

I began hinting at this from the beginning of the chapter. Lest you think all streaming services are pretty much the same, since they all provide some degree of personalization and are offered for about the same $9.99 per month, that is where the similarities end. Let's walk through several of Spotify's more prominent features for their listeners, and then later we will get into the details of how they work.

The listener experience

There are two types of Spotify subscriptions: free and paid versions. An individual premium subscription is $9.99 per month in the US and there is a range of lower-cost student plans and higher-cost family plans depending on the market. The free subscription includes access to all of the same library of music and audio content as the paid version; however, the user can only play their music on shuffle and has to listen to advertisements. Free users cannot download their music for offline playing.

Everywhere, anywhere, any time

If you have an internet connection you have Spotify. Actually, even if you don't have an internet connection, if you are a premium customer you can download up to 10,000 songs to listen to offline. We have a cottage in the "middle of nowhere Nova Scotia" that uses a 3G network (yes, they are still around) and the sound quality is actually pretty amazing. In the city on our home Wi-Fi network, I have two other music streaming services that I pay for: Pandora and Apple. Only Spotify allows me to play through every type of listening device in the house: my iPhone, my laptop, our three Google Home speakers and our Sonos speakers. If my coffee mug had a Wi-Fi connection, I suspect it would play through that as well. This is all thanks to a feature introduced in 2013 called Spotify Connect that allows you to play the catalogue of music over virtually any Wi-Fi-compatible audio product.

But this is just the warm-up. Let's focus on how Spotify makes this concept of a "personalization flywheel" a reality.

Rethinking personalization

First of all, it is important to understand that although the interface is the same for every user, Spotify doesn't deliver one single user experience, it delivers a unique experience to *each* of its more than 500+ million monthly subscribers. Although Spotify curates personalized playlists from songs you have selected or liked, their approach to personalization techniques such as collaborative filtering is far more sophisticated. As the user continues to stream, "like," and save tracks, the recommendation algorithm learns their preferences and adds content that it predicts they will enjoy. The more the user interacts with the app, and reacts to the tracks recommended, the more accurate the algorithm becomes. This builds a virtuous cycle between the user and Spotify. The more content I stream, the better Spotify gets to know my preferences, and hence the more I stream, and the first of a series of virtuous flywheels begins to turn.

To keep the cycle spinning, Spotify leverages the five dimensions of engagement by inviting the user to become co-creator of their personalized experience. Spotify sees its customers as both listeners of the service and producers of playlists, and with that comes even more data to drive even greater personalization. This is what turns a virtuous cycle into an actual flywheel that gets even more powerful over time and generates same-side and cross-side network effects, which we will discuss later.

The minute a user subscribes to the service, Spotify creates a "data double" of that user that effectively places them into categories that filter their experience with various media content. The goal is less about predicting the future and more about driving engagement with the app, and with it, keeping the user absorbed, retained, and continuing to stream the "soundtrack to your life." To achieve this, Spotify's recommendation algorithm considers behavioral data such as how long a user plays a song for, adds it to a playlist, or skips it. Without even necessarily "liking" a song or podcast, the algorithm is silently learning about the user's tastes and preferences from their behaviors.

In 2014, a group of MIT Media Lab engineers decided to build on Pandora's Music Genome Project that analyzed a song like a DNA sequence, tagging each "gene" in terms of its tempo, timber of the singer's voice, and what instruments were played.[16] The Media Lab team instead broke down music into a series of "events." This meta-data was similar to a "gene" but

> 66 *Spotify leverages the five dimensions of engagement by inviting the user to become co-creator of their personalized experience.*

captured things like a song's "danceability" as well as applying semantic analysis on any digital discussion about the song from tweets to music reviews to better match a person's cultural tastes to the music content they would find most appealing. They formed a company called Echo Nest that Spotify acquired and incorporated into their personalization team. Going forward, this allowed Spotify to not just make suggestions based on melodic or genre preferences but also to factor in a socio-cultural matching. If a subscriber demonstrated an affection for songs associated with heavy metal, the Echo Nest algorithm would predict that not only would they like a song with similar musical elements but also songs that their heavy metal peers were discussing via social media and online blogs.[17] All of the data is then used to construct a user's "taste profile"—their "data double" mentioned earlier—that is weighted based on this combination of preferred music "events," demonstrated content preferences, and probabilistic predictions from the social sphere of data that can be associated. This taste profile becomes more refined as the subscriber interacts with the app.

To increase the algorithm's accuracy even further, Spotify knows that a person's context affects listening patterns. When I'm writing, I am less likely to turn up the volume on Metallica, and in fact, if I did, it would be an outlier as the truth is, my metal days are mostly behind me at this point. Using a method to determine "listening modes," Spotify uses "big data and clustering algorithms to figure out how the totality of music we consume breaks down into clusters of artists."[18] As a result, they are able to personalize the experience based on both aural consistency and cultural consistency that are the sum of many interests and preferences to provide a more holistic view of the user to base their recommendations on.

When you open the app, it is easy to find playlists such as *Time Capsule*, a list of songs curated by Spotify that will remind you of previous life experiences, or *Release Radar*, a playlist of both artists you follow but also new singles picked for you from their algorithm. *Podcasts & Shows* queues up podcasts they predict you will find interesting. The more precise the recommendations, the more absorption and engagement with the "soundtrack to your life."

> I use [Spotify] every single day, to listen to music when I'm getting ready in the morning on my phone, when I'm going places in my headphones, on my computer when I'm doing homework—it's great—we have a very loving, mutual relationship.[19]

Raising the bar

Spotify users know that every Monday they receive their *Discover Weekly* playlist. This is a playlist based on a hybrid recommender system that draws data from the events, cultural, and contextual indicators referenced above, but also factors in crowdsourcing from other users' playlists. *Discover Weekly* was developed by two Spotify engineers during their "spare hack time." It began life as an internal feature that only Spotify employees had access to but gained popularity quickly so that senior leaders eventually took notice and realized this could be a feature worth launching.[20]

Customer feedback to the playlist was immediately positive and quickly gained traction.[21] *Discover Weekly* works at an enormous scale given the user base of listeners. It takes your taste profile and the specific songs you listen to, then it looks for other playlists where that combination of the same songs is included. Spotify uses deep learning and neural nets to identify patterns in huge data sets that improve the probability that the listener will like the playlist it assembles.

Once it has been trained on enough data about other users' playlists, the algorithm constructs your personalized *Discover Weekly* playlist that includes songs that are similar to your taste profile, remembering that taste profiles are generated based on music preferences, cultural similarity, and mood context. As one Spotify user admitted, "Sometimes I feel like Spotify knows me better than I know myself."[22]

And in the spirit of Oskar Stål's previous statement around matching artists to listeners, *Discover Weekly* becomes a channel for a relatively unknown artist to reach a subscriber who may never have have learned about them otherwise.

Spotify has playlists that are sponsored by partners and others based on genre, mood, or time of day. You can turn a playlist into a station and the algorithm kicks in to add songs that fit with your taste profile. Again, the goal is to engage users as both listeners and creators.

From listening to creating

With an abundance of content to draw on, users create their own playlists and are able to either keep them private or share them with friends. Similarly, they can follow friends on Spotify and listen to the same playlist together as a group. A user can invite collaborators to create shared playlists and listen to the same playlist simultaneously. There are Spotify users with hundreds of playlists and when the user becomes a producer—basically a DJ of their own musical experience—then Spotify has become more than a streaming service, it has become a form of social expression that exemplifies the fifth dimension of engagement: identification.

Researcher Ignacio Siles published a paper that explored the relationship between Spotify "heavy users" and affect theory, the idea that feelings and emotions are the primary motives for human behavior, with people desiring to maximize their positive feelings and minimize their negative ones.[23] His findings included three insights about the process of creating playlists that reinforce this dimension of identification but go even further.

First, users often saw the process of creating and sharing playlists as a ritual that created meaning for them individually and contributed to important social constructs: "I'm in charge of music at home... I try to create an environment so [that everyone] is tuned, on the same page."[24]

Second, users took enormous care and pride in the playlists they produced as it said something important about them: "I like to be as creative as I can because I believe music represents a lot of one's personality."[25] Music has often been described as a "technology of the self," allowing us to consider our various identities as inspired by the moods and emotions it evokes. In her book *Music in Everyday Life*, author Tia DeNora suggests that "music can be used as a technology for spinning the apparently continuous tale of who one is."[26]

Finally, Siles suggests that "playlists can enable the formation of 'intimate publics' when a fantasy of social belonging emerges through the moods and emotions they evoke."[27] Many of his subjects commented on the number of followers their publicly shared playlists had attracted and how Spotify had assisted them in their creation through aspects like the "similar" feature, which added a song they had not listened to but was consistent with the mood and emotions they were attempting to produce.[28]

Not all Spotify users would fall into this category; however, in our previous research into customer ownership, it didn't take an enormous number of customers with this level of commitment to a brand to generate significant impact in terms of retention and advocacy. Customer owners proactively promote the brand to friends and family and Spotify's social sharing features make this a natural extension of the experience.

> " Spotify has become more than a streaming service, it has become a form of social expression that exemplifies the fifth dimension of engagement: identification.

Same-side network effects

This concept, from the world of platform strategy, forms the final piece in the Spotify listener experience puzzle. It states that the value of a platform increases when the number of users increases. For example, Facebook is valuable in part because so many people that I would like to connect with have adopted the platform as well. When I asked one Spotify user, our neighbor next door in her second year of law school, why she left her previous streaming service for Spotify, she didn't hesitate. "Everyone I knew had it." Besides the cost advantage that the student pricing afforded her, it made it easier for her to listen to the same playlist with friends, to share songs through any social media app, and to poke fun at her roommate's surprising obsession with ABBA. Spotify goes to enormous lengths to make it easy to invite friends to listen together, create a shared playlist, and share a song with a non-subscriber that by default encourages them to download the free app to hear the whole track. As Spotify likes to say, "the head-bopping never stops."[29]

Spotify for Artists

Until now, we have been talking about user engagement and how Spotify seeks to personalize the experience for every single subscriber. But that is only one half of the story. Spotify's mission is:

> To unlock the potential of human creativity—by giving a million creative artists the opportunity to live off their art and billions of fans the opportunity to enjoy and be inspired by it. [30]

Note that their mission statement doesn't start with the listeners, it starts with artists. To manage this balancing act between listeners and artists, in December of 2013 Spotify launched *Spotify for Artists* to provide the other side of the platform with a way for artists to better understand how to grow their audience and increase their income on Spotify. The site provides a feature-rich portal for both artists and their production teams to track their streaming performance on the app and drill into the details of their listeners. An artist with a growing list of monthly listeners can learn how their volume is growing or declining and where they are located. The same data is available for their followers, which includes demographic breakdowns.

At the highest level, each quarter Spotify publishes their *Fan Study from Spotify for Artists*, "a quarterly exploration into fandom around the world.

With each edition, we analyze millions of data points and uncover new insights to help your team develop the fanbase you need to reach your goals."[31]

Profile customization tools help an artist stand out from the crowd and new creative tools allow artists to add 3D graphics, video, and mixed media to their songs when they are played rather than just the static album cover artwork. The result is better brand awareness for the artist, feedback on what material resonates and what doesn't, and what geographies might represent the best opportunities for touring. As we said with the importance of brand authenticity, *Spotify for Artists* allows the performer's followers to get beyond the music to the artist's life story.

Artists can also submit a song for playlisting. If their pitch is selected, it will be heard by potentially millions of users. And it isn't just for the Dua Lipa's of the world—more than 150,000 artists were playlisted for the first time across 2020 and 2021.[32]

ARTIST INTERVIEW: CAPITOL RECORDS RECORDING ARTIST: EVAN GIIA

Brooklyn-based artist Evan Giia has over 1.8 million monthly listeners on Spotify. Her breakout single "Westworld" and self-directed video propelled her to number one on Hype Machine. A classically trained opera singer who graduated from the Berklee College of Music, she has performed at festivals including Coachella, Firefly, and Bonnaroo.

What do you like about Spotify for Artists?

I love the main page. I love the "Artist Pick" feature, which allows me to pick the song that I would like my fans to listen to that week and I can write a little blurb about it. I love the visual aspects. I can put visualizers behind my songs. So, while my fans are listening, my mini music video is playing. That part of my music is very important to me, I want people to be able to visualize my music.

The Spotify for Artists app is my favorite feature. It is very easy to use and insightful. For example, "Rabbit Hole," my new single, was just released. Every time someone streams the song, my phone vibrates. It's very addicting to watch the numbers climbing, it feels very good as an artist. And then every week I get to see the data from the last seven days. It'll show me how many listeners are online, how many times the song was streamed, and how many followers I gained.

I also find the graphing very helpful. My top song, "Westworld," peaks on the graph every Saturday. This helps me see that people are listening to it on the weekends. It allows me to understand where they are, what they like to do, when they listen.

Does it inform what you write in terms of new music?

It does. For example, after seeing the Spotify for Artists data on my song, "Westworld," it was clear we needed another college party song because it was working in that market. We then hone our skills in that area and hope to write another song in that world. Feedback from my listeners absolutely influences what I write and produce.

How do Spotify playlists help you build a fan base?

I love the editorial playlisting. It's tough to get in those playlists, but it really, really works. You can see the results on the Spotify for Artists backend platform. It'll show you a little tick when your song gets added to a Spotify editorial playlist. Once your song is added you can see your followers go up, page views go up, listeners go up. It is a direct correlation to growth.

How does the financial model work for an artist at your stage in your career?

I would definitely say the main value of Spotify for me is as a promotional tool. The "monthly listeners" portion, which is right under the artist's name, is the biggest and most important part because it shows brands, opportunities, interviewers, live show promoters etc. that I have a following. They see the numbers and go, "Wow! OK, over a million monthly listeners? She's legit."

So, it's very important for promotion and also bringing people to shows. Once they find me on Spotify, they are so much more likely to buy my tickets or follow me on my social media platforms.

What could be improved?

Currently, the five songs that are listed at the top of an artist's profile are the artist's five most streamed songs. But instead of most streamed, I would love for them to be artist curated. I wish I could pick the five songs that are featured because there are some songs in my catalogue that I feel represent my brand more and I want them to get their time to shine.

Spotify Advertising

In 2021, Spotify changed the name of their advertising division from *Spotify for Brands* to *Spotify Advertising* to appeal to small to medium-size companies as well as large brands like McDonald's and Coca-Cola. In their Q1 2022 earnings report, Spotify announced their "largest Q1 ever for ad-supported revenue (11% of total revenue)."[33] This was important news for the third leg of their business model and relevant for their future growth.

The streaming service offers three advertising pillars: 1) branded playlists, 2) paid ads, and 3) podcasting. A study by PwC reported that 2021 podcast advertising revenues would almost triple by 2024 to over $4 billion.[34] In 2020, Spotify finally passed Apple as the "most commonly used apps for listening to podcasts among podcast listeners in the United States" at 25 percent and 20 percent respectively. To widen their lead even further, the company acquired Megaphone, a leading podcast advertising and publishing platform, and has gotten creative with the audio experience with innovations like Video Podcasts and Music + Talk. It is continuing to introduce content with the acquisition of website and podcasting network The Ringer and exclusive partnerships with some of the world's most influential voices, including a controversial exclusive contract with commentator and podcaster Joe Rogan.

Spotify Ad Studio

Spotify provides its ad developers with a broad array of self-service tools to design, record, and share audio and video ads. What is different from other ad models is both the design of the ad and the context of the user. If the ad is placed in a playlist that has evoked a set of emotions in the listener, it has the potential to leverage that emotion and positively influence that listener's behavior. For example, "Pizza Hut ran an audio-first campaign to keep delivery services top of mind for pizza lovers listening on Spotify. The QSR brand targeted their core audience segments, including Gen Zs, families, and people interested in gaming, TV shows, or sport."[35]

Finally, in early 2022, Spotify introduced the *Spotify Audience Network*, an audio-first marketplace that connects advertisers with listeners using audience-based targeting tools, which has been well timed with the addition of new third-party podcast publishers, effectively tripling their podcast inventory.[36]

The details

As sophisticated as Spotify's personalization technologies are, they don't ignore the influence of human curation on playlist recommendations. Algotorial is a term they invented that speaks to the merging of human editors with machine learning algorithms to create playlists that do more than just provide a "fix" in the moment. But to do this at scale while leveraging common features and avoiding duplication requires some tight organization. For Spotify, this is based on a three-tiered architecture that starts with data.

1 Data

There are three types of data that Spotify includes at this level of the architecture. *Use data* is what they are able to discern from what their users listen to, the playlists they typically play or create, or stations or podcasts they select. *Content data* is data Spotify will receive from the internet or data from their suppliers. Finally, there are the *audio profiles* of a song or podcast. At the top of the data hierarchy at Spotify is something called "Golden Datasets," which is stored in an open-source tool called "Backstage." This is the most strategic data that they want to have easily accessible and where high data quality is paramount. They have also invested in reusable user interface designs that make it easy for Spotify developers to build, test, and execute interactions without reinventing the wheel. This is called "client instrumentation" and includes predefined links between various events that also inform their downstream recommendation algorithms.

2 Shared models

At this level, Spotify's developers have access to commonly used machine learning models for a variety of use cases, like clustering algorithms that may take 20 artists and reveal their similarities. Spotify has a massive digitally mapped file structure created from collaborative filtering. It is like an uber "taste profile" but for all of the music they publish that forms clusters of artists.

3 Features

Finally, at the top of the architecture are the features themselves, many of which we have discussed earlier, like your *Start Page* or *Discover Weekly*. All of these features draw on the data and shared models available to the developers but applied as required by each individual feature. For example, in a typical feedback loop, a feature may consider the intent: Is this playlist for a party or a workout? How about the *context*? Is the user streaming on their phone or on their laptop? Is it early in the morning or 10 o'clock on a Saturday evening? And finally, what does your taste profile tell Spotify about your preferences? From this comes a set of five or more tracks they believe you will find appealing, and they record your interactions. Do you listen to them? Skip them after a few seconds? And depending on the use case, is it about discovery of new artists or is it about relaxing with familiar songs? The outcomes provide updated training to the algorithm, so it does a better job next time.

Spotify did some research to understand what really informs a strong recommendation. Not surprisingly, relevance was the most important attribute while popularity mattered much less than expected. Diversity of content was also quite important, and this data provided Spotify with a clue as to how to create the balance between the familiar and the new to deliver on their brand promise of the "soundtrack to your life." As Oskar Stål has stated:

> We're not just optimizing for the current moment. We're not optimizing for the thing that is most likely to get clicked… or streamed or optimizing for just driving more listening time in the moment. Instead, we want a healthy journey for a lifetime of fulfilling content.[37]

Spotify wants to ensure that by focusing beyond the next logical "click" and getting that balance right, you will see Spotify as a membership rather than just a subscription service that you continue to renew each month. For example, they may inspire the user who joined Spotify to get them through their morning workout to also turn to the service while studying. This is about balancing your wants (immediate rewards—next) and your needs (delayed rewards—future) as you traverse your "journey of discovery" and how Spotify can help you incorporate a more satisfying "content diet."[38]

> ❝ *Spotify did some research to understand what really informs a strong recommendation. Not surprisingly, relevance was the most important attribute while popularity mattered much less than expected.*

To accomplish this level of personalization, Spotify applies a technique called "reinforcement learning."

Reinforcement learning

This involves employing contextual bandits, which is a machine learning algorithm that "can test out different actions and automatically learn which one has the most rewarding outcome for a given situation."[39] At Spotify, this involves maximizing the "future accumulative rewards"[40] for the listener as well as something we have already learned about from behavioral science, *nudging*, that tries to optimize that more satisfying "content diet." To do this, they take note of users that over time are self-navigating their journeys, expanding their *taste profile* and listening to more diverse and relevant content. They also apply machine learning to predict customer satisfaction by modeling "state changes" for their users from which they build *survival models*. These are scenarios that predict probabilities of how users will move between various states, such as what they are listening to and when, or if they have upgraded to Premium, or downgraded to Free—any number of state changes.

Given the amount of data from more than 500+ million users, these probabilities become quite accurate. This allows them to create a model that defines the user's relationship with their audio content. So, are you extremely satisfied listening to diverse content with high levels of frequency, or are you just playing your favorites at specific times of day or on a weekend evening? This leads to the development of an encoder that includes the unique aspects of the user's current state and then generates learning into a decoder that tracks the effectiveness of Spotify's resultant recommendations to "nudge" the user into new, more satisfying (long-term) states.[41] But prior to actually making recommendations, Spotify generates a simulator that leverages their scale from millions of similar users to run scenarios of recommendation mixes that predict how the user will respond. Depending on the results, they retrain the algorithm against the simulator over and over until they land on the combination of recommendations which is most likely to achieve greater user satisfaction.[42] Finally, they take these algorithms and conduct A/B tests with real users to compare algorithms (or agents) using more effective versus less effective simulators to improve the performance of the simulators themselves over time.

This more holistic approach to machine learning goes far past your "next likely click" to guiding you along your "journey of discovery," which creates more relevant and diverse audio. A 2019 research paper highlights the value of reinforcement learning at Spotify:

> Our findings reinforce the insight that when we optimize for a metric of user satisfaction, it is important to go beyond clicks. By focusing on the post-click experience, we can capture the "intent" of the content, as shown with "genre" affinity being the most significant factor in impacting the bandit algorithm. We are also able to capture that users are different regarding how they consume content, as we see that "playlist affinity" is often the second most significant factor. Using clicks alone cannot surface these important components when measuring satisfaction.[43]

The concept of a personalization flywheel now becomes more amplified by providing these insights to content creators—artists, podcasters, and third-party app developers—to create more meaningful content that serves all members of the Spotify ecosystem. As Spotify's VP of Engineering and Head of Machine Learning, Tony Jebara, has stated: "That's really an exciting next frontier, machine learning that's beyond just clicks and clickbait and going after the long term."[44]

The heart of the matter

Like Lemonade, understanding how Spotify separates from the pack in terms of personalization requires us to dig into their business model more deeply, which when your direct competitors include Amazon, Apple, and Google, needs to be about as robust as they come because you aren't just fighting them as alternative streaming services; each one could provide product/service bundles that include their streaming service at a loss if they wanted to. Hence the race to attract and retain users is really a sprint and though 500+ million users seems like a lot, in terms of the global addressable market with their device ubiquity afforded by *Spotify Connect* in hand, there is a lot more room for growth.

Audio-first strategy

A recent *Harvard Business Review* case study stated, "Spotify viewed podcasts as a particularly lucrative format because it did not have to pay royalties for streams and could profit off of inserted ads."[45] When interviewed by CNBC in February 2022, CEO Daniel Ek commented, "We've really expanded the opportunity also on the top line for the company so we're now talking publicly about getting to over 50 million creators of this company and over a billion users and I feel more confident than ever with our audio first strategy that we will get there."[46] Let's consider the digital assets that Spotify have linked together that may provide a glimpse into what may give Mr. Ek such confidence.

Advanced personalization

Spotify's commitment to personalization demonstrates that as their customers use the service more and receive even more relevant and diverse music and podcast recommendations, greater use of social sharing, conversion to premium subscriptions, and creation and sharing of their own playlists will follow in greater numbers.

Spotify Connect

There are now partnerships with over 2,000[47] hardware companies, suggesting Spotify's market prediction of 1 billion users is hardly aspirational.

Spotify Ad Studio

As we discussed earlier, the growth in advertising—in part driven by the company's audio-first strategy—does not appear to be slowing down. The simplicity and pricing model of the Ad Studio portal to create and publish effective audio and video ads reduces any friction that might exist to add this channel for both small businesses and large brands. Also, Spotify shared, "In the coming weeks, we'll be introducing podcast ad buying to Spotify Ad Studio, our easy-to-use, self-serve channel. We're starting in the US with plans to expand to more markets in the future."[48]

> " *We're now talking publicly about getting to over 50 million creators of this company and over a billion users.*

Streaming Ad Insertion (SAI) and the Spotify Audience Network

If there was icing to add to this cake, then the combination of the Streaming Ad Insertion technology with the Spotify Audience Network represents a lot of butter cream. Remember, the Spotify Audience Network is a first-of-its-kind audio advertising marketplace which will give advertisers the ability to reach Spotify's audience of hundreds of millions of listeners—at scale—both on and off Spotify.[49] When added to the Spotify Ad Studio above, consider the additional advertising revenue this should generate.

The personalization flywheel

As we have dug into the details, I think we can agree that what began as a Personalization Flywheel between listeners and artists has actually grown. Let's consider the concentric circles of direct and indirect network effects that these linked digital technologies are enabling:

- Users and users: As my law student neighbor said to me, "Everyone I know subscribes to Spotify." This is a classic same-side network effect. Basically, the more people that subscribe, the greater value there is to individual users who want to share and collaborate with others on the platform.

- Users and artists/podcasters: There is also a cross-side network effect at play in that the more listeners subscribe to Spotify either as free or paid subscribers, the greater likelihood there is that artists and podcasters will want to provide content and vice versa—the more artists and podcast content the user can access, the more value there is to the listener.

- Artists and artists: One way an artist increases their number of monthly followers is to collaborate with other artists within and across genres. The more artists that publish on the platform, the easier it becomes to reach like-minded fellow artists that would be interested in expanding their reach through a mutually beneficial collaboration.

- Personalization and engagement: As we have illustrated, as listeners use the platform, the better the algorithms become at providing more relevance and diversity in its recommendations. The better these recommendations, the greater engagement and commitment to the platform from users. Artists also benefit from learning about what elements of their music are generating greater *Monthly Listeners* and other data that can inform future content creation, but also generate other forms of monetization on and off Spotify.

- Users and advertisers: Much like Facebook and other social platforms, the more users, especially the more users that can be precisely targeted based on more than just demographics, but also from their musical tastes, podcast preferences, and other behavioral data, the greater the number of advertisers and the more personalized those ads can be, the greater the value provided to users *and* advertisers.

Now, as these five network effects grow, it becomes clear why achieving scale is so important. Beyond the competitive threat, the more data Spotify can collect, the more refined tools like collaborative filtering and reinforcement learning become. If there is a touchstone to which all of these virtuous cycles owe their origination, it is the core idea of providing the "soundtrack to your life" through machine learning and algotorial curation.

Business model: the Core Foundation

Spotify's business model begins with what they describe as the *Core Foundation* that we have been unpacking throughout this chapter, centered around music streaming. These include:

- Ubiquity: As we have said, Spotify distinguishes itself from competitors by the number of devices on which you can stream the service. This isn't just about convenience, it's also about growing engagement as the higher the engagement, the lower the likelihood of churn. In fact, 89 percent of Spotify premium subscribers use Spotify on multiple devices, up from 75 percent in 2018.[50]

- Personalization: This has been the focus of this chapter so its role in creating engagement is obvious. Spotify reports that more than 81 percent of listeners attribute personalization as the reason they stay with the service.[51]

- Freemium: This combination of free, ad-supported membership with well-placed "nudges" to upgrade to a paid premium subscription has been central to Spotify's success in scaling to over 500 million members, especially in new markets where they have displaced competitors.

Getting under the hood: the Spotify Machine

During their 2022 Investor Day presentation, Spotify executives revealed the next iteration of their business model that stands on the shoulders of this

Core Foundation in music streaming. What they refer to internally as the Spotify Machine.

The *Core Foundation* generates revenue through reoccurring subscriptions, advertising, and marketplace offerings to content providers. The music streaming business is supported by a very specific backend operating model based on the revenue share of a royalty pool that requires custom integrations to facilitate payment to labels, publishers, and artists. As discussed previously, Spotify expanded from music into podcasting through a series of acquisitions and exclusive partnerships with high-profile content creators. Podcasting represents a very different business model from music streaming, driven mostly by advertising and direct creator upload.

It begs an obvious question. With 500+ million customers, how could Spotify take this single-user experience, introduce new vertical offerings, but design the backend complexity inherent to each of them without exposing it to the customer? If you could solve this problem, and create a single-user experience that would provide access to additional audio and video content without changing apps, across the ubiquity of devices, how powerful would that be?

The answer: pretty powerful. Spotify's Chief R&D Officer Gustav Soderstrom explains:

> Our strategy to adopt a single consumer experience enables us to accelerate our entry into new verticals and formats. This allows us, and creators, to capitalize on a compounding user base—rather than several separate ones. Second, behind the scenes, our strategy is to build dedicated backends that serve separate industries, different business models and different creator groups. This enables us to power the world's biggest music creator stack, the world's biggest podcast creator stack, and soon, hopefully, the world's biggest audiobook creator stack.[52]

This is easier to say than do. For example, adding podcasts to the user experience is one thing, but when considering audiobooks, the differences for the user experience are significant. To address this, Spotify developed the *Adaptive User Experience*, which introduces specific features required for each vertical. For example, audiobooks may seem a lot like podcasts, but they aren't. They have chapters rather than episodes and as such, the listener will expect to hear them in order, rather than tune into the latest podcast

> **❝** Behind the scenes, our strategy is to build dedicated backends that serve separate industries, different business models and different creator groups.

episode.[53] This is just one of dozens of user interface designs that the *Adaptive User Experience* practices must address to optimize the user experience. But that is not the most important point to take away from this paragraph. The bigger point is this:

> Adding audiobooks to the single-user experience doesn't just add a new feature for the user. Given Spotify's subscriber base, it redefines the boundaries of the audiobooks industry.

Think about it. Spotify can take what today is a relatively small market of audiobook listeners paying à la carte and expose it to more than 500 million potential listeners. In addition, once *Discoverability* applies what they already know about their millions of users, they can recommend content with a high likelihood of conversion. Much of this to people who may never even have been exposed to audiobooks in the past.

Today, audiobooks command about 6–7 percent of the $140 billion global book market, but in more mature markets it is closer to 50 percent.[54] With one major player dominating the category, this appears to be an attractive opportunity to grow the industry and with it, Spotify's position. Even better, it has more attractive gross margins (approximately 40 percent), and as more users broaden their use of the service, engagement goes up, churn goes down, and annual revenue per user (ARPU) increases right along with customer lifetime value (CLV). As audiobook authors and publishers experience the exponential growth generated by the *Core Foundation* of *Ubiquity*, *Personalization*, and *Freemium*, the extent of their reach and data they will be provided with about the preferences and behaviors of millions of customers sets a new vertical flywheel in motion.

As Daniel Ek emphasized:

> We see the opportunity to continue to imagine and explore new verticals across our platform—within audio, but also beyond. And for each vertical, we will develop a unique set of software, services, and products and business models that's going to be tailored for that specific ecosystem. But again, all of these will live in one consumer experience.[55]

Vertical growth flywheel

We've looked at each of the players in Spotify's ecosystem, so how specifically does this "personalization flywheel" translate to their business model?

Spotify describes this as five steps that repeat themselves as new verticals are added:[56]

- Value proposition: As you would expect, it starts with attracting new customers and removing any friction to join by offering free subscriptions with its ad-supported model and then introducing different subscriber offerings once they have started using the service.

- User intake and engagement: Next, once you have started interacting with the service, be it music, podcasts, video podcasts, or audiobooks, *Discoverability* kicks in and that rich "content diet" set of recommendations based on the *Reinforcement Learning* and *Contextual Bandits* increases engagement, especially as the number of devices to access Spotify grows, increasing retention.

- Grow advertising: As the number of users grows in the vertical, this attracts more advertisers, simultaneously increasing ARPU.

- Subscription growth: With engagement growth comes higher conversions to premium subscriptions, including incrementally more multi-user accounts, expanding monetization opportunities for additional verticals as the subscriber base grows.

- Open à la carte: The fifth step literally takes the ceiling off of ARPU as it provides new paths for additional spending on "à la carte purchases" by subscribing to specific creators, or purchasing one-off offers specific to the vertical.

While the R&D team works behind the scenes to develop the backend business model for the next vertical, the design team applies *Adaptive User Experience,* so the user isn't learning a new way to interact with the service. Once it launches, the flywheel repeats itself with all participants in the ecosystem, growing monetization opportunities and, most importantly for Spotify, increasing CLV.

Customer lifetime value and the value economy

One of the things we advocate and assist our clients with is calculating customer lifetime value for each customer segment they choose to serve. Without it, it is virtually impossible to know how much investing in the customer experience will pay off for all of your stakeholders. Put simply, CLV is the financial benefit that a customer will generate over their lifetime of purchases, discounted to today's net present value (NPV) of those cashflows. There are many ways to calculate CLV and we will walk you through an example when we discuss how to build a business case in Chapter 13. But Spotify's version takes advantage of their machine learning competency, allowing them to extend CLV from a static number to a continuous learning framework driving several types of decision-making. As Tony Jebara, Spotify's Head of Machine Learning, has stated: "Our vision is to have it (CLV) be the primary driver of all of our business decisions as it allows those decisions to be automated, personalized, and scalable, something that wasn't possible before."[57]

Spotify can reliably predict retention, acquisition, and even a user's future survival rate on the service based on their "dynamic consumption behavior"[58] and other factors such as their location. They then append a financial value that each user represents to both Spotify and its creators, measuring gross profit contribution, unifying profitability, and lifetime into a single metric. With this insight they can forecast each user's lifetime value and run scenarios to predict the impact of changes that recommendations, additional content, or ad loads might have on increasing or decreasing CLV, with the goal of optimizing the right balance and increasing ARPU over time.[59]

This is consistent with the company's strategy of encouraging a "healthy content diet" over the customer life cycle. Daniel Ek extends this concept as the transition from the "attention economy" to the "value economy":

> It's important to note that this is not an attention economy—where content competes for the user's attention in the moment. It's actually something quite different. It is a value economy—where the content competes to give users the most long-term value, that makes them want to stick around for as long as possible.[60]

This level of rigor, made possible by their investment in machine learning, means Spotify can understand things like how much financial value a specific software feature roll-out contributed to the platform and their users.[61]

> " Our vision is to have it (CLV) be the primary driver of all of our business decisions as it allows those decisions to be automated, personalized, and scalable, something that wasn't possible before.

A new vision: the world's creator platform

Daniel Ek believes that over the next decade, the Spotify Machine has the potential to generate $100 billion in annual revenue, with a 40 percent gross margin and 20 percent operating margin,[62] rapidly transitioning to a platform that will "entertain, and inspire and educate more than one billion users"[63] by providing the infrastructure and resources enabling 50 million artists to become the world's creator platform.

Results

We have reviewed many of its more recent results over the course of this chapter, but it is worth mentioning that for Q1 2022, Spotify reported revenue growth of 24 percent and premium revenue grew 23 percent. But perhaps these results are best explained by some of their millions of customers:[64]

> "My best app on the phone. It's flawless, reliable, and quick. I am in love with Spotify—I use it every day. I highly recommend. They have such an amazing product. I use premium and it is worth every penny."—Asyem

> "I love that Spotify has a Discover Weekly and Daily Mix just for me and also being able to save so many albums! The website is very easy to handle, especially for someone that is not tech savvy."—Josephine

> "I love Spotify because it helps me listen to full albums. I have the free streaming service, but I am still able to stream music from my computer. When I use it via the app on my phone it will play an artist of your choice in shuffle mode. You are allowed six song skips. You will also have to listen to ads but that's not a big deal. You can create playlists and share them via several social platforms as well."—Vanessa

Summary

Selecting an example for this design strategy was challenging as there were several strong best practice companies to choose from. So many companies are applying machine learning to generate better recommendations and personalize the customer experience. But the way Spotify has thought about personalization, to go beyond the "next likely click" and short-term conversion optimization, to playing the long game around customer loyalty, is a best practice worth really understanding. Let us recall the five ways in which personalization can drive engagement:

- Enthusiasm: An individual's strong level of excitement or zeal and interest in a brand.
- Attention: A customer's level of focus, consciously or sub-consciously.
- Absorption: A customer's level of concentration and inclination toward a brand.
- Interaction: Customers exchanging the ideas, thoughts, and feelings about their experiences with the brand.
- Identification: Customers tend to relate with some brands over others. This happens because they tend to relate themselves to brands by matching their self-image with the brands.

With these as our criteria, Spotify tends to separate from the pack. Creating the "soundtrack to your life" requires a partnership between Spotify, the listener, and content providers. As hard as Spotify works to get it right, they aren't perfect, but the multitude of mechanisms, from playlist creation to song sharing and "liking" favorites, helps the listener receive greater value and Spotify a richer set of data to apply their technology assets. For artists, the data provided about their listeners and the real-time updates they receive immediately after a concert, as Evan Giia shared with me, is "addicting."

And let's not forget the unique emotional and psychological connection that music has in our lives and the depth which a company like Spotify can reach in terms of achieving the *Identification* level of engagement.

Now as the "Spotify Machine" extends the company's growth strategy to additional verticals using the same single user interface, we will have to watch and see how these investments in a truly digital-first experience will pay off for all of their ecosystem partners and stakeholders.

Key insights

- Effective personalization strategies consider how to drive all five elements of customer engagement.
- Putting in place regulatory-compliant policies that conform to privacy and security laws and standards is the point of entry when considering personalization strategies.

- Staff the role of a chief privacy officer.
- Consider how to amplify the level of personalization delivered by involving customers in co-creating experiences that are unique to them.
- Create a robust data-collection strategy that informs backend machine learning techniques.
- Develop machine learning algorithms that go beyond just predicting "next logical click" but consider how to predict and generate experiences that inform customer lifetime value.
- Build reusable UI frameworks to avoid duplication and ensure consistency in the customer experience.
- Ensure personalization technologies inform and integrate with other digital tools and human processes that serve customers better than competitors do.
- Where possible, apply machine learning to enhance customer lifetime value to set priorities around improvements to the customer experience.
- Consider looking beyond digital strategies that enhance attention to those that create more value for customers over time.

What's next?

This is a perfect set-up for our next strategy because the more an experience can be personalized, the easier it is to increase customer commitment by providing them with both choice and control, as exemplified by CEMEX Go.

05

Design Strategy 3: Strengthen customer commitment by providing choice and control

"The largest advantage that CEMEX has is alignment. If you provide hard evidence that what you are creating delivers value in the experience and reduces churn, you get a lot of momentum, a lot of excitement from senior leadership."[1]

JESUS CAVIEDES MONDRAGON, CHIEF COMMERCIAL OFFICER, CEMEX

The person who taught me the most about this design strategy was Maxine Clark, the founder and former Chief Executive Bear at Build-a-Bear Workshop (BABW). What Maxine put into approximately 2,800 square feet of retail space was a Disney-like experience that provided any eight- or nine-year-old child the opportunity to create their own new "best friend." Watching my own daughters go through the experience, from choosing the skin to selecting sounds and accessories, taught me firsthand the power of providing choice and control. I mean, what nine-year-old doesn't yearn to be in charge? This strategy gets to the core of our human desire for agency and autonomy.

We moved house recently and we tasked both girls with sorting through their possessions to give away toys and books that had served their purpose. They did a fine job of letting go of the many artifacts from childhood that would then find their way to the donation center. I wasn't surprised, however, to see the stuffed animals that they created at Build-a-Bear Workshop safely stored for moving to our new home.

Behavioral scientists call this the "Ikea effect" and it is evident when invested labor in the assembly or creation of a product leads to an inflated product valuation by the owner.[2] We feel greater emotional attachment to things we help create.

What the science around choice and control comes down to is what is often described as "consumer empowerment," which we will revisit later when we consider how Nike creates immersive experiences. It would be easier to simply acquiesce to the standard economic theory that surmises helping consumers choose what they want, when they want it, and on their own terms is obviously a benefit.[3] But in a digital-first world, it is not as simple as that. Sometimes when we are given too many choices, we find it overwhelming and simply close the browser and move on. Or we make one choice that seems relevant, but then it leads us to a second choice that felt like we were being baited to buy something we didn't want. Understanding the type, sequence, and number of choices you provide to customers really matters and may explain some of the cart abandonment or bounce metrics some companies experience.

Here is the good news. Recent research into the effect of channel integration on consumer empowerment in omni-channel retailing uncovered some important insights.[4] The researchers found:

- Consumer empowerment was positively related to consumer perceptions of channel integration: "Through channel integration, retailers eliminate the constraints and barriers in single-channel retailing, and no longer can control consumers for their own benefits. For example, when there are integrated prices between the online and offline channels, consumers are no longer constrained to shop in whichever channel has the lowest price. Also, when the natural borders between channels disappear, consumers have more freedom and choices in their shopping processes."

- Consumer empowerment had a positive effect on consumer satisfaction: "Although some researchers have argued that more consumer empowerment may lead to decision difficulty, choice paralysis, and confusion, our empirical results show that empowered consumers still had positive satisfaction and trust toward integrated retailers."

> " *Invested labor in the assembly or creation of a product leads to an inflated product valuation by the owner.*

- Consumer empowerment had a strong direct effect on consumer trust: "Empowered consumers have more control during the shopping process where they can conveniently gather information, reduce information asymmetry and uncertainty, and enhance their trust."

This makes sense for retail, and in the wake of the COVID-19 pandemic, understanding how to adapt your customer experience to reduce physical contact became an urgent requirement for stores and restaurants everywhere. But retailers were not the only businesses impacted. The construction industry, which has seen only 1 percent growth in productivity over the last two decades from digitization, is another sector defined by labor-intensive physical contact for employees and customers.[5] Could a digital-first experience provide an almost touchless experience while also positively influencing consumer empowerment through greater choice and control?

CEMEX Go

CEMEX, our best practice example of this design strategy, has literally set a new standard for delivering a touchless, digital experience that puts the customer in complete control of their journey. CEMEX is headquartered in Monterrey, Mexico. In 2022 it delivered $15.6 billion in sales from its four core businesses—cement, ready-mix concrete, aggregates, and urbanization solutions. With more than 46,000 employees and trade relationships with 96 nations, it is one of the world's top traders of cement and clinker.

In 2017, CEMEX launched CEMEX Go, a multi-device offering that provides a seamless experience for order placement, live tracking of deliveries, and managing invoices and payments.

The experience

The company's commitment to customer centricity drove their effort to digitize the commercial business in 2016, which would become CEMEX Go, to provide a seamless digital-first solution that would both transform the industry and deliver a significantly superior customer experience while optimizing internal processes.

As he shared with us at the beginning of our interview, Homero Reséndez, CEMEX's Vice President of Digital Enablement, elaborated on this point: "One thing that I think is very important is that we had a clear command from our CEO and executive committee. One of the first company priorities was customer centricity and a lot of changes were made in our processes, starting with the digital transformation of the commercial business."

Obviously, CEMEX could not foresee how advantageous providing a touchless experience would become given the coming pandemic. But having it in place proved clearly advantageous. Let's take a quick tour of how it works before we get into the details of how they got there.

CEMEX Go—the industry's first integrated digital solution

STEP 1: PREPARING TO BUY

After becoming a customer and registering via either a tablet or mobile device, the customer can manage job sites and delivery locations in real time to improve visibility and accuracy of places where CEMEX will be delivering to their construction projects. The complete list of current contracts and quotations is easily viewed and can be filtered by job site to see detailed information for things such as open volumes, products, prices, and payment terms, data which the customer can choose to view and filter. The purchase order integration feature means information is directly updated into CEMEX's backend systems, making the placement of future orders or reconciliations easier and faster.

STEP 2: PLACING ORDERS

By visiting the online order and product catalogue the customer can select the type of product they want to buy—ready-mix, cement, or multi-products—and the delivery mode required. Most customers order ready-mix (delivered by trucks ready for pouring ready-mix concrete) and in that case, they can specify type of concrete, quantity, requested date, frequency of deliveries, and any other relevant information such as security requirements or site access conditions. Once the order is complete, the customer receives confirmation. To be clear, the customer still has not talked to a single CEMEX representative about their order.

STEP 3: MANAGE DELIVERY AND FULFILLMENT

CEMEX Go allows the customer to then track the status of their orders and deliveries either via the web using their laptop or on mobile devices such as a phone, tablet, or even a smartwatch. A ready-mix customer can see the delivery and pouring speeds to ensure seamless coordination between CEMEX

FIGURE 5.1 CEMEX screenshot

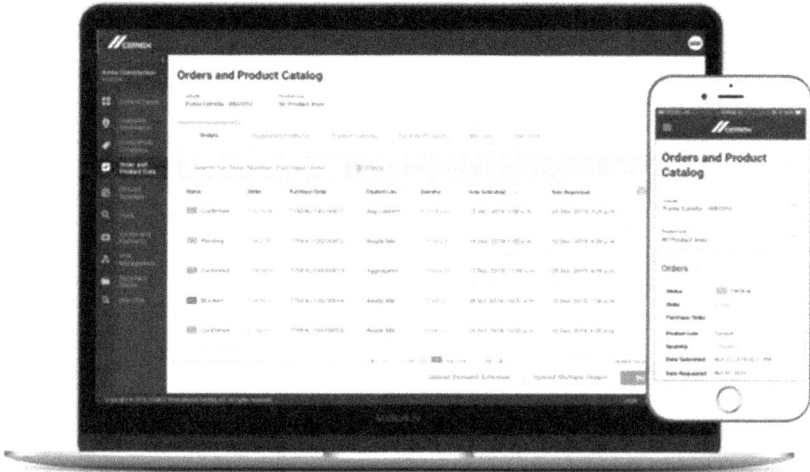

and the job site supervisor. They can also track the truck waiting time and compare their pour planning against the final outcome. This is an enormous improvement in productivity because every minute a truck is not delivering ready-mix is a minute it isn't creating value, and given conditions on construction sites, getting these delivery schedules right can be challenging. However, with CEMEX Go, the customer can manage order changes such as adding or reducing order quantity, or requesting to put the order on hold and resume it in real time. (Recall how we talked about "pause and resume" functionality previously.) The customer can do all of this digitally without the need to call a dispatcher or the service center and the CEMEX bot can usually handle any additional customer questions about their order. Finally, CEMEX Go also provides the customer with electronic proof of delivery to notify CEMEX that the customer received the product and the delivery was a success.

The other side of the same coin, however, is the driver experience. Ask any truck driver how much time they spend just trying to find the right entrance to a site, or who to contact when they arrive, or how they decipher the handwritten scrawl on a work order around what time they need to arrive by, and you will have a long conversation. CEMEX Go changes the driver experience as much as it changes the customer experience. Everything is digital and triggered safely by alerts when the truck is stopped. This includes making it easy (and touchless) for both customers and drivers by utilizing scanning and

FIGURE 5.2 CEMEX bot

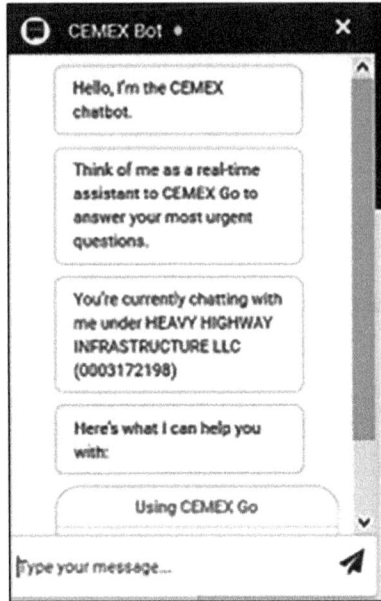

e-signatures to confirm delivery at the site. Homero Reséndez explains. "We are applying data science to improve the experience for our drivers as well. Our driver mobile app has a lot of capabilities, such as measuring the different sensors from the truck, tracking their speed and location, as well as some features designed to minimize accidents."

Jesus Caviedes Mondragon, CEMEX's Global Head of the commercial business, emphasizes the importance of the driver experience:

> Our drivers have embraced CEMEX Go. They play such an important role in the experience and now with the paperless initiative it greatly simplifies things

> ❝ We are applying data science to improve the experience for our drivers as well. Our driver mobile app has a lot of capabilities, such as measuring the different sensors from the truck, tracking their speed and location, as well as some features designed to minimize accidents.

FIGURE 5.3　CEMEX Go—e-signature

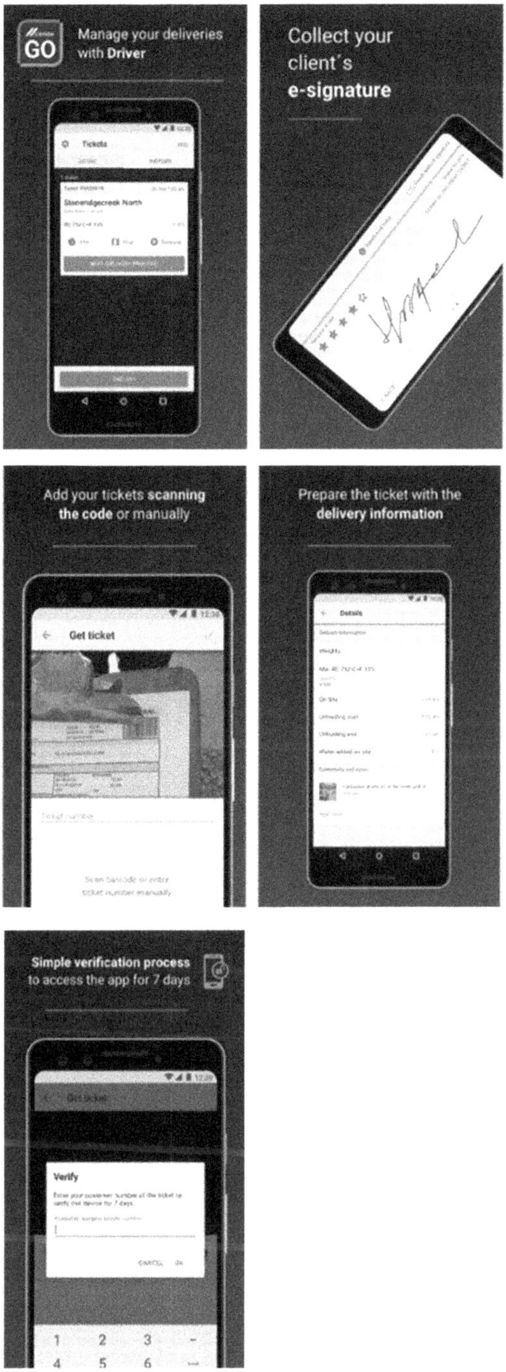

for them. They have more visibility on their round trips. They can review their tickets and manage their overtime, and in countries where overtime is not allowed, this provides a level of compliance that is required.

STEP 4: MAKE PAYMENTS AND REVIEW TRANSACTIONS

Finally, for invoicing and payments, CEMEX has developed a single source of information so the customer can review real-time credit limits and balance data to get a complete overview of all of their invoices and the documents related to them. By visiting the document section, they can review their invoices, credit and debit notes, and payments. Imagine the amount of paperwork associated with any bill of materials on a large construction project, all of which needs to be stored and itemized for budgeting purposes but also for passing inspections. The CEMEX Go dashboard can be customized to include any additional information the customer might need, such as documents relating to contracts or purchase orders linked to invoices. CEMEX Go also allows the customer to make advance or online payments, with an email confirmation sent to the customer.

The CEMEX Go platform is supported with a learning hub, especially helpful for new customers as it addresses every step in the process with extensive online and offline instructional tutorials.

What makes this case example so compelling is not just CEMEX's innovation in their industry, but the fact that they executed CEMEX Go globally.

FIGURE 5.4 CEMEX Go dashboard

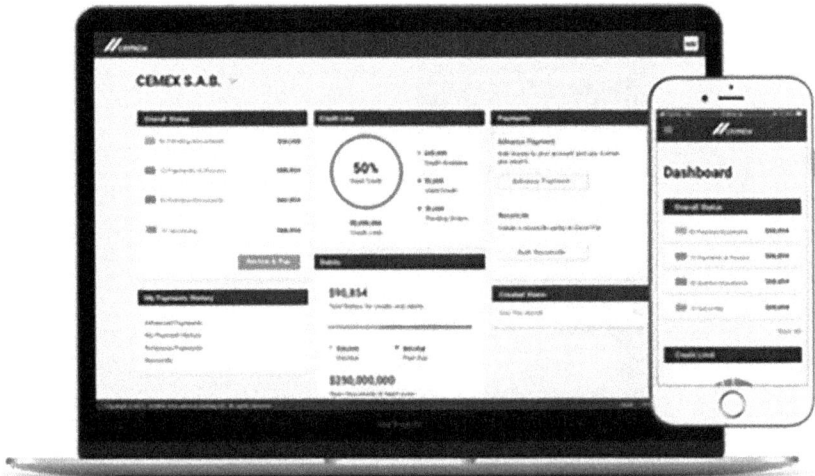

Just consider the implications for design of the user interface from language set to language set. CEMEX's Head of UX and Product Design, Jonathan Holden Hernández, explains:

> It's one thing to design one web or mobile application for one country but when you go globally you have to deal with more than translation challenges. For example, the German language has longer words, so we needed to redesign the site navigation to accommodate for that. In Israel, their whole language goes from right to left. It is important not to underestimate the task of localization for each country.

Let's go behind the scenes to uncover the details that have made CEMEX Go the new standard for customer experience in the construction industry.

The details

CEMEX applied a variety of tools and approaches to include the customer in the design of the solution in combination with innovations in technology. Their eventual competency in Lean and Agile methods served as a strong foundation as they iterated prototype after prototype to test and learn with customers. But the transition from "waterfall-based" software development to Agile project management is challenging for any IT group. Several tools helped the designers focus on customer pain points, including journey mapping that identified both challenges customers were having and areas that would serve to differentiate CEMEX from competitors. While developing CEMEX Go, however, CEMEX departed from the traditional Agile method of developing "minimal viable products" as this approach did not support their goals. Eventually they landed on the concept of testing a "minimal lovable experience." Homero Reséndez explains why:

> We eventually started calling protypes of CEMEX Go "minimum lovable experiences" because we wanted them to give us feedback about both the digital and analog experience since what we were delivering was truly omni-channel and we needed to ensure that our customers were really satisfied with the changes we were testing. We were working to exceed their expectations, not just meet them.

> *Eventually they landed on the concept of testing a "minimal lovable experience."*

Their approach followed three stages:

- Stage 1: Identification of the latest customer relationship and technology trends with the goal of keeping CEMEX at the forefront of the industry as the customer's preferred supplier. An internal team was chartered along with other external stakeholders that included customers, consultants, and academic experts to better understand cutting-edge digital technologies and practices from other industries. This is a standard CEMEX practice. A decade earlier when CEMEX decided to provide a service guarantee to ready-mix customers in Mexico City, they didn't benchmark other cement companies; they studied US taxi and courier companies to better understand how they managed real-time routing through busy urban centers. Jesus Caviedes Mondragon emphasizes how important this was at the beginning but also as part of their ongoing continuous improvement effort:

  > We started doing benchmarking based on the functionality we wanted to add to CEMEX Go. We looked outside of our industry quite honestly. For example, with respect to onboarding of customers, we went to one of the world's largest banks that had the highest adoption rate of onboarding and retaining new clients to understand how they did it. In fact, next week I'm visiting American Express and DHL just to understand their best practices with respect to how they manage their service centers.

- Stage 2: Understanding the problem included listening to the voice of the customer through dozens of interviews and co-creation design sessions. They applied design thinking tools including empathy maps, customer journey maps, and service blueprints, three tools we will describe in Chapter 14, to reveal both the problems customers faced and the touchpoints in the journey where the interaction with the customer could exceed their expectations with digital solutions. Jonathan Holden Hernández elaborated on the value of prototype testing:

  > We started using many new tools in addition to journey mapping, including wireframing for protypes and tools for high-fidelity prototypes, before developing software in order to show these potential solutions to customers to validate if they would actually eliminate the pain points that were described in the customer journey maps.

- This led to a final "digital business model design" created by CEMEX in collaboration with their contracted technology partners.

- Stage 3: Development. The CEMEX Go team took all of these insights and rapidly developed a minimal lovable experience for testing and iterating with customers. More than 500 programmers located in three cites—Monterrey, Mexico, Prague, Czech Republic, and Chennai, India—were involved to staff 40 scrum teams to dramatically reduce time and waste. The first version released to the market took two years to develop but was well received and was followed with feature updates in subsequent releases that added the mobile app's live delivery truck tracking capability among other features. Conducting rapid experimentation, as we will discuss later, allowed the development team to ensure the choices and the options presented by the user interface were relevant and built commitment from their early adopter customers.

Comments from CEMEX Go customers were extremely positive:

- "My favorite thing about CEMEX Go is the fact that it's a one-stop shop for everything we need in the concrete industry. The process is extremely seamless… what differentiates CEMEX is the personal approach and their willingness to go into the future with these technology advancements. The ready-mix industry is one that's not going to be stuck in the Stone Age, it's going to be looking for ways to continue that improvement."

- "What I like best about CEMEX Go is how easy it is. Ordering cement is just one of the hardest things that I do in the day, it's not something I want to spend a lot of time on. CEMEX has improved my business because it's made it easier for me to order. I just get on my computer—'What do you need?' Boom, I order it and I'm done!"

One of the benefits of a digital-first experience isn't just the impact that results from the initial deployment, it is what follows: both incremental improvements, introduced through additional releases to the platform, and step-change innovations that take the platform—and its broadening ecosystem of customers and partners—to new levels. CEMEX is no exception to the rule.

As CEMEX Go began to scale globally, they continued to drive greater digital transformation through their Digital Innovation in Motion ecosystem, launched to apply their digital platform and advanced artificial intelligence tools to production, management, and commercial operations. Two examples of this include:

- Improving cement production mills through artificial intelligence: Traditionally, mill operations are controlled by human operators and rely on manual processes. By applying AI, these operators become supervisors, fine-tuning the AI's behavior. Model-based optimization uses machine learning to generate models that predict the performance of the mill, reducing the amount of energy consumed while at the same time producing a higher-quality product more efficiently.

- PartRunner: This is an advanced on-demand delivery solution platform that optimizes route planning for "last-mile" delivery specializing in handling "big and bulky" items. It connects building materials suppliers, expanding the reach of CEMEX Go beyond cement and concrete to delivery of tools, machinery, and materials from their e-commerce site and retail operations: Promexma and Construrama stores. All of this was made possible through CEMEX's open innovation practice and their corporate venture capital arm, CEMEX Ventures.

MARKETING AND CEMEX GO

A conversation with Edson Santos, Global Head Digital Marketing, CEMEX

Edson, how would you say your marketing efforts have changed as a result of CEMEX Go?

Before CEMEX Go, our marketing strategy was quite traditional. We conducted activation programs and campaigns in a few markets. Our buildings were properly painted, our trucks were properly painted with our logo with our brand. But that was as far as we went. CEMEX Go was really the catalyst to rethink marketing completely and so we decided to focus entirely on a digital marketing framework that included segmentation, channels, technologies, operational mandates, and architecture—all aligned to the customer journey.

That is interesting, so digital marketing isn't just about lead gen and conversions?

Far from it. When you create so many digital touchpoints to interact with customers, a few different things become possible. First, you learn a lot more about your customers through analyzing both their online and offline behavior, so we are able to hyper-personalize our digital messaging to them. Secondly, we apply machine learning to the database of customers with similar profiles and predict future purchasing needs and align our promotions and offers based on predictive analytics versus just past purchasing behavior. Third, with so much data, it is much easier to weight what we promote in different regions based on a variety of factors, from product market share to operational constraints. Finally, what I think many companies may not realize is that when you aggressively pursue a digital-first customer experience, you learn a lot about your customers, but the reverse is true also: they learn a lot about you. So, we have invested in digital interaction tools that make it really easy for customers to provide us feedback that both improves their experience and how we market to them.

Is it fair to say you spend more on digital marketing now than before CEMEX Go?

Oh significantly. I mean, before CEMEX Go, we probably allocated about 10 percent to digital marketing. Today that number is closer to 80 percent. But it makes sense, not just because of how we digitalized the customer experience; it also helps us with our social media strategy in support of our net-zero commitment. We have very aggressive targets and really innovative green products that help our customers achieve their own ESG goals. Digital channels allow us to control the narrative and are by far the most effective way to get that messaging across.

Edson, can you point to any results from digital marketing you are particularly proud of?

Sure, a couple stand out. One is that because of CEMEX Go, we are able to serve a customer segment that includes smaller contractors which had been underserved by the bigger cement providers as they tend to focus on larger customers. CEMEX Go makes it possible for us to deliver and support those customers profitably. This is actually quite an important innovation on our industry. Secondly, our digital marketing efforts contributed an incremental $250 million revenue to the company over the past four years against an investment of approximately $5 million in digital marketing. So that is something I feel particularly proud of, besides the amazing digital marketing team we have assembled that work on behalf of our customers around the world.

Going further upstream

CEMEX didn't stop there. They have gone even further, bringing the power of digital transformation to build the "connected quarry" allowing for truck and machine efficiency optimization with the use of telematics data. Imagine drones fitted with high-definition cameras surveying every corner of the quarry. This allows CEMEX to create a "digital twin" of the quarry by overlaying topographic information with machine learning data, increasing productivity by 15 percent and net profits by 50 percent.[6]

Not ignoring the back office

Working Smarter, announced in late 2021, is CEMEX's initiative to digitize mission-critical business services in its finance, customer support, human resources, and information technology operations. At the core of this program is the redesign of its shared services operating model, implementing virtual fulfillment centers that accommodate a remote workforce, retaining high-quality talent pools regardless of their geographic location. Homero Reséndez elaborates:

> We looked at our internal processes and it was clear we needed to make some changes. At the beginning we called these "manually assisted." Let's say a customer of ready-mix ordered 49 cubic meters and wanted it delivered at 7:00 in the morning. To ensure we delivered on this expectation, our first version of CEMEX Go needed to establish service level agreements (SLAs) for our service center representative to handle this request behind the scenes and then communicate directly with the customer. So, beyond the customer interface associated with CEMEX Go, our work to automate these processes has been an extraordinary amount of work. The digital confirmation feature is a good example of this. Where in the past the request above would have required a service representative to intervene, now even complex requests can be confirmed almost instantly through a digital channel of the customer's preference. But we aren't finished, and the vision is never completed.

There is a lesson from CEMEX that should not be missed by any organization pursuing a digital-first customer experience effort. Even though their service center processes were not part of the original feature set, they established SLAs to ensure staff could fulfill a customer's digitally generated requests. This avoids investing in improvements that customers do not truly value while ensuring their expectations aren't missed when introducing new digitally migrated interactions. But at some point, those backend processes need to catch up. As Jesus Caviedes Mondragon explains:

> Transforming our 17 global service centers to fulfillment centers is our next big transformation. It is massive. As digital interactions with customers increase, it requires more coordination, better integration of systems, more visibility into supply chain capacities for remote dispatching. You need to design new

chatbots, new call routing and reskilling, so that one person can handle different lines of business. But this creates capacity so staff can take on more fulfillment duties. It is a total metamorphosis that will take time but is essential.

Like all of our best practice examples, the CEMEX Go story is worthy of its own book. Given we don't have that luxury, here are just a few of what CEMEX executives shared with us regarding the key factors that have contributed to their success.

COMMITTED TO SUSTAINABILITY

Like their alignment around delivering a digital-first experience, CEMEX's commitment to net-zero is industry-leading. "We conceive of sustainability as the only safe way to do business... Sustainability is embedded in CEMEX's strategy, and thus, it is linked to all functions across our business lines."[7] This also extends to product development. Recently, CEMEX introduced a new product line called Vertua, their first net-zero CO_2 concrete offering developed by their research and development team. This product:

- reduces the carbon footprint of concrete by up to 70 percent;
- neutralizes the remaining 30 percent of carbon through offsetting efforts;
- generates less heat and fewer cracks.

SOURCE https://www.cemex.com/sustainability/future-in-action/sustainable-products-and-
         solutions

Critical success factors

A number of factors have contributed to CEMEX's success, all grounded in a commitment to customer centricity.

TOP MANAGEMENT SUPPORT AND INVOLVEMENT

It cannot be emphasized enough how big a difference the CEO and leadership team's commitment and involvement made in the launch and scaling of CEMEX Go globally. But this commitment built on the previous CEO's commitment to technology. Jonathan Holden Hernández explains:

Lorenzo Zambrano, the former CEO, was an advocate for technology, so at some point the company already had the seed to take this step into digital. So, that combination of a focus on customer centricity on top of our foundation in valuing technology helped a lot. The new CEO really set the example. He visited the scrum teams in Monterrey, in Prague. He met with the service design leads and the Agile leads to learn about what their challenges were.

EXECUTIVE EDUCATION

To ensure that this support was felt throughout the organization, CEMEX invested in educating the top 100 leaders in what digital transformation was about and the change management strategies that would underscore successful implementation. The company partnered with the Massachusetts Institute of Technology (MIT) to customize and facilitate a five-day residential program. Homero Reséndez explains the impact achieved from the program:

> We launched a program to train all the executive committee and all leaders of the whole operation from the different countries where we operate, but mainly the commercial leaders and the country presidents. All attended a five-day program that was designed with MIT to understand digital transformation but also addressed change management. After that training, you cannot imagine the number of requests we started to receive from different people with more specific use cases referencing relevant technologies.

CEMEX executives believe the investment in the program paid off in spades. With a more profound understanding of both the "what" and the "how" of digital transformation, CEMEX's senior leaders provided more direct support to the design and Agile team leaders across all three stages.

TECHNOLOGY THAT SOLVES PROBLEMS

Often the final technology stack you end up with is quite different from the one you imagined, even after the research and prototyping steps. CEMEX Go was no exception. Jonathan Holden Hernández describes a typical example:

> We needed to apply technology to solve a real customer pain point. For example, we tested several new technologies including a chatbot we call Olivia that we launched with some artificial intelligence and machine learning behind it. It was a good experiment, but in the end, it really wasn't addressing a customer pain point, so now it is used to handle basic support questions. We have learned that the latest technology only matters if it solves a real customer problem.

> **❝❝** *We needed to apply technology to solve a real customer pain point.*

REINFORCING FEEDBACK

Like any journey, it is important to look for milestones that reinforce you are on the right path or should consider pivoting as incoming data suggests. In the case of CEMEX Go, early on in its implementation, management monitored the digital channels customers were being offered and discovered adoption rates grew rapidly. Cost-to-serve metrics for some interactions improved as much as 50 percent over previous analog methods. In some cases, person-to-person interactions were still preferred, and their results became more consistent as they developed integrations that kept a service representative in the middle of the interactions when required.

CUSTOMER MEASUREMENT

As CEMEX Go rolled out, it became clear that different parts of the business measured customer satisfaction differently. There was little consistency and the roll-out of CEMEX Go presented the opportunity to change that. Homero Reséndez explains:

> Over the past five years we have created a standard measure: net promoter score. NPS has been adopted by all countries using the same methodology with the same time frame. We added some of the attributes associated with the CEMEX Go into what we were measuring, and it was embedded in the actual experience.

As a result, NPS has improved significantly and CEMEX's NPS score is in the 68–72 range, allowing CEMEX to command premiums in most of the markets in which they operate.

IT ORGANIZATION

Speaking of details, one of the most important was the fact that CEMEX restructured their IT organization to remove any barriers between service designers and software developers. As Homero Reséndez told us:

> I have been in IT many years, but I never thought I would have service designers and user researchers reporting to me. This is a totally new practice that we have been maturing over the past five or six years now. The other example is our global data science team. At one point in my past, I was a statistics and mathematics professor, but I honestly never expected I would lead a team of statistical experts, mathematical experts. However, what I can tell you is that they are very much needed.

As we will discuss in Chapter 15 on executing to scale, involving your IT organization at the beginning of such an initiative isn't a good idea, it is an imperative. CEMEX went a step further and eliminated any potential communications failure points by integrating the design and IT teams together.

CEMEX GO GOVERNANCE

Lastly, a global implementation as comprehensive as CEMEX Go obviously required some extensive governance. There were eight different dimensions, with specific key performance indicators (KPIs), each with different maturity levels depending on the region or business line. Every quarter their results were reported to the CEO and financial resources allocated to support the effort in "working with leading consultants or subject matters as needed. This allowed us to speed up decision-making so we could move fast."[8] Secondly, CEMEX created customer experience offices in every region. These teams of 5–10 members coordinated CEMEX Go locally, as well as customer complaints, measurement, and service center projects.

Now, if we broaden our gaze, we can see how CEMEX Go has provided CEMEX with a unique position in the global construction industry.

In 2021 CEMEX announced it had joined a global initiative to develop OpenBuilt, a new platform designed to securely connect fragmented construction industry supply chains. Through OpenBuilt, the participating companies, which include IBM, Red Hat, Cobuilder, and others, aim to offer new digital solutions to help innovate and drive more efficient, sustainable, and safer construction projects. OpenBuilt is designed to allow companies across the globe to securely connect their current technology platforms and digital solutions to partners, suppliers, or subcontractors in their supply chain via a single integration hub. Again, Homero Reséndez explains:

> We realized that CEMEX Go was really only solving 2 percent or 5 percent
> of the pain points that those customers were experiencing day-to-day, so with
> OpenBuilt we hope to create something much bigger. And that is also the idea of
> CEMEX Ventures. Taking the digitalization of our internal processes, commercial
> operation, production, supply chain transformation and solving some significant
> pain points in the industry. CEMEX Ventures is looking for innovations in many
> dimensions in the construction supply chain, but not around how we deliver
> ready-mix or cement. But OpenBuilt and CEMEX Ventures are two of the ways
> we are working to address the pain points of the industry.

CEMEX VENTURES

CEMEX Ventures is CEMEX's corporate venture capital arm that invests in innovative construction startups globally to drive "the construction industry revolution."[9]

CEMEX Ventures brings together the main ecosystem of players, including startups, entrepreneurs, universities, and other stakeholders. From their website (https://www.cemexventures.com/) they offer promising startup companies support in:

- capital investment: smart money to promote your continued growth and connect with potential investors;

- commercialization and expansion: access to construction leads and industry decision-makers to pilot and test new markets;

- advisory and deep industry expertise: feedback and insights from our expert network, from industry experts to the CEMEX Ventures team;

- the CEMEX global network: access our extensive network, R&D and marketing teams, and physical spaces around the globe.

If you are a startup in the construction industry, a visit to the CEMEX Ventures page could be a serious game changer for your future success. This is one of the most robust, clearly defined approaches to helping bring to life innovative ideas and companies in any industry. CEMEX Go is nothing short of extraordinary and represents the promise of not just moving the company and its customers to new levels of prosperity but the entire construction industry with it.

The heart of the matter

We talked about how providing customers choice creates greater customer empowerment, but let's dig a little deeper. At the root of this is what behavioral science describes as choice architecture: the practice of influencing choice by "organizing the context in which people make decisions."[10] This addresses many of the issues we discussed earlier around things like choice overload[11] (having just too many options), regret (choosing a single option means rejecting the rest), and self-control (giving into impulses to consume what we know we shouldn't).[12]

Three mechanisms[13] have the potential to mitigate some of these issues:

- Control of the choice set composition: To create a truly empowered consumer this mechanism suggests that it is less about the number of options and more about defining one's choices. For example, having control to reverse a selection after it was made would increase my feeling of control. Also being able to select from a number of categories that may be of interest prior to choosing would potentially produce greater empowerment.

- Progress clues: We experience this every time we see a progress bar across the top of a web page or mobile app, a process timer, or clear definitions of the steps being selected and feedback on when those steps are completed. The language app Duolingo is masterful at designing a mobile experience that does both of these things.

- Information about other consumers: Being able to see the choices others have made can help the consumer increase their confidence if their selections are affirmed by other consumers with similar needs. Think of how Yelp or travel site reviews about a potential hotel stay influence decision-making.

Putting these three mechanisms together may give the customer the ability to make a gradual commitment across a sequence of decisions that once invested in would reduce the likelihood of attrition. There are other behavioral science heuristics at play in the CEMEX Go choice architecture:

- Default options: These are pre-set courses of action that take effect if nothing is specified by the decision-maker. If there are regular orders to be generated each week to supply a large project, the customer can easily reorder, keeping their previous information and merely adjusting for any changes.

- Anchoring (heuristic): This is a particular form of priming effect whereby initial exposure to a number serves as a reference point and influences subsequent judgments. In CEMEX Go, once the pricing has been presented from the product catalogue, it sets the precedent for future pricing.

- Automation bias: As we discussed in the Lemonade example, this is an over-reliance on automated aids and decision support systems. In the case of CEMEX Go, this is a positive effect given the accuracy, efficiency, and real-time nature of the platform.

- Habit: Habit is an automatic and rigid pattern of behavior in specific situations, which is usually acquired through repetition and develops through associative learning, when actions become paired repeatedly with a context or an event. "Habit loops" involve a cue that triggers an action, the actual behavior, and a reward.[14] As you read the CEMEX customer testimonials, you clearly see habit-forming behavior. Put yourself in the shoes of a CEMEX competitor and ask yourself, "How would I compete with that?"

Results

CEMEX had grown the user base of CEMEX Go to well over 42,000 in 2021,[15] and at a year-on-year rate reported 16.9 percent growth in its revenues for the first quarter of 2021, to $3.4 billion, and improved net profit over the same period to $665 million. But that is not the whole story. CEMEX obtained efficiencies in both customer-facing and internal processes, including:[16]

- reduced time in customer ordering;
- reduction of the time spent by the sales representative on the management of invoices and payments;
- reduction in the number of calls received in the call center to track the delivery truck;
- reduction in the time spent by the sales representative/dispatcher who monitors the delivery truck;
- reduction in the number of credit notes;
- improvement in working capital;
- cut in the courier service for physical deliveries of product delivery tests.

The company's NPS for the fiscal year 2021 was 68, with a target to get to 70 by 2030, which they have already surpassed.

Summary

The CEMEX Go experience speaks to a company with a strong foundation of leadership, innovation, and a relentless focus on their customers, their employees, and sustainability goals. It underscores that a successful digital-first customer experience transformation is about far more than technology, and if careful attention is paid to its implementation, a company can do more than just delight customers, it can set a new standard for its industry. Where will

CEMEX Go be in 20 years? We asked that very question to Jesus Caviedes Mondragon. Here is what he said:

> In 20 years, projects will all be managed digitally. The physical part—the trucks, the holding, the warehouses—they may never be fully integrated, so I don't know if it's more a digital challenge or a physical challenge. CEMEX will participate but it will be part of a conglomerate of solutions. It will be a full integration of four or five mega levels of functionalities with an open platform and APIs. That is, for me, the ultimate.

Key insights

- Giving customers choice and control creates customer empowerment that positively influences customer satisfaction and trust.
- Designing a choice architecture that considers the types, sequence, and number of choices will produce a superior customer experience by avoiding choice overload, regret, and loss of self-control.
- Tap into multiple channels to capture the voice of the customer.
- Engage customers as co-creation partners, beginning with a minimal lovable experience from which to iterate, improve, and update with a continuous stream of releases based on customer feedback.
- Apply Lean/Agile project management as well as design thinking tools including empathy maps, customer journey maps, and service blueprints.
- Spend time upfront exploring what is possible in terms of new technologies and approaches to your customers' pain points.
- Once proven and scaling, leverage your digital experience platform to extend to other functions (back office, etc.).
- Consider how your digital-first experience can extend to your industry to create even more value through an ecosystem of participants.

What's next?

Now let's stay in the world of B2B as we consider our next strategy, foster ownership through customer community and co-creation, as we learn from enterprise software leader VMware to uncover the power of getting past the hype and literally putting the customer in the center of your business.

06

Design Strategy 4: Foster ownership through customer community and co-creation

"My story's still being written. I am so happy to be part of this community. I am so happy to be around all of these incredible minds. And I look forward to what my next steps are in the world of technology."[1]

LINDY HERRING, MY JOURNEY AS A VMUG LEADER PRESENTATION

Listening to Lindy Herring's story of her journey, starting with her family's immigration from Thailand during the Vietnam War, to becoming a leader of a local VMware Users Group (VMUG) chapter isn't just inspiring, it underscores what fostering ownership by building an engaged customer community is all about. Presenting at a VMUG "UserCon'—VMware shorthand for a local user conference—in just over 10 minutes, Lindy described her journey from working in the meat-processing industry to joining the IT support department of a company that used and resold a variety of technology solutions including VMware. When I interviewed Lindy, she told me, "I uncovered that our own people didn't really understand what VMware was. It was just a component to this private cloud that we were building." VMware's technology was both broad and deep and for a person coming from her last role in human resources, it seemed like the climb ahead to master the technology it encompassed would be quite steep. That was about the time she heard about VMUG.

I took it upon myself to get educated and through that education discovered VMUG. In September 2016, I went to my first VMUG meeting and realized,

"Wow, this is very unique." You didn't have this where I'd come from in HR. I was immediately taken in by this group of individuals who invited me to their table. I told them my story, that I was new and where I was from, and they were so encouraging. They helped me learn that the only way to be completely integrated into the technology was to be a part of the VMUG community.

Talking with Lindy for even a few minutes, it becomes clear this is a person who has stared down more than a little adversity in her life. Refusing to be deterred by the learning curve ahead, she dove right in.

I sat down with the president of the company and I said, "You know, here's what I'd like to do," and I presented this business case for becoming the VMware platform specialist, understanding that I was going to be learning, and eventually coaching a team of players who really didn't understand VMware's products. I presented that in December of 2016. In January 2017 I was promoted to VMware platform specialist. So yes, to answer your question, I did get promoted because of VMUG.

In 2008, I co-authored *The Ownership Quotient*[2] with Professors James Heskett and W. Earl Sasser, Jr, of Harvard Business School, a book that detailed the best practices of firms we described as "service profit chain leaders." The companies we studied applied service profit chain concepts to generate high levels of employee and customer ownership. Since past behavior is a good predictor of future behavior, we defined a customer owner as:

- offering constructive complaints;
- recruiting new customers;
- testing and recommending new products and services.

Lindy Herring represents the model of a "customer owner." In fact, she was such a customer owner, she eventually joined VMware and transitioned into becoming an "employee owner" whom we defined as:

- offering ideas about how to improve processes;
- recruiting potential employees;
- testing and recommending new products and services.

"They are our harshest critics and our strongest advocates." That is Jean Williams, Senior Manager, VMUG program at VMware. "We work closely with VMUG on a number of different areas around feedback about our products and our product roadmaps. I think to have such an engaged user community to provide so much value to VMware in a number of areas, including collaborating around products, solutions, and our other core processes, has been simply invaluable."

What creates the motivation for customers to become owners? What attracts them to volunteer the time required to help ensure the success of new products or to improve existing processes?

A study that focused on B2B companies found that a participant was primarily driven by opportunity- or goal-related motives. Further, this study demonstrated that peer-influencing behaviors shaped customer interest in participating in value co-creation.[3] Additionally, the wider an organization's customer base, the more interactions between them, the stronger the product ecosystems. Customers wanted to recommend products as the ecosystem became stronger. This study also extends the understanding of peer-influencing behavior affecting co-creation when employees move to another organization.

A second study by leading academics from the Faculty of Economics at the University of Porto revealed additional insights into the motivation of customers that complete co-creation activities with technology providers like VMware:

> The most important motivators for users' participation are knowledge acquisition and intrinsic motivations. Socialization with other users sharing common interests also emerged as a relevant determinant, while being rewarded for their participation was not among the most important in this study... Additionally, our findings suggest that regular contributors recognize benefits attained with co-creation more intensively than occasional users... and, thus, will exhibit higher willingness to engage in collaborative innovation. This may generate a reinforcing "feedback loop" effect (users more willing to engage will participate more and this, in turn, may generate higher engagement).[4]

With this backdrop, let's examine how VMware has structured an engagement platform that has achieved such an extraordinary level of customer ownership from its members, and the specific practices in which stories like Lindy's are made possible.

A study that focused on B2B companies found that a participant was primarily driven by opportunity- or goal-related motives.

VMware

VMware was founded in 1998 by five technologists who had a different idea on how to scale enterprise computing. In 2002 they were granted their first patent for a system and method for virtualizing computer systems. The rest, as they say, is history. Today, the company holds more than 5,000 US patents and at almost $13 billion in revenue for fiscal year 2022 is a leading provider of multi-cloud services, "enabling digital innovation with enterprise control."[5] You may recall that Dell Technologies acquired VMware several years ago but then spun the company out, completing the transaction on November 1, 2021.[6] Dell remains a strategic partner and the two organizations work closely together on go-to-market activities. Just a year and three days later, on November 4, 2022, VMware stockholders voted to approve a proposed $61 billion acquisition of VMware by Broadcom, Inc. and the deal was expected to close in 2023.

In an open letter to the VMUG community, Broadcom's President and CEO, Hock Tan, shared with VMUG members his thoughts about the value of the VMware community:

> In the months since we announced our transaction with VMware, I've been meeting with many members of the VMware ecosystem to hear more about the intricacies of the business and what matters most to the VMware community. As I've listened and learned, one theme stood out to me: the value that the VMware user group brings to the broader ecosystem. The passion, talent, and dedication of VMUG's members—whether its end-users, partners, or VMware employees—speak to precisely what excites us about VMware and the vast potential we see in this combination. Broadcom recognizes the important contributions of the VMUG community and the value inherent in this independent, customer-led organization to the broader VMware ecosystem.[7]

The experience

"People naturally want to hang out and communicate with people that are doing similar things, especially if it makes them better at something they care about." Those words are from VMUG past president, Steve Athanas, whom I had the good fortune to spend some time with to get an inside look into what has made the VMUG community so successful.

It starts with the product

Some business applications are straightforward. Most people can navigate their way through setting up their Microsoft 365 configuration, but VMware products are a totally different deal. As Lindy Herring quickly learned when she accepted her new role as the VMware platform specialist, the complexity and breadth of the VMware product portfolio are much more challenging. A DevOps or systems engineer who might be proficient with one VMware product will still have lots to learn about another. Second, and this is less obvious today, but when VMware products were introduced, the capabilities they afforded their customers were embraced by the technical community as real breakthrough solutions. For example, the ability to have a server, including its applications and data, move from one piece of hardware to another without an end-user even knowing something had changed was pure magic at the time. These users were super excited about using these products and mastery of them became central to their role as systems engineers in the companies they worked for.

But becoming proficient on one VMware product was one thing, achieving mastery across the portfolio another. A lifetime could be spent reading manuals, but the internal complexity of IT configurations made anticipating problems and the needed workarounds difficult. What these customers needed was access to other customers who could relate to their environment and share their best practices and knowledge across this very broad spectrum of capabilities.

Who they are and what they value

Steve Athanas went on to explain, "VMware figured out very early on that people were craving that connection and so were very smart to create the forum for these people to come together." The user group was formed to serve exactly that, VMware product users, people that actually had to learn and deploy their products, not the IT directors or CTOs. This was important as it made the format and agenda for the early meetings straightforward. A new member who had just finished their certification on one VMware product would come to a UserCon and hear a member talk about another product set or, even better, join a table of customers with expertise in a complementary area. Practical advice from someone who had deployed a similar configuration was simply invaluable. The interactions were reciprocal. Being part of a group where you could help someone and they could help you was of real value.

A virtuous cycle

The result of this focus on networking and knowledge building led to a powerful virtuous cycle, as Steve described it: "Help me achieve a level of mastery with the software, I will then have an affinity for it and evangelize it in my company, and we will get more done with it because I have developed those competencies and am growing in both my skills and my career. Eventually, I may get promoted to a role that allows me to evangelize even more where I can have a greater impact, therefore we buy more of it, have more impact, and the cycle continues." This shared benefit, between the individual, their company, and VMware, isn't a new idea in the software industry, but what is new are the conditions VMware put in place to help it flourish. That virtuous cycle worked to grow VMUG's membership exponentially. One person that got so much value out of VMUG told two people who signed up, told two people, etc. until 12 years later there were more 150,000 members.

Enabling rather than owning

Where many companies go astray is in treating their user group as a marketing tool to keep pitching products, or worse, promoting it as a low-cost channel to provide product help desk support. Steve explained that VMware had a very different idea. "To VMware's credit, once it got to a point that it was self-sustaining, they backed off and said, 'Our best interest here is to let this community grow and mature and we will be a participant in the platform but not own the platform,' which I think was just brilliant—very few companies have that presence of mind."

VMware has two seats on the VMUG board of directors and are involved in the group's strategy as board members, but the VMUG leadership team run their own programs, manage their own events, and are responsible for their own P&L. Steve continued, "By taking their hands off of it, they let the

> ❝ *That virtuous cycle worked to grow VMUG's membership exponentially.*

community grow and they let people have conversations—even with competitors. VMware was confident enough to say, 'If you are here, you probably aren't looking at a competitor, but if so, that's fine.' Because it had freedom in conversations, the community grew even faster. VMware assists with product support and participates in user conferences, but one thing that VMUG members are assured of going to an event is that you aren't going to get a high-pressure sales pitch."

VMUG membership is free to anyone. You don't even need to be a VMware customer, and for $200 per year you can sign up for an advantage membership that includes discounts on VMware education, VMware Explore (formerly VMworld) admission, webcasts, and access to an annual license of the EVALExperience that includes a portfolio of VMware products for personal use (i.e. home lab) in a non-production environment. It is amazing value by any standard.

Executive involvement

Something as successful as VMUG can never be attributed to one single factor. However, one thing that can reduce the effectiveness of any customer community is a lack of executive support. At VMware, the support for VMUG comes from the whole executive team, starting with the CEO. In fact, once a year, just before Labor Day in the United States, VMware hosts VMworld, the annual conference that brings together customers and partners and attracts over 20,000 attendees. One year, VMUG members were encouraged to wear a lime-green, neon T-shirt to stand out in the crowd. Halfway through his opening keynote address, VMware's CTO at the time opened his shirt to reveal that very same lime-green T-shirt. Of course, the reaction was overwhelming, and the message was heard around the world: VMUG wasn't a line item on a marketing director's program list, it was a central tenet of VMware's focus on the customer.

CEOs including Paul Maritz, Pat Gelsinger, and the CEO at the time of writing, Raghu Raghuram, have attended VMUG events, spent time with their members, answered questions, and fostered a "you are part of the family" mentality to all VMUG members. Over the years, VMware has invited the VMUG leadership group, about 135 members from around the world, to the Palo Alto, California, head office to participate in a week of leadership training. The focus is on networking, best practice sharing, technical knowledge, but also career development in support of the virtuous cycle described earlier. One year, every VMware presenter was given a "I

HEART VMUG Leaders" T-shirt to wear just before the group arrived. All employees were informed of the VMUG leaders' visit and were invited to meet them at various cafeterias across the campus. Talk about feeling part of the family.

VMware Explore

For many customers in the enterprise software industry, VMware Explore is the most important event in the calendar year. The biggest exhibitor hall booths at this event are reserved for the firm's larger strategic partners like Dell and AWS, and of course they are always impressive. But as impressive is the VMUG booth, which stands at about the same size as any of the largest partners and is important for two reasons: 1) many times, would-be VMware customers are given free passes to VMware Explore as part of the selling process, so it is a way for VMUG to grow the member base by giving people a taste of what it is like to be a member through seminars and other events, and 2) for long-time VMUG members, this is homecoming week, an annual ritual to connect with fellow members and strengthen their shared commitment to the community and the company.

VMWARE EXPLORE

After 18 years of VMworlds and hundreds of thousands of global attendees, VMware is evolving its flagship conference, VMworld, to focus on its multi-cloud future by unveiling its first in-person event in over two years with VMware Explore. VMware Explore 2022 will be the company's first large in-person conference since the global COVID-19 pandemic, with huge expectations of becoming the industry go-to event for all things multi-cloud.

"I'm super excited about VMware Explore 2022," VMware CEO Raghu Raghuram said in a statement. "It's going to be a unique event—a 'gathering of the tribes' for the multi-cloud community. I can't wait to welcome all the innovators who are leading the way in defining the multi-cloud era, including our customers, our ecosystem partners, and influencers from around the world."

VMware held its first-ever VMworld in 2004 in San Diego, with about 1,500 attendees, according to a VMware blog. Over the next 15 years, VMworld's attendance would soar to over 21,000 people for the mega technology event, with the majority of live US events taking place in Las Vegas and San Francisco. However, the global COVID-19 pandemic would halt in-person VMworlds in 2020 and 2021.

Now, VMware is looking to reimagine and reinvent its flagship event with VMware Explore, which kicks off in the US in late August in San Francisco, followed by a European VMware Explore event in Barcelona, Spain, in November. VMware expects to announce official VMware Explore events in Brazil, Singapore, Japan, and China later this year.

VMware's goal with revamping VMworld into VMware Explore is to include more technologies and ecosystem and developer communities that help shape the multi-cloud universe. There will be an option for people not wanting to attend the VMware Explore in person. VMware said it will offer unique on-demand content as well as replays from the events in the US and Europe. Access to the VMware Explore US content will be free but will require a VMware ID.

SOURCE These excerpts are reprinted from: Goodbye VMworld, Hello VMware Explore "Multi-Cloud Universe" Event[8]

Direct feedback

As Jean Williams told us: "VMUG can be the company's harshest critics." She has been involved with VMUG since 2005 and understands first hand the value the group provides to the company through its many feedback channels.

One of these is around direct customer feedback. Some of this is informal, as when a product team arrives at a UserCon and spends time hearing customer feedback and ideas for improvement, but VMUG also has a formal Voice of the Customer Program that channels feedback from members right into the company.

For example, at one point VMware introduced a new licensing policy on their vSphere 5 product and the user group was quick to respond. As a result of their feedback and other factors, VMware changed the policy. This is instructive for many reasons, not the least of which is if you want to increase your customers' response rates to things like customer surveys and requests for feedback, earn their trust by actually taking action on what they tell you. Nothing increases response rates like actually being responsive.

A one-way door

Setting up a user community with this level of autonomy and freedom might appear risky. What if the wrong leadership were elected? What if the group derailed into a lobby group to negotiate better prices or became enamored with a competitor? As Steve commented to me, "I think one of the dangers is, once you set free a large enough customer community, it is a one-way door. If you try to pull it back or worse kill it—a community with so many people that has a life and a soul of its own—they will hate you for it. For VMware, I think their stewardship of VMUG has been a big contributor to its success and the impact it has produced."

The details

As we get into some of the details of what generates such a high level of customer ownership at VMware, let's isolate the insights that may inform how your organization might pursue launching or improving a customer user group or ongoing customer community to create a greater quotient of customer owners.

The product itself generates enthusiasm

This point has been made a few times, but it is worth repeating as central to the success of VMUG. By 2010, VMware's product offering had become diverse and technically robust enough that simply studying the manual was not going to be adequate to gain a level of competency across the portfolio. First and foremost, serve the growth and development of community members: this is perhaps the most important insight to take away from this section. Lindy shared with me that she attended a technical user group of an up-and-coming SaaS solution just before she joined VMUG but she didn't stay with it: "It was completely different. They talked about a lot of the cool things that they were doing and what they could do. But then when I went to the VMUG user group, it was more technical. It felt like there was more that I could bring to the table and there was going to be a lot more that I was going to be learning that could really enhance my career." Jean Williams would agree: "The users have this opportunity for networking and professional growth and development. They have a chance to solve problems together, to help each other advancing their careers."

Effective leadership and governance

This might fall under the category of the "not so obvious" things that VMware has done. As Steve said, at some point they realized that for the community to thrive, it would best be run by the members who would stay squarely focused on advancing their agenda. Although VMware holds two seats on the VMUG board, VMUG runs its own show. Having said that, each local chapter around the world has an assigned VMware representative, usually from the systems engineering organization that interfaces with the local VMUG leaders and acts as the liaison between VMware and the chapter. This "hands-off" but "hands-ready" approach has proven to be a winning formula. "I think it's just built up over the years," Jean Williams reflected, "these relationships, whether it's among the board members or the local VMUG volunteer leaders who are so passionate about VMware products and the impact they have in their respective organizations. They get to know me and the other people within VMware and trust us. There's just an enormous amount of mutual respect."

Design programs that accelerate the "virtuous cycle"

Remember, at the heart of this is the "virtuous cycle" that Steve talked about. As membership in VMUG grew, a natural exponential effect took place, as Steve described. But VMware was able to support both membership growth and career development of individual members through some specific programing. One of these, the discounted EVALExperience program, provided VMUG members with a way to get experience across much of VMware's portfolio. Lindy confirmed to me that this was one of the key resources she used to dial up her skills and expertise, and she became so proficient at it that VMware approached her to lead a podcast called "Hello from Your Home Lab," during which she interviewed VMUG members from around the world to showcase how VMUG members were applying the different applications. The show went viral and Lindy shared with me, "At the last VMworld, a gentleman come up to me and said, 'I watched every one of your episodes. You know, you were my inspiration. Would you take a picture with me?'"

> ❝ This "hands-off" but "hands-ready" approach has proven to be a winning formula.

A second program that Lindy instigated was V-Ladies. Right from the start, Lindy was determined to bring more women into VMUG. VMware didn't hesitate to assist and Mandy Botsko-Wilson, Kim Delgado, and Betsy Sutter, VMware's Chief People Officer, worked with Lindy to develop a platform to increase female participation in VMUG, to the point where Lindy was traveling to different chapter meetings as part of the program roll-out, including a trip to Japan. "Hands-off" but "hands ready."

Know your audience

This can't be emphasized enough. I suspect it is why many user groups or customer communities just don't scale. Viewing your customer community as a source for sales leads takes the role of the community in a different direction. It may not be a bad one if your goals are to use it on a short-term basis to drive revenue, but I suspect it may have the opposite effect long term.

We have talked a lot about the value that VMUG members received from their membership. Let's turn the tables and focus on the value it generates for VMware. As Jean Williams shared with me, "There's this ongoing dialogue between the user group and our business units, whether informal or formal. It's touched a number of different products."

There are three formal structures that VMware have in place that effectively harness the power of VMUG.

USE CASES

A lot of VMware's innovation comes from an end-user with a user case where a client couldn't achieve what they needed to accomplish with a VMware product. If they share it in the community, VMware will pair them up with a group called the "ACE Team" whose entire job is to find those "purple unicorns"—business problems that could represent a step-change improvement in performance of some kind. "And a lot of times these uses cases get solved in a next release," Lindy commented. "We are well known for making revision version releases based on client interaction."

PRODUCT INNOVATION

When a product team wants to involve customers in a product development effort, they will turn to customers and partners who want to help shape VMware decisions. These customers have opted in to provide feedback to the company on a variety of topics including product development. For example, when the VMware cloud services team wanted to innovate and improve the design of their product through a series of Agile iterations over the course of eight weeks, they turned to these customers to participate at different steps across the process. VMware also embraces open-source software (OSS) development. Open-source teams are guided by hypothesis-driven design, starting with a set of assumptions and validated with user testing through learn and iterate cycles. Feedback channels within the development community help identify key issues to solve and set priorities. Co-creation of these products with the community is characterized by transparency, dialogue, feedback, and voting to form a learning-rich, collaborative environment.

TALENT ACQUISITION

In some ways, it is no surprise that a VMUG leader as active and engaged as Lindy ended up working at VMware. The truth is, VMUG is a rich source of potential talent for VMware, should a member be considering a career change. Lindy explained how this came about for her: "At the end of 2019, I found myself looking for a job. The VMUG community started a hashtag: #vmwarehirelindy. I kid you not. I was interviewing for three different positions within VMware and every time I started the interview process, the manager was like, "You were probably the most highly recommended person that we've ever interviewed.'"

Executive involvement and organizational commitment

We have covered this at length, but it is worth reinforcing. Both involvement and commitment to VMUG run to every level of the organization and are demonstrated in both words and actions. The size of the booth reserved for VMUG at VMware Explore is just one of many examples of an organization that "walks the talk."

Aspire to a higher purpose

It isn't clear that VMware started out with this intention, but after spending time with Jean, Steve, and Lindy, the overwhelming insight that you can't help but be impressed with goes far beyond VMware and its products. When Lindy Herring showed up at that first VMUG meeting and was invited to sit at a table, where she had the opportunity to explain her story (and perhaps her trepidation over what she signed up for), this group of VMUG members embraced her and saw the chance to support a new member in their career aspirations. I asked her how she would have grown her career had she not discovered VMUG. Would she have had to go back to college to pursue a computer science degree? Go back to her former employer where she worked in HR and convince them to give her a role in the IT department? Here is what she said:

> There are so many people I've talked to within the VMUG community who have been in the same boat as I was in, you know, and they just pushed and pushed, and they never gave up on themselves. And they also had a community that never gave up on them either.

I don't know about you, but to me this is powerful stuff. Here is a talented person with no formal computer science training who was able to advance her skill set and knowledge in a highly technical field. How did she do it? Clearly, it started with her own focus and motivation, but it became enabled through the support of a technology company that had the foresight to create a customer community where members are able to help each other grow, and to provide just enough support for it flourish on its own. Jean Williams underscored this very point:

> VMUG does a great job on helping, supporting, and providing opportunities for professional development of its members/leaders. I've seen first hand the transformation of VMUG leaders as they have grown professionally, becoming leaders not only within their communities but in their organizations.

> ❝ *The overwhelming insight that you can't help but be impressed with goes far beyond VMware and its products.*

THE NEW DIGITAL FRONTIER

The VMware "Digital Frontiers" study explored consumer trends and sentiments during the pandemic and the rising demand for better digital experiences across all industries. The "Digital Frontiers" global research effort explored the links between tech innovation, people, and society. More specifically, it looked at how technology helps push exceptional digital services and experiences— and whether consumers feel organizations are doing it right. To get a pulse on global consumer trends and sentiment during the pandemic, YouGov and VMware surveyed more than 13,250 people worldwide.

Highlights from the study include:

- Fewer than half of people surveyed believe the companies they interact with deliver an improved digital experience now compared to before the pandemic.

- Over half of all respondents would switch to a competitor if their digital experience didn't live up to expectations.

- 51 percent would welcome the use of virtual reality to enhance the buying experience.

- 66 percent trust connected devices (e.g. smart speakers/thermostats) will be used to benefit society in the next five years, though 35 percent don't trust businesses or governments to use algorithms to benefit the customer (rather than the business).

SOURCE https://news.vmware.com/technologies/digital-frontiers

The heart of the matter

Given the amount of data that exists to support the value of B2C customer co-creation and community engagement, our focus here is around B2B communities. The data in terms of behavioral science is compelling. When inviting customers to participate in co-creation and community it is important to consider:

- How do you create opportunities for knowledge acquisition and career development?

- How do you design socialization mechanisms that will allow participants to expand their professional network and create positive, helpful mentoring relationships?

- What could be done to create onboarding processes that would ensure new community participants feel welcomed and invite contributions that inform new product/service development but also set in motion a virtuous cycle with reinforcing feedback loops?

In an interview featured in *Strategy & Leadership* entitled "Venkat Ramaswamy—a ten-year perspective on how the value co-creation revolution is transforming competition," Prof Ramaswamy said:

> The main components of co-creation are engagement platforms, experience domains, and capability ecosystems. The task of enterprises is to collaboratively design and build platforms of engagements so that these interaction environments create outcomes of value to all participating stakeholders. In short, the co-creative enterprise is not so much about "build it and they will come," but much more about "build it with them, and they are already there."[9]

"Build it with them, and they are already there." Could there be a better summary of VMware and VMUG than that? I once flew out to the University of Michigan to spend a day with Professor Ramaswamy, who is one of the world's leading experts on customer co-creation, having co-authored *The Co-Creation Paradigm* among other notable works on the future of competition. One of the examples he shared with me when we met in his office that day was the story of LEGO. Few will recall that in the early 2000s LEGO was on the verge of bankruptcy. Sales had fallen in a hyper-competitive toy market and the company had lost touch with both its core competency and its core customer. Resolute in his goal to return the company back to profitability, CEO Jørgen Vig Knudstorp turned to its customer fan base LUGNET (the LEGO Users Group Network) for help. "At LEGO, we stumbled across the phenomenon of customer co-creation, which is now becoming a major innovation practice."[10] For example, in 1998 they introduced Mindstorms, which allowed kids to make robots out of the familiar LEGO bricks. It turned out over half of the product's users were adults who actually wrote new computer code to extend the capabilities of the product into functional robotics, sharing their designs on websites and creating a new ecosystem community of users. Sales increased and profitability returned, in part because of the extraordinary contribution of the customer community to co-invent products. Knudstorp acknowledged the impact from the customer co-creation efforts: "While we have 120 designers on staff, we potentially have probably 120,000 volunteer designers we can access outside the company to help us invent."[11]

> ❝ *While we have 120 designers on staff, we potentially have probably 120,000 volunteer designers we can access outside the company to help us invent.*

Results

VMware increased its 2022 annual revenue by 9 percent over fiscal 2021 to $12.85 billion and the combination of subscription and SaaS license revenue was $6.33 billion, an increase of 13 percent over the previous year.[12]

VMware customers commenting on their involvement in the VMware cloud service team Agile product development process we referred to earlier said:[13]

- "Offer more of them :-) But seriously, perhaps a time to meet online to brainstorm or whiteboard together. Maybe interactive sessions between the members or members and staff."
- "The design teams are fantastic. Very helpful, attentive, and do a magnificent job. I am very happy to contribute to the product development process."
- "This is a great idea and I look forward to more opportunities to offer feedback in a focus group like this... I also would like to see a summary of responses and graph of votes after a week's activities so you can see the learnings of the larger group... Finally, it would be very nice to have more feedback and interaction with the VMware inner circle administrators."

A recent blog post describing this effort reported, "Most importantly, the biggest value uncovered from this initiative was that the customers felt they had a stake in this project and a sense of ownership over the product. Because of that constant iteration, VMware built a partnership with the customers and made them feel valued."[14]

Summary

Early on in this section, we talked about the power of harnessing customer community and the drivers of what motivated people to participate in co-creation and community activities which included knowledge building, social connection and reinforcing feedback loops. We looked at how VMware has effectively modeled each of these factors. We learned from Prof. Ramaswamy that "the task of enterprises is to collaboratively design and build platforms of engagements so that these interaction environments create outcomes of value to all participating stakeholders." VMware stands out as a company that demonstrates a sophisticated understanding of how to enable such a platform to produce value-added interactions, but also how to harness the benefits of this investment through a commitment to processes that places the customer in the center of all they do.

This design strategy begins with the word "foster" for a reason. To foster is to "encourage or promote the development of (something, typically something regarded as good)." Great companies don't look at their customer community as a sales lead engine. To sustain true community that has lasting impact requires a mindset that goes beyond what your company can get out of it. Best practice firms like VMware see it as an invitation to become "part of the family," collectively working together to bring the firm's brand promise to life and advance the wellbeing of their members.

Key insights

- Strong customer communities are characterized by offering knowledge acquisition, intrinsic motivation, and socialization opportunities.
- In B2B user groups, aim to foster a "virtuous cycle" between the company and the community members.
- Executive involvement and organization commitment are essential to grow and sustain an effective customer community.
- The value derived from an effective customer community ranges from the co-creation of new products and services to sales and marketing support, talent acquisition, and more.
- The task of enterprises is to "collaboratively design and build platforms of engagements so that these interaction environments create outcomes of value to all participating stakeholders."[15]

What's next?

The power of this example speaks to what can happen when you put the customer in the center of your business. Brands that create that level of customer intimacy may very well have the opportunity to design rituals into the experience that accentuate and even celebrate the shared meaning that their brand promise delivers. In the next chapter, we do a deep dive into the difference between a "habit" and a "ritual" while we take a guided tour of how Starbucks has designed rituals into the heart of its business for both customers and employees.

07

Design Strategy 5: Inspire rituals that create shared meaning

"We're reinventing the company, but we're not reinventing what we do. We're just reinventing how we do it."[1]

HOWARD SCHULTZ

The charitable organization Habitat for Humanity has helped make the dream of home ownership possible for thousands who never imagined it would happen for them. Today, more than two million Habitat volunteers a year build, advocate, and raise awareness about the global need for shelter, including former US President Jimmy Carter and his wife Rosalynn, who over 30 years have worked alongside nearly 103,000 volunteers in 14 countries to build, renovate, and repair 4,331 homes.[2]

There are many touching moments that occur in the process of building a new Habitat home, but one that is relevant for this discussion around building rituals is the Mortgage Burning Ceremony when the homeowner pays off their mortgage. As reported by one Habitat recipient:

> The day came and I was rushing around, I was rushing around because I was doing something at church, and just rushing, rushing, rushing, rushing. But when the time came to light the fire, this overwhelming feeling came over me. And I said I wouldn't, but I actually started to cry. I just felt so, so important because I'd paid this mortgage off, and Habitat is still around me, helping me celebrate this moment.[3]

This is a powerful example of the three conditions that constitute a ritual. Let me explain.

It has been said that we humans are "creatures of habit." Think of your typical morning routine after you silence your alarm clock. Whatever it is, your "morning ritual" really isn't that at all. It's a habit, which is technically defined as "the choices that all of us make at some point, and then stop thinking about, but continue doing, often every day."[4] Those behaviors that we all do automatically are simply a "natural consequence of our neurology"[5] and though they can be changed, are pretty much ingrained.

For our purposes, it is important to distinguish between a habit and a ritual.

To constitute a ritual, a set of behaviors must include characteristic physical features (e.g. rigid, repetitive action sequences) as well as certain psychological features (i.e. the user must interpret the ritual to have a purpose or meaning). Moreover, the meaning inherent in a ritual is often acted out through overt symbolic expression.[6]

A habit and a ritual on the surface may look the same, but the ritual is different because it carries with it an inherent personal or shared meaning that is not present in a habit. The singing of a national anthem before a game isn't a habit; if it were, it would just be the performance of a song with little meaning or consequence. However, when thousands of people stand, many with their hands over their hearts, and recite each line of the anthem word for word, they are participating in a ritual.

The same researchers who posited the definition above explored three underlying regulatory forces that underpin the structure of rituals: a) emotions, b) goals, and c) social connections.

- Emotional regulation: Several studies have demonstrated that rituals can relieve emotional distress, which leads to increases in ritualistic behavior. The rigid, physical, sequenced activities of a ritual may also increase endorphin production to induce pleasurable feelings, reduce stress, and help a person cope with anxiety, "... this overwhelming feeling came over me."

- Goal regulation: Rituals also play an important role in preparing a person for a performance goal, such as the ritual sequence a team follows prior to a championship game, or the tuning of the orchestra before a performance, "... I just felt so, so important because I'd paid this mortgage off."

- Social regulation: Rituals that are shared with others are experienced as social events or actions that mediate two processes. One is around enhancing the affiliation with fellow group members that reinforces the group's loyalty and trust. The second, when observing a group demonstrating a ritual, helps the observer learn and share cultural knowledge related to the social norms most important to the group, "... and Habitat is still around me, helping me celebrate this moment."

In a digital-first world, the power of ritual is not to be ignored, much like our discussion of customer communities. In the same way that creating a platform for customers to collaborate with a brand to co-create shared value, so does inviting rituals that create the opportunity for both company and customer to experience the shared meaning of the brand promise. To deliver an experience that customers truly love means not just exceeding their expectations but creating a "container" for what your brand stands for and recognizing its shared meaning for you and your customer.

Now what we think of as "consumption rituals" is similar to but slightly different from what we describe as "ritual" above. Here we think of it as:

The linkage of the episodic event strings in an exact, fixed sequence, where the ritual tends to be performed in the same way each time it is observed over a time period and has meaning compared to habits.[7]

Again, it represents a higher order than a habit, but may more closely appear as one, especially if viewed on a daily basis. In a business environment, rituals typically involve three elements and can act as an effective tool for enhancing meaning:[8]

- physical: actions (including movements and words) that are repeatedly performed as part of a group ritual;
- psychological: the psychological meaning that participants derive from a group ritual;
- communal: the perception that a group ritual is being shared with others.

Let us consider three questions before we move much further along this path of inquiry about rituals:

- To what extent does your company invite customers to perform a ritual that creates shared meaning between them and your brand promise?
- To what extent does your company invite employees to demonstrate behaviors or habits that model your brand promise?

> " To deliver an experience that customers truly love means not just exceeding their expectations but creating a "container" for what your brand stands.

- To what extent does your company create the opportunity for customers *and* employees to participate in a ritual that creates shared meaning, bringing your brand promise to life?

Maxine Clark, the founder of Build-A-Bear Workshop, is fond of talking about the company's heart ceremony,[9] which was invented by an employee. It happened at a point in the experience when their guest, usually a nine-year-old child, would pick a red heart from a bowl, touch it to their head, then their heart, and place it in their new "best friend" to reflect the values they wanted them to personify that they were making with the help of a Bear Builder. With the design of the new store experience, the heart ceremony changed to a digital format with an interactive kiosk, but the emotional impact remained. In fact, Build-A-Bear Workshop is an excellent example of a company that has been successful in delivering an experience that customers love and that has adapted it to a digital-first world.

But without question the company that learned how to inspire rituals to create shared meaning is Starbucks.

Starbucks

The Starbucks experience combines a series of intentionally designed brand elements that include the aroma that invades your senses when entering a store, the greeting that welcomes you, the selection of furniture, lighting, art, music, and the store layout. The brand built its retail business on the idea of providing its customer with a "third place" between work and home. Howard Schultz, Starbucks' founder, has said, "I've never thought of the third place just as a physical environment. For me, the third place has always been a feeling. An emotion. An aspiration that all people can come together and be uplifted as a result of a sense of belonging. This is the cornerstone of our business."[10]

If I had a dollar for every time I sat in a Starbucks, enjoying my favorite grande latté (non-fat, extra foam) and catching up on email or putting the finishing touches to a presentation, well, I might not be a millionaire but I certainly could have covered a car payment. I once met Food Network star Bobby Flay in a Starbucks in Manhattan who kindly agreed to a selfie with me and an autograph on a Starbucks napkin. That was quite a memorable connection.

In 2015, Starbucks recorded a video compilation of several customers commenting on their experience. One couple shared that:

> We go to Starbucks pretty much every day. It's sort of our special place because this is where we used to go for a date…. We've been together for almost 23 years and Starbucks is a huge part of that. People who are welcoming and it's kind of nurturing. It's not just a cup of coffee, it's memories… It's about relationships. Starbucks is kind of like a second home.[11]

Or a third place? A second Starbucks customer commented:

> Not only are you recognized, but you feel valued. Not only am I just a face you remember, but you actually remember something about me. When they know you, and they already have your drink—I love that. You get that perfect first sip. This is just the way I like it. This is a chance to really engage. And when you have that it's beautiful. They love working here. I love coming here. It's a really nice feeling to feel that connection.[12]

This is not a habit, this is a ritual. "That first sip" (physical), "a chance to really engage" (psychological), "they love working here, I love coming here" (communal). And consider the fact that Starbucks has done this in a category defined by attributes associated with speed and convenience. In fact, the truth is, Starbucks created a category and with it, a pricing premium for coffee that consumers were gladly willing to pay as a result.

My colleagues from the Harvard Business School would describe interactions like the ones shared by these two customers as a demonstration of the satisfaction mirror, a process that generates a learning relationship between customers and frontline employees as exemplified by companies like Southwest Airlines, Ritz-Carlton Hotels and Resorts, or Wegmans Food Markets.

However, as the second customer stated at the end of her testimonial, "But not every Starbucks has that."

In Q2, 2022, Starbucks' North American stores achieved revenue of $5.4 billion, up 17 percent from the prior year, driven by a 12 percent increase in comparable store sales that included a 7 percent lift in average ticket and 5 percent growth in transactions.[13] Not exactly the sort of numbers reported by a company facing a crisis. But a crisis, nonetheless.

The company that had taught the world how a global brand could be built by delivering an employee and customer experience that promoted coffee from a beverage to a ritual, that was delivered by baristas that often remembered your name and your favorite customized order, that invited its customers to find refuge in a "third place" between work and home, this company was feeling the impact of a post-pandemic reality.

FIGURE 7.1 The satisfaction mirror adapted from The Service Profit Chain Institute Power Service Program

CUSTOMER   **EMPLOYEE**

More Repeat Purchases ← → More Familiarity with Customer Needs and Ways of Meeting Them

Stronger Tendency to Complain About Service Errors ← → Greater Opportunity for Recovery from Errors

Higher Customer Satisfaction ← → Higher Employee Satisfaction

Lower Costs ← → Higher Productivity

Better Results ← → Improved Quality of Service

Jeffrey Hollender, the cofounder of the American Sustainable Business Network, was quoted in a recent *Fast Company* article as saying:

> In my opinion the customer experience has deteriorated significantly over the last two to four years. AI is not going to change that. If the people who are serving the customer are not happy, committed, and passionate about what they're doing, the whole experience is going to suck.[14]

> ❝ *If the people who are serving the customer are not happy, committed, and passionate about what they're doing, the whole experience is going to suck.*

Starbucks had begun its digital transformation efforts long before COVID, but the pandemic, plus other factors including a change in demand from hot to cold beverages, often with more complex ingredients, sent store teams that had already returned to full capacity into a frenzied level of service delivery. A labor force that had joined Starbucks to build relationships with customers through the "ritual of coffee" were suddenly finding themselves pushed to the limit. One Starbucks partner remarked, "We're short staffed, but you can't stop. You have to keep moving."[15] Although it represents less than 1 percent of the company's US employee population, over 240 of Starbucks' 9,000 US corporate stores petitioned to unionize and 46 won elections.[16]

Starbucks, however, is by no means the only retailer facing a generation of retail workers reevaluating their employment status, influenced by a global pandemic that created unprecedented stress, including health risks in serving customers as lockdown restrictions relaxed. Retail employees at the REI Co-Op in its Manhattan SoHo store voted in 2022 to join the Retail, Wholesale and Department Store Union (RWDSU). All workers at the store, including full- and part-time sales staff, will now have union representation. REI president and CEO Eric Artz commented, "I do not believe a union will serve our REI employees' best interests. The presence of union representation will impact our ability to communicate and work directly with our employees and resolve concerns at the speed the world is moving." He also added during a podcast with employees, "The fact that we're in this spot in SoHo in this moment means something didn't work. If a group of employees needed to seek different representation for their interests and to speak for them, then I failed in some fundamental way. I know that. I see that, I take responsibility for that, and I own that."[17]

Apple was also facing unionization efforts, according to reports from *The Washington Post*. Workers in two of the 270 Apple stores had already filed to hold a union vote with the NLRB and six more were in "advanced" stages of filing.[18]

The Bureau of Labor Statistics reported that from May through December 2020, each month ended with more than one million retail job openings. This after 7.7 million retail workers walked off the job the previous year. Forbes Senior Contributor Pamela Danziger summarized what we are seeing accurately when she commented, "Retailers have not faced such an employment crisis in recent history and the retail workers who remain can't help but feel the balance of power is shifting."[19]

When Starbucks' former CEO Kevin Johnson retired after 13 years with the company, Howard Schultz returned in April of 2022 as interim CEO to lead the company in an effort to reimagine its future and put in place a Reinvention Plan that would ensure its continued growth. His first order of business was to travel the country to participate in a series of co-creation sessions with a mix of frontline partners and managers in different regions, including the company's five roasting plants. These sessions had three parts. The Opening was about listening and candid discussion of the issues facing partners in serving Starbucks' guests. The session would begin with a "partner play-back" of the themes of what the partners were saying from several data sources. The second part of the agenda centered around Partner-led Ideas to address immediate issues but to also imagine what the new Starbucks could look like. Finally, the Closing allowed the group to reflect on the day's discussion and idea generation. Howard Schultz and other senior leaders took the opportunity to emphasize that the reimagination of Starbucks was being co-created with other groups just like this one and included in the final plan. Though Howard Schultz and the other leaders listened more than they talked, during one of these sessions the interim CEO fully acknowledged the burden that partners had carried.

STARBUCKS PROFILE

Our mission

Our mission is to inspire and nurture the human spirit—one person, one cup, and one neighborhood at a time.

Our values

With our partners, our coffee, and our customers at our core, we live these values:

- Creating a culture of warmth and belonging, where everyone is welcome.
- Delivering our very best in all we do, holding ourselves accountable for results.
- Acting with courage, challenging the status quo, and finding new ways to grow our company and each other.
- Being present, connecting with transparency, dignity, and respect.
- We are performance driven, through the lens of humanity.

SOURCE https://www.starbucks.com/careers/working-at-starbucks/culture-and-values/

We are co-creating together, and we are going to fix the near-term problems like maintenance people not showing up on time… we're going to fix the bigger issues of training, wages, and the other issues facing the company and the challenges that partners are having… I've realized that there's been many short-term decisions that have adverse long-term effects on the company. We're going to reverse that.[20]

I decided to go back and pull the Q2, 2021 Earnings Transcript in which then CEO Kevin Johnson reported:

Our work in AI is providing Starbucks the underlying predictive models, enabling us to fuel the great human reconnection by freeing up partners to do what they do best, connect with customers and deliver a world-class customer experience.[21]

Really? What got missed? And if something like this can happen at Starbucks, one of the most progressive companies in the world, is any company immune? As we said in the Introduction about digital-first: Is it filled with promise or peril?

Today, standing inside almost any Starbucks café, watching the line of pick-up orders generated by pre-ordering with the Starbucks app, it is easy to see why Howard Schultz reported on his first earnings call upon his return, "Our customer base is getting younger, they're digital natives, and they expect Starbucks to be as relevant outside of our stores as we are inside."[22]

So how will Starbucks meet the expectations of this younger customer demographic? Most likely, they have been dating over the metaverse rather than in the company's cafés through the pandemic. Perhaps they are working from their apartment rather than in an office tower across from Grand Central Terminal and are more interested in reading their Twitter feed than *The New York Times* while waiting to pick up their order. However, this description exaggerates the point, as seven years later I would be willing to bet that the couple cited from the testimonial compilation earlier will still be meeting at their favorite Starbucks and experiencing their "third place— second home" ritual.

> ❝ *We are co-creating together, and we are going to fix the near-term problems.*

For Starbucks, this means serving both that longtime couple who you can bet knows every barista by their first name, while not becoming irrelevant to the rapid pick-up customer who may represent a larger average ticket from food items added to their beverage purchase and additional drive-through transactions that will deliver a substantial amount of future earnings. All while staying true to their mission and values.

In his best-selling book *It's Not About the Coffee*, longtime Starbucks executive and leadership expert Howard Behar stated:

> Early on at Starbucks, we quickly figured out that when there was pain—
> economic pain, conflict, or disappointment over a failed idea… our values
> were still our values and sticking with them was the most important thing we
> could do. We knew if we broke that trust with ourselves and our customers, we
> wouldn't be who we are; we wouldn't be on the right path.[23]

Has Starbucks strayed from its path? To answer this question, let's rewind the clock to when Starbucks' celebrated digital transformation strategy had started to take flight.

The experience

It was 2016 and Starbucks had launched a five-year plan they called "the digital flywheel" that consisted of four competencies that cut across the business: rewards, personalization, payment, and ordering.[24]

Rewards

The Starbucks Rewards loyalty program drives approximately half of all sales in the US and the company has been putting significant digital resources into broadening the reach and depth of engagement in the program, which has grown to a membership of approximately 60 million customers around the world.

Personalization

The company has invested significantly in AI to better personalize the experience based in part on the data Starbucks Rewards captures about customer preferences and behavior. The company reported about 30 million digital connections[25] feeding into its personalization systems. Everything from data about what times of day people usually order to which drinks they typically like, which can then be combined with other data like the geolocation and time of year to provide personalized recommended items and offers. The company combined its consumer insights, partner analytics, and marketing analytics functions into a single center of excellence called Deep Brew to mine the data from these connections and refine them into more personalized experiences for customers.[26]

Deep Brew applies machine learning to personalize mobile offers. It captures order histories, customer location, and even your birthday. This data informs "nudges" to influence customer behavior with the goal to better match capacity to demand. For example, if the store you are visiting is really busy, it may suggest you prepay before arriving, or offer you a digital coupon for a simpler but similar beverage rather than your more complex personalized cappuccino. It also helps the company schedule staff based on demand, and manage inventory levels and machine maintenance. During the pandemic, mobile ordering jumped 8 percent, also contributing to the capacity crunch felt in the stores. It has become quite advanced—for example, if the customer goes to the drive-thru, Deep Brew will now display personal recommendations on the digital menu board.[27]

Payment

Starbucks has always been an innovator when it comes to its mobile payment ecosystems, and recently added Bakkt, a cryptocurrency exchange and payment platform in which they took an equity stake. You can now pay for your latté with Bitcoin and it will link with your Rewards points. Also, Starbucks created an incentive by not letting those points expire if they're tied to a prepaid card or a Starbucks Rewards Visa credit card.[28] Add to this the fact that, as of the time of writing, $1 billion[29] is loaded on Starbucks gift cards that has yet to be spent and it paints a very positive picture of future demand with a cost of customer acquisition of zero.

Ordering and delivery

Though the wide adoption of mobile ordering has put significant pressure on capacity within the stores, for the Starbucks customer the app makes ordering and pick-up amazingly convenient, with notifications sent to tell you when your order is ready for collection. With Starbucks Delivers, a partnership with Uber Eats that seamlessly integrates into the Uber Eats app, you can also have that latté or frappuccino delivered to your home or office.[30]

Starbucks and Amazon Go

In November of 2021, Starbucks introduced their first Starbucks Pickup with Amazon Go, leveraging Amazon's Just Walk Out™ technology.[31] The store highlights new, wider tables with USB ports, allows customers to order ahead and pay using the Starbucks app, and integrates Just Walk Out™ technology to bypass the checkout. The first store, located in midtown Manhattan, features the full Starbucks menu and additional food items from the Amazon Go lineup. Katie Young, Senior Vice President of Global Growth and Development at Starbucks, commented:

> Our goal with this new store concept is to give our customers the ability to choose which experience is right for them as they go through their day, whether it is utilizing the Starbucks and Amazon apps to purchase food and beverages on the go or deciding to stay in the lounge for the traditional third place experience Starbucks is known for.[32]

A digital screen alerts customers to the status of their Starbucks order when they arrive and after using their Amazon mobile app or credit card (or in some cases, a biometric reader) to enter the Amazon Go marketplace, items are added to a customer's virtual cart and the linked credit card or Amazon account is charged when they leave the store.

As such, Starbucks is striving to deliver a "self-regulating" experience to every type of customer: to the couple who connect to Starbucks' "third place" and cherish their visit as their "second home," but also to the busy commuter looking for quality, convenience, and speed.

The "bloom comes off the rose"

Fast forward to September of 2022.

> " Starbucks is striving to deliver a "self-regulating" experience to every type of customer.

We have a trust deficit. We have a trust deficit with our partners, not all our partners, but far too many of our partners, green apron partners, in particular, in our stores, we have not lived up to the highest level of obligations.[33]

So stated Frank F. Britt, Executive Vice President, Chief Strategy & Transformation Officer, early on in the 2022 Investor Day conference to a room full of financial analysts and institutional investors, keenly interested in how Starbucks would respond to the headwinds facing the company.

At the heart of the Starbucks Reinvention Plan unveiled at the meeting are improvements focused on the partner, the customer, and the store, with the premise that "these three elements need to work individually better, and they need to work as a system in kind,"[34] as Mr. Britt emphasized.

Since Howard Schultz's return, they have committed over $1 billion to improving and elevating the partner experience.[35] This commitment represents an important shift in mindset from thinking of partners as part of a cost center to a value creation center, from labor to talent including broadening their reach to where talent can be sourced. The company unveiled their Thrive initiative that includes support for helping partners grow at work, individually and as a team. Specific improvements (co-created between the company's partners and management) include:[36]

- a shift from fixed schedules to anytime shifts to meet the individual needs of partners in creating a work schedule that works for them;
- personalizing the partner experience to provide career paths that are specific to them individually;
- improvement to job design to simplify workflows and leverage technology to truly free them up to make those emotional connections to customers;
- the reintroduction of the Coffee Master and Black Apron programs for partners that achieve the highest level of coffee knowledge;
- the launch of a new partner app to create one digital community for all 240,000 US partners;
- additional training, including doubling the amount of training time for new baristas and new shift supervisors;
- incremental wage investment to $17/hour (eligibility based on whether there was labor activity at the store at the time of the announcement, not implementation);
- enhanced benefits including increased sick time accrual, a new savings program, and solutions to help partners refinance student loan solutions;

- introduction of credit card/debit card tipping as ways for customers to further recognize their favorite Starbucks partners;
- updated recognition programs and the expansion of a portfolio of upskilling and career mobility programs.

Future innovations will take on wage innovation, new wellbeing benefits, and recognition and connection programs. A Partner Experience Innovation Center was announced as a mechanism for co-creating solutions with partners to enrich their careers and drive constant value creation in the partner experience. To that end, a new Partner Lifetime Value Equation was revealed that quantified the financial benefit delivered to partners, customers, and shareholders from focusing on attracting and retaining employees.

FIGURE 7.2   Thrive initiative reproduced from Starbucks 2022 Investor Forum

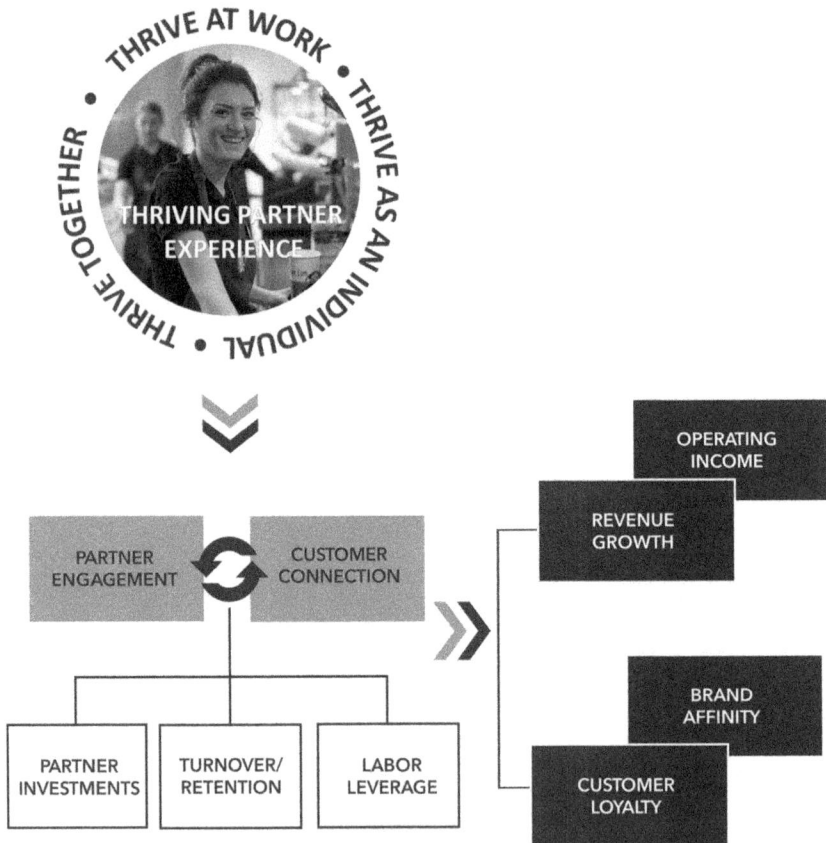

As Mr. Britt pointed out, "A partner that is thriving is the catalytic force that drives the value chain of Starbucks. It's that simple. It is the ignition for the flywheel of Starbucks financially and in terms of brand equity."[37]

Of course, it was not lost on this observer how closely the Thrive model mirrored the service profit chain introduced by my former business partners many years ago. Sometimes in life, "everything old is new again."

Highlights from how partners responded on social media and internal channels to the changes were immediate:

- "So excited that we're bringing back more coffee knowledge, coffee master, more training for our partners!!!!"
- "Yes, Coffee Master! The heart and soul of Starbucks!"
- "I love the investments that are being made, they are thought out. Especially the training/retraining. It's imperative."
- "This is the Starbucks that hired me, and I remember. Thank you."
- "Investing in partners = investing in customers = investing in shareholders."
- "(This is) a historic moment in the history of Starbucks. I am so proud to be a 27-year partner."

In terms of the customer experience, the Reinvention Plan[38] is:

- expanding the concept of the "third place" to not be constrained by the four walls of the store, but to bring that feeling of connection and caring across drive-thru, digital, licensed stores, and delivery channels. Starbucks CMO Brady Brewer has emphasized that "the flywheel of Starbucks begins with that connection. It is our differentiation;"
- extending the Starbucks delivery business in partnership with Uber Eats, which grew 20 percent year on year to include a second delivery partner, DoorDash;
- with respect to Starbucks Rewards, introducing new features that will allow members to link up with other popular rewards programs, from airlines to other retailers, to earn and redeem additional benefits at the tap of a button;
- launching the much-anticipated Starbucks Odyssey, a "digital third place" that will offer Starbucks Rewards members and Starbucks partners (employees) in the US the opportunity to earn and purchase digital collectible assets (NFTs, or non-fungible tokens) that can be sold or traded in a built-in marketplace, that "unlock access to benefits and experiences, never thought possible before."[39]

As referenced in Chapter 1, new technologies that underpin the next level of the internet, referred to as Web3 or Web 3.0, appear to represent the path to a "digital third place." Web3's embedded blockchain architecture will allow Starbucks to eventually list an unimaginable number of artifacts that are or can be rendered as digital files. Volumes have been written on the legions of Starbucks brand advocates who collect Starbucks cups and memorabilia, and the introduction of these assets as digital products could represent an adjacent business all its own with few edges. NFTs also provide an obvious way to frame digital communities around the Starbucks brand and with the added bonus of serving as an access pass into specific online groups. If NFTs are new to you, visit https://opensea.io/ to get a glimpse of an NFT marketplace. But don't scoff, as NFTs appear to be emerging as a legitimate digital marketplace:

> Until October, the most Mike Winkelmann—the digital artist known as Beeple—had ever sold a print for was $100. Today, an NFT of his work sold for $69 million at Christie's. The sale positions him "among the top three most valuable living artists," according to the auction house.[40]

Today, most NFTs are part of the Ethereum blockchain, which stores extra information about the digital file. NFTs can really be anything digital such as drawings, logos, music, or digital art.[41] Sound familiar?

It doesn't appear the new "digital third place" will resemble the current one. I most likely won't meet Bobby Flay there unless he bids on my digital rendering of the autograph he gave me on that Starbucks napkin (note to self: where did I put that napkin?), but it may represent a significant opportunity to provide a way for customers to connect and celebrate their affiliation to the brand through a new kind of digitally enabled community, while creating even greater shareholder value. I am not sure it will meet the standard of a ritual, but time will tell. What creates meaning for you will be different from what creates meaning for me, and perhaps that is the point.

The details

However, it is the third element of the Reinvention Plan that more profoundly answers the "what was missed?" question. Several new proprietary technologies will increase store capacity and throughput, simplify the workload

> " What creates meaning for you will be different from what creates meaning for me, and perhaps that is the point.

of partners, and increase speed of service dramatically. Retiring Chief Operating Officer John Culver spoke plainly about it:

> Three key levers that we're focused on, simplifying the engine to drive greater throughput through our stores, leveraging automation, so that we can simplify the tasks and reduce the complexity of the work. And, as we think about our stores for the future, how do we design more efficient, more purpose-built stores to meet this moment?

Starbucks had already implemented automated ordering across all stores for food as well as merchandise. The increase in the product mix of cold beverages added more complexity and required greater time to produce them, and the surge in volume had caused bottlenecks along with the time it takes to deliver warm food. The Siren system is designed to simplify tasks across both beverage and food platforms. This improves quality and consistency while creating the capacity to meet the growing demands for customization across both hot and cold beverages as well as warming food products. It reduces the production of a frappuccino from approximately a minute and a half to about 30 seconds, with no bending, replenishing ice containers, and reducing most manual production steps. The new food production process ships food products in pre-packaged containers that are simply handed to the customer from a warming oven. Production steps eliminated? All of them!

But beyond cold beverages and food, the new Clover Vertica system is able to freshly grind and brew a cup of coffee on demand in 30 seconds with a single touch of a button. Not only does it improve quality, it also reduces waste. In addition, the Cold Pressed Cold Brew technology reduces the process for creating cold espresso products from 20 steps to 4, from 20 hours to a matter of seconds, completely reinventing the experience for Starbucks partners and customers.

Finally, you will see an increase in convenience-based Starbucks retail formats, including pick-up only and drive-thru options, described as "purpose-built" stores designed to be more efficient, create a strategic advantage for Starbucks to deliver the accelerated revenue and margin growth set as guidance at Starbucks' 2022 Investor Day. Over the next three years, they expect net new stores to grow approximately 3–4 percent.[42]

The heart of the matter

Isn't it curious that in a digital-first world, for many companies it turns out getting the customer experience right requires understanding the impact on the employee experience first? As we learned from the CEMEX Go example and others, when it comes to introducing digital transformation into the customer experience, you must "get the kitchen ready before you go changing the menu."

Core to the Starbucks experience is a fundamental commitment to seeing coffee itself as a ritual. As author Joseph Michelli wrote about in his book *Leading the Starbucks Way*, the first thing a new hire at Starbucks does is undertake a tasting of the store manager's favorite coffee. Michelli writes, "It demonstrates the store manager's passion for coffee, and thus displays the desired behavior to the new recruit."[43] In fact, in the recent partner co-creation sessions described earlier, true to the brand, they each began with a coffee-tasting ceremony.

Over several weeks of training, a new hire is required to taste and document their reactions to all the coffee blends Starbucks offers. Even executives at the company regularly undertake rituals to remind themselves of the centrality of coffee to their business.

But Starbucks understands the difference between a ritual and a habit.

In his best-selling book *The Power of Habit: Why We Do What We Do in Life and Business*, author Charles Duhigg devotes an entire chapter to Starbucks. And well he should because the reason that so many millions of Starbucks customers are inspired to find their own ritual when visiting a Starbucks café is because of the way Starbucks has turned the willpower of their partners into a habit. You don't need to have worked at Starbucks to see the emotional toll an eight-hour shift can have on a partner. Not every customer is as polite as we might imagine, and some can be downright snarly. It takes a lot of self-discipline to maintain the firm's legendary service standards, especially during peak periods, when any normal person's reactions would be tested. "What they needed were institutional habits that made it easier to muster their self-discipline."[44]

And that was what they did. They developed training to help their store partners develop a habit, an automatic response, which was cued during challenging times in the store. Clearly, the skills taught and demonstrated by Starbucks partners prior to the pandemic were simply not enough to prepare them for what was to come: a store operating model unprepared to deal with the demand generated by a change in product mix and digital ordering facing off with a power shift in the employee–employer social contract spurred on by the pandemic and what has been called "the Great Resignation."

Back to my provocative question: To what extent does your company create the opportunity for customers and employees to participate in a ritual that creates shared meaning, bringing your brand promise to life?

Prior to the pandemic, this was something that Starbucks had arguably done better than any other company over the years. The mantra at Starbucks, as stated in the past by both Howard Schultz and Howard Behar, has been: At Starbucks… we're not in the *coffee* business serving *people*, we're in the *people* business serving *coffee*.[45]

Underlying their Reinvention Plan, Howard Schultz has cited four principles, developed with partners, to guide the company forward:[46]

- Safety, welcoming, and kindness for our stores. In a world that is increasingly isolating and often divided, we can operate in a way that knits together the fabric of our neighborhoods. We can expect to protect each other, respect, and include each other, and work together to create the kind of safe and welcoming environment we need at work.

- Advancement and opportunity for our partners. Starbucks can be a stepping-stone to betterment—the gaining of skills that matter, roles that pay equitably, and paths to more growth and opportunity.

- Wellbeing for one another and for our communities. The uncertainties and challenges in our communities are degrading our mental, physical, and financial wellbeing. Starbucks wants to make a deposit back into society—to help each of us heal, recenter; not just cope, but thrive. Starbucks is investing in the mental, physical, and financial health of every partner through our practices, policies, and benefits.

- Shared power, shared accountability, shared success. We built this company on the power of partner ideas and voice. Our Reinvention must even more deeply unleash power within each of us, more deeply share accountability in building a shared future, and benefit all of us when the company succeeds. We aim to be a wholly new kind of company in our industry, setting a new standard.

Howard Schultz also announced a new CEO, Laxman Narasimhan, to start in October of 2022 to take over from Howard Schultz in April 2023. When he introduced him to the investor audience, Mr. Schultz said, "His deep sense of humility, his understanding of the human connection at Starbucks, his understanding of people who wear the green apron and work so hard on behalf of the company, I just think he's the perfect person for the job."[47]

Clearly, history will be the judge as to whether his prediction is right, but this is the subject for a different book.

Results

Specific to Starbucks' digital successes, it is worth noting that in 2022, mobile order and pay increased 400 percent over the past five years and grew 20 percent over the previous year. Starbucks' $500 million delivery business rose 30 percent over the last year and the Starbucks Card grew to nearly 120 million holders, while in 2021 customers prepaid for their purchases to the tune of approximately $11 billion.[48]

Summary

Designing rituals that celebrate your brand promise may be the hardest design strategy of all to engineer. You may say, "Hey, we sell auto parts, we aren't building new homes for people in need or creating a 'third place' for our customers." There is some truth to that. But does Starbucks just sell coffee? Does Habitat for Humanity just build homes? Suspend your disbelief until we get a bit further along. You may be surprised at what can be designed when you collaborate with customers and employees to co-create experiences—including new rituals and habits—that enable customers and employees to celebrate your brand promise—together.

One final thought before we move on. This is not the first time Starbucks has reinvented itself, and I doubt it will be the last. Mr. Schultz told the firm's investor analysts during the Q2, 2022 earnings call, "Love and responsibility brought me back to Starbucks. My love of the company and my deep responsibility for our partners and shareholders."[49]

The person who showed us that you do not have to compromise in doing what is right for the employee and the customer while doing what is best for the corporate shareholder left his fellow partners with one other important message:

> You know, Starbucks has been about love. Starbucks has been about humanity, about joyousness, and certainly about community. The human connection and

> 66 *Love and responsibility brought me back to Starbucks. My love of the company and my deep responsibility for our partners and shareholders.*

the emotional relationship that we have built over these many years with you, and you have built with your customers—we are going to get back to that.[50]

I wouldn't bet against him.

Key insights

- Even established companies with strong brand awareness and deep resources can struggle with connecting the customer experience with digital transformation.
- Rituals and habits are not the same thing. A ritual is regulated by emotions, goals, and social processes that have important meaning to the individual.
- Leading organizations inspire customers and employees to share rituals that bring the brand promise to life.
- Designing rituals in a digital-first environment should consider new technologies that can connect customer communities in ways that were not possible in the past.
- Be prepared to increase capacity quickly and reliably should demand from the introduction of new digital channels drive up transactions faster than anticipated.
- Ground zero for linking customer experience and digital transformation requires a profound understanding of the impact on both the customer and the employee experience.

What's next?

These 7 Design Strategies have the potential to generate step-change improvements in both attitudinal and behavioral brand loyalty. It sets the stage as we are about to consider embedding immersive experiences which can fully envelop the customer into your brand promise. Lace up your sneakers because we are not taking a break. Rather, we are going to sprint ahead to examine how Nike combines digital and physical assets to create immersive experiences that deliver a new vision for what retail is quickly becoming.

08

Design Strategy 6: Empower customers through immersive experiences

"Digital is fueling how we create the future of retail."[1]

JOHN DONAHOE, PRESIDENT AND CEO, NIKE

Think of a time when you had an experience that completely overwhelmed your senses. Maybe it was your first ride through Disney's Space Mountain as a kid or attending your first Broadway musical. Or maybe you can recall seeing your beloved baseball team send a game-winning home run over right-field bleachers to defeat their archrival. The anticipation of the pitch, the crack of the bat, the moisture in the early evening air that served as a container for the suspense until the ball's trajectory met the spectator's gaze—all rise and cheer—the game is won!

Moments like these are memorable not only because of the meaning they hold for us but because so much of our mind and body are fully immersed in the experience. As we discussed previously, what we tend to remember is the emotional peak or the finale of an experience.

Digital technology creates the opportunity to shape highly immersive experiences for customers. They range in intensity from the virtual fitting room mirror found at many retailers to complete virtual reality experiences that use head-mounted devices (HMD) to generate digital reconstruction of physical objects and spaces through their three-dimensional representation.

Immersion can be thought of as "the pleasurable experience of being transported to an elaborately simulated place" and "the sensation of being surrounded by a completely other reality that takes over all of our attention and our whole perceptual apparatus."[2]

The Interaction Design Foundation (interaction-design.org) defines augmented reality as:

> Augmented reality (AR) is an experience where designers enhance parts of users' physical world with computer-generated input. Designers create inputs—ranging from sound to video, to graphics to GPS overlays and more—in digital content which responds in real time to changes in the user's environment, typically movement.[3]

Tim Cook, CEO of Apple, believes that "augmented reality is going to change everything."[4]

This design strategy explores how you can embed immersive experiences that create customer empowerment in ways customers truly value. But it begs the question: given the level of investment you may need to consider providing for these sorts of experiences, would they positively impact retention, spending, and advocacy?

Social scientists use a method to measure these sorts of things: the stimulus–organism–response (S–O–R) model describes how perceived stimulus/stimuli evoke consumers' internal feelings, which subsequently produce their actions and behavior. It is particularly useful in considering the degree to which technology-mediated immersive experiences have a positive impact on consumer behavior. A study explored this question associated with "phygital" experiences (not a typo—"phygital" has been defined as "a retail experience combining physical features and digital features in the same point of sale"). The researchers wanted to better understand whether cross-channel integration (both physical and digital) influenced consumer retention. What they discovered was that consumer empowerment plays a key role, especially in retailing, and it has the potential to facilitate the customers' ability to control their purchase choices and navigate the customer journey as they like. Also, a cross-channel experience will typically provide more options, and as we learned earlier, giving consumers choices that are relevant, provide progressive cues and are informed by a social context contributes to greater empowerment.

> ❝ *Augmented reality is going to change everything.*

Their findings validated that cross-channel integration does significantly affect customer retention and blending digital and physical touchpoints while initiating communication offers multiple benefits to both retailers and customers.

> In the phygital environment, retailers can empower customers by making their selections offline while knowing about promotions through a digital medium. Consumer empowerment (CE) as we know is all about providing customer avenues to connect with the retailers actively to shape the nature of transactions, to connect and to collaborate by sharing information; praise; criticism; suggestions; and ideas about its products, services, and policies… The salient point is that retailers interested in retaining customers should always look to empower them… allowing customers to participate, choose and deliver products helps increase customer involvement.[5]

The magic words: "What makes a brand powerful is the emotional *involvement* of customers" (Beers). Let us now discuss our best practice example of an immersive experience in action: Nike, Inc.

NIKE, Inc.

Way back in 1984, Nike signed what would be a historic endorsement deal with basketball superstar Michael Jordan that launched the Jordan brand. At the time, Nike anticipated that Jordan's endorsement would generate between $3 million and $4 million. It didn't. It actually generated over $100 million in the first year and heralded the birth of a whole new industry. If you need a reference point for this, visit a website called stockx.com. StockX is an online trading platform that has now expanded to other luxury items like watches and handbags but got its start in 2016 in the sneaker resale market and today is valued at $3.8 billion in an industry projected to grow to $30 billion by 2050. At the time of writing, you could bid on a pair of Nike SB Dunk Low x Ben & Jerry's "Chunky Dunky" shoes for around $1,300, but that might not be enough to secure the purchase as they most recently sold for $1,640. But these appear to be a bargain compared to the Nike Dunk Low Pro SB "Paris" that sold for $62,000.

It is not unusual for Nike and other leading brands to release limited-edition sneakers to generate interest and exclusiveness from their most ardent fans or collectors. With the introduction of Nike's SNKRS mobile app, these releases have moved into "online drops" using a simple raffle to purchase them. There, third-party resellers follow a similar process.

This context is important for one specific reason: what Nike presents in terms of an omni-channel, immersive experience is impressive. There is much to learn from Nike, keeping in mind that they are the market leader in a high-involvement, premium category with additional cross-sell opportunities to similar higher-margin products—aimed at a demographic that skews younger (15–45 years)[6] that are, for the most part, digital natives. It does not mean we can't take more than a page or two out of their playbook, it just means we must always remember, influencing consumer behavior is a big challenge for every company, and we must measure what is most effective based on the target market we are focused on growing and what would and would not be of value to them.

With that disclaimer, let's "Just Do It" and see how this company engineers an immersive experience that merges physical and digital together, centered around their mission: "To bring inspiration and innovation to every athlete* in the world." (*If you have a body you are an athlete.)

The experience

Writing about the Nike customer experience is a bit like trying to describe the first time you attended Dvořák's New World Symphony at Carnegie Hall, or a Major League Baseball game at Fenway Park, or a Wimbledon final between Roger Federer and Rafael Nadal. No matter what you write, it will never truly describe the experience. So, as you read the following section, I invite you to put yourself in the shoes of a Nike customer, especially a Nike Member, and immerse yourself in the experience.

Here is how it may begin: When a Nike Member enters a Nike store, all of their data from past interactions, purchases, app usage, events, and activities is used to enable virtual assistants to provide a personalized, immersive product experience through recommendations and content based on their captured preferences.

> " When a Nike Member enters a Nike store, all of their data from past interactions, purchases, app usage, events, and activities is used to enable virtual assistants.

Store formats

Today, Nike boasts several store formats, including Nike Live, Nike Rise, Nike Unite, and Nike House of Innovation. These concepts have a high focus on showcasing the best of Nike and giving importance to local communities by leveraging data analytics. Thanks to insights into their customers' behaviors and buying patterns, every week the stores display new footwear and apparel assortments to answer local needs. Each of these retail formats merges digital and physical channels, including interactive displays, self-service checkout, and other services enabled via the Nike app, including the Nike Fit technology and access to physical and digital events.

Delivering an immersive experience

At the store in New York's SoHo district, customers, assisted by a personal coach, can try on shoes in several simulated sporting environments (e.g. a basketball half-court, soccer trial field, and outdoor track) to determine their favorites. Training treadmills and indoor courts allow shoppers to test shoes and assess their movements to educate customers before they purchase. In addition to innovative product tests, Nike creates a retail environment that feels like an art gallery in celebration of athletic performance, with some stores focused on very targeted customer segments. For example, the company has opened women-dedicated stores that provide bra fit consultations as well as female-focused consultations using data analytics and expert personnel. Running assessment technology (powered by treadmills and smart cameras) in numerous stores allows Nike retail athletes (how Nike describes their frontline employees) to recommend the shoes that best fit the customer based on the results of the test.

Taking it "to the basket"—Nike's House of Innovation

To the untrained eye, entering the 68,000 square foot House of Innovation (HOI) on Fifth Avenue in New York City may appear like a digitally turbo-charged athletic/fashion meets high-tech art gallery. But to a Nike Member, this is about as immersive as retail experience gets. Upon entering the store, the member is greeted with a "Welcome to Nike New York" screen on their mobile device to begin their curated experience. All of their color preferences, favorite sports, shoe size, etc. are already poised to personalize the experience for the customer.

The inside spaces are digital, agile, and able to interact with consumers to deliver personalized and engaging experiences. Moreover, New York's HOI features customizable internal walls and floors that can be rearranged to host new configurations, dedicated to special launches and events.

- Interactive displays: A main object of the store itself is to provide an engaging shopping experience that responds as quickly and personally as its digital counterpart. For example, the ceiling at the entrance is angled at exactly 23.5 degrees, which is the inclination of the Swoosh logo, and each dressing room showcases the career of a particular Nike athlete via digital displays that shoppers can control to access different features.

- Digitally connected mannequins: Nike learned that consumers really like mannequins, but they get frustrated when they can't find the product that's on display. In the HOI, the Nike member simply scans the QR code and all of the products displayed are listed on their smartphone and can be selected for the customer to try on, in their size and with a few selections, queued to be delivered in a few minutes to a fitting room assigned to them.

- A digital-enabled fitting room experience: Speaking of fitting rooms, this part of the retail experience has traditionally been one of the lower emotional peaks. The HOI seems to have solved this problem. Once your selected products have been delivered, you can view them in different lighting modes, including "yoga studio" or "indoor gym." Better lighting makes them more conducive for taking selfies, which Nike learned their customers like to do.

- Reserve, pick-up, and instant checkout: A store this popular can get quite busy. For the customer who knows what they want, they can purchase their product of choice online and have it ready to be picked up at a locker when they arrive. They go to the Instant Checkout station, scan the product QR code, and off they go.

- Speed Shop: The Nike Speed Shop, located on the ground floor, uses data based on local SKU sales to stock its shelves, based on the community's buying patterns. It ensures frictionless access to city favorites, without local customers having to visit the whole store to find them.

- Sneaker Lab: The Sneaker Lab is a place dedicated to the brand's newest shoe models and provides a museum-like experience to sneaker enthusiasts. It includes exclusive launches, limited colorways, a women's zone, and the Sneakers Lounge, an area devoted to "sneakerheads" where the most popular products are released.

- Product testing experience: HOI and other Nike retail concepts have implemented numerous trial zones, such as the Kids Pod in Paris, treadmills, and a temporary basketball half-court in NYC to get live feedback from customers on products.

- Community: One key aspect that emerges from every activity of the brand is its commitment to creating an inclusive community based on respect and people empowerment. The messages that Nike is spreading through its campaigns are reflected inside the stores. One example of this is the range in mannequin sizes, heights, and body types.

Sustainability

As a part of its Move to Zero program, Nike stores use recycled materials. For example, the staircase in NYC is made entirely out of recycled shoes. Moreover, the stores are actively promoting Nike's sustainable technologies and collections, such as Next Nature footwear, and are implementing the Nike Refurbished program and Nike Reuse-A-Shoe program. This program collects end-of-life Nike shoes to create Nike Grind, a product that comes from manufacturing waste, unused materials, and end-of-life product that Nike has been incorporating back into product, retail spaces, workplace environments, athletic facilities, skateboards, and more for nearly 30 years.

Heidi O'Neill, President, Consumer and Marketplace, had this to say about Nike's approach to reinventing retail:

> I can serve you better at Nike House of Innovation in New York because I know what you prefer through your experience on the Nike app. If I know you're training for a marathon, I can better serve you... But it starts with the consumer. The ecosystem is working to be your personal shopper, but also to be your personal trainer, your running coach. People want more from Nike than buying stuff.[7]

The metaverse

As immersive as the store experience is, Nike is also using the Roblox platform to invite customers into the metaverse through NikeLAND on Roblox, an avatar-enabled environment where fans can meet, socialize, and find promotions that also translate into the physical world. Each visitor becomes a custodian of their own "yard"—a personal virtual space within NikeLAND that allows them to share their collectibles and designed to reflect their personality, taking and extending the Nike brand into virtual spaces.

> According to Nike, as of March 2022 nearly 7 million visitors had spent time in NikeLAND since it launched in November 2021. While there, they have been able to enjoy celebrity appearances from sports stars, including LeBron James, as well as buy exclusive digital products to decorate their avatars with. The items are not restricted to NikeLAND and can be worn as their avatar travels to other Roblox environments—essentially turning the visitors into digital brand ambassadors. They can also test their reactions and strategy skills with a number of games, with the opportunity to win even more products and rewards.[8]

In December of last year, Nike purchased RTFKT Studios, a maker of "next-generation" NFT collectibles. They sold 600 pairs of NFT sneakers in just six minutes, for a total of $3.1 million.[9] Building on the RTFKT platform, in Q3 of 2022, Nike launched Nike Virtual Studios, Nike's channel to extend their best-in-class digital experiences and develop Web3 products and experiences to scale this virtual community.[10] President and CEO of Nike, Inc. John Donahoe believes that it is "another step that accelerates Nike's digital transformation and allows us to serve athletes and creators at the intersection of sport, creativity, gaming, and culture."[11]

Extending their Web3 presence further, in November of 2022 Nike announced the launch of .SWOOSH, "a web3-enabled platform that champions athletes and serves the future of sport by creating a new, inclusive digital community and experience and a home for Nike virtual creations… SWOOSH will allow Nike Members to learn about, collect, and eventually help co-create virtual creations, which are typically interactive digital objects such as virtual shoes or jerseys."[12]

NIKE BY YOU

For those Nike members who wish to create their own pair of Nike sneakers, the Nike By You website provides a variety of styles to customize a pair of lifestyle or performance shoes to their preferences, including a personal ID in some cases. The shoes take two to five weeks to arrive depending on the style selections chosen.[13]

The details

Nike, Inc. is by far the world's largest athletic footwear, apparel, and equipment brand, with FY22 revenues of $46.7 billion.[14]

Setting bold goals

As part of its Consumer Direct Offense, Nike. "doubled down" on scaling its digital investments, announcing the "Triple Double Strategy" in 2017: doubling the impact of innovation, doubling their market speed, and doubling direct connections with consumers. In 2020, John Donahoe introduced the Consumer Direct Acceleration, a "new digitally empowered phase to unlock long-term growth and profitability,"[15] focused on growing the company's app ecosystem, product innovation, and speed initiatives.[16]

Nike also doubled its investments in professional development for women and ethnic minorities internally while operating with a substantial reduction of greenhouse gas emissions, wastes, and freshwater usage. You can see the role that brand authenticity plays here. Those values are promoted externally through many events and products including Nike's BeTrue and Converse Pride Collections featuring LGBTQIA+ athletes and celebrating the power of the team across the world of sport.

A dedicated team and reduced channels to market

To execute the strategy, the Nike Direct organization was formed to unite its platforms (website, retail, mobile, and digital services), reducing the number of styles of its products by 25 percent, followed up in 2020 with the announcement of their Consumer Direct Acceleration that included a reduction in the number of retail distributors to ensure great retail experiences and strengthen brand authenticity and consumer empowerment. Among those retailers that didn't make the cut were Amazon, Zappos, Belk, Dillard's, and Bob's Stores. Strong partners like Foot Locker, Nordstrom, Dick's Sporting Goods, JD Sports, Intersport, and others that aligned with the Nike digital/physical experience quickly became important partners in their distribution ecosystem.

Smart products

Nike developed multiple models of self-lacing shoes such as the Nike Air Mag (inspired by the *Back to the Future* movie) and the Nike Adapt BB. The shoes

> ❝ In 2020, John Donahoe introduced the Consumer Direct Acceleration, a "new digitally empowered phase to unlock long-term growth and profitability.

electronically adjust to the pressure generated by the feet thanks to smart sensors in the sole and can be controlled via smartphone to calibrate narrowness. Imagine being able to adjust the tightness of your shoes without missing a stride.

Multiple apps

Nike mobile apps have evolved over the years and are a key element of their omni-channel experience. There are four that can be downloaded from either app store: the Nike App, Nike Run Club (NRC), Nike Training Club (NTC) and SNKRS targeted at their most loyal Nike fans and collectors. Any of these apps will enable a customer to participate fully in the digital/physical immersive experience described.

THE LEBRON JAMES INNOVATION CENTER

The LeBron James Innovation Center is part of Nike's world headquarters in Beaverton, OR. This 750,000 square foot building in the center of the firm's campus includes the Nike Sport Research Lab where athletes' performance data is collected and analyzed. It is also a hub for athletes to share their wants and needs by participating in testing, prototyping, and co-creating solutions with Nike innovators and designers.

Janett Nichol, Nike's Vice President of Apparel Innovation, states, "Our focus is really delivering the best of innovation to athletes everywhere. We believe that if you have a body, you are an athlete. So, my first philosophy around innovation is that the athlete is at the center of everything that we do because they really are the ones that help us solve these problems."[17]

The Nike Sport Research Lab features a full-size NBA basketball court, a 200-meter fatigue track, a 100-meter track with two lanes of track and field surface and a lane of concrete, a one-third-size regulation soccer field with artificial turf, and outside the building, a 500-foot-long, 15.63 percent incline ramp. The capturing of data comes from 400 motion-capture cameras and 97 force plate pits, the world's largest array of either.

As they gather data, the goal is to become predictive such that Nike innovators, designers, and engineers can build products that solve problems that matter to athletes. "We don't start with 'we have to build a new shoe', we start with 'let's change injury in running and see where that takes us,'" Dr. Matthew Nurse, Vice President of the Nike Sport Research Lab, says. "Products and services will come out of that."[18]

Data analytics, computer vision, AI, and personalization

The company has been strategic at acquiring technology firms that extend their personalization capabilities. For example, two of these, Zodiac[19] and Celect, provide predictive analytics capabilities, but the former is a market-focused platform that aligns the right marketing offers to the right individual customer, while the latter represents the other side of the same coin, allowing Nike to optimize inventory based on hyper-local demand predictions. Both "onstage" and "offstage" activities are synchronized to ensure supply can be fulfilled as demand is generated. Two other acquisitions, Invertex[20] (computer vision innovator) and Datalogue, extended the firms' abilities to exploit the data collected from mobile apps, websites, and retail stores to understand customer habits and predict purchase behaviors and create cutting-edge technology, such as Nike Fit.

The Nike Fit app uses augmented reality-infused technology to take a picture of your feet (stand back to a wall wearing plain socks that contrast with your floor) and measures them to determine your exact shoe size. It takes just a few seconds but achieves a better result than the standard sizing tools we have all experienced in a shoe store because it considers the entire morphology and anatomy of your feet, rather than just length and width.[21] To accomplish this, the app taps into your smartphone camera and applies computer vision, machine learning, and recommendation algorithms. Once scanned, Nike provides "best fit for you" suggestions: a product personalization program so that once you search for shoes to buy, you will only see your size for any given pair of sneakers they carry.

The combination of these linked digital assets represents the way digital and physical come together to generate a deep level of immersion into the customer experience. The adoption of any one of their mobile apps makes it possible for Nike to engage with and sell directly to customers, offering a fully customizable, personalized buying experience based on both stated preferences and actual customer behaviors (such as type and frequency of workout routines). As a result:

> ❝ *The adoption of any one of their mobile apps makes it possible for Nike to engage with and sell directly to customers.*

- What the store experience may mean for one customer can be completely different for another as personalized recommendations and offers can be generated in real-time.

- Innovations like audio-guided runs in the Nike Run Club (NRC) app and the run statistics captured through the Apple watch allow Nike to gain additional, permission-based data about their opted-in customers' work-out preferences. NRC members can interact, share information, and unlock exclusive content (for example, recording their mileage so that the app can recommend shoes based on specific running behaviors of the user) as well as participate in special events.

- If the customer opts in to allow the app to track their activities, Nike can further recommend products or suggest events for them to participate in based on their location.

This was perhaps best summed up by Nike CFO Matthew Friend during the Q2 2021 Earnings Call when he responded to a question about predictive demand and inventory strategies:

> We're investing in technology in the supply chain, so that we can better predict where to put inventory, where we think consumers want the inventory, and the benefits for us are in gross margin. It's more full-price realization, it's lower cost to fulfill, and frankly, it's better for the environment because it's less shipping and it's less moving stuff. We're investing in technology, to create O2O (online to offline) capabilities in the marketplace.[22]

MOVE TO ZERO

Move to Zero is Nike's global initiative aimed at achieving zero waste and zero carbon. Key Move to Zero initiatives[23] include:

1 Nike will power owned-and-operated facilities with 100 percent renewable energy by 2025.

2 Nike will reduce carbon emissions across its global supply chain by 30 percent by 2030, in line with the Paris Agreement of 2015.

3 Nike diverts 99 percent of all footwear manufacturing waste from landfills.

4 Additionally, Nike diverts more than 1 billion plastic bottles per year from landfills to create yarns for new jerseys and uppers for Flyknit shoes.

5 The Reuse-A-Shoe and Nike Grind programs convert waste into new products, playgrounds, running tracks, and courts.

Nike's 2021 Impact Report takes the reader through a detailed explanation of the company's broad ESG practices including examples of closed-loop recycling:

> While our first aim is to reduce waste in the footwear creation process, we also want to create opportunities for reinserting the waste we create back into footwear product. Our goal is to leverage at least 25% of Tier 1 factory waste back into footwear. We work closely with the Nike circular economy team to identify closed-loop opportunities in manufacturing centers and with our creation teams and suppliers to enable the conversion of the waste into new materials.[24]

Yanko Design reports, "The new Nike capsules include popular silhouettes such as the Air Max Moti, Tech Pack, Nike Pro, Nike Sun Club, and some of the classics reimagined such as the Nike Dunk Low Next Nature, Nike Blazer Mid '77 Next Nature, and the Nike Waffle One Crater Next Nature. The latter actually boasts 25% recycled synthetic leather on some details and 100% recycled polyester twill upper. Even the Crater Foam midsole, heel clip, and midsole are made of at least 10% recycled materials as described. Nike has maintained the iconic styles but with a twist. There is less impact on the environment as some 20% of the materials are utilized."[25]

The heart of the matter

As with our previous best practice examples, several behavioral science heuristics and processes are present at different touchpoints in Nike's immersive customer experience:

- The IKEA effect: A close relative to the "endowment effect" which suggests that mere ownership of a product increases its value to individuals, the IKEA effect is evident when invested labor leads to above-market product valuation. When a customer leaves Nike's Customization Lab with a pair of Nike sneakers that they designed and produced, the value associated with those shoes will be significantly higher than their actual commercial value.

- Identity economics: Identity economics describes the idea that we make economic choices based on monetary incentives and our identity.

A person's sense of self or identity affects economic outcomes. As we noted earlier, Nike defines an athlete as anyone with a body. It associates the brand with both LeBron James and your neighbor who decided to join the Nike Running Club to shed a few pounds before that 25-year high school reunion. Who doesn't feel like an athlete when sporting the same training gear that Serena Williams wears when staring down an opponent at Wimbledon?

- Incentives: Nike's membership program appears to influence sales, but these incentives also promote healthy behaviors, and with it, a virtuous cycle that helps grow revenue for the company and greater value for their customers.

- Scarcity (heuristic): When an object or resource is less readily available (e.g. due to limited quantity or time), we tend to perceive it as more valuable.[26] Marketing messages with limited quantity appeals are thought to be more effective than limited time appeals, because they create a sense of competition among consumers.[27] Nike is a master at introducing limited-edition silhouettes, often co-branded with an athlete, celebrity, or other popular brand, to increase their appeal to a target audience, which also fuels the resale market for these products.

- Nudge: As referenced previously, a nudge is any aspect of the choice architecture that alters people's behavior in a predictable way without forbidding any options or significantly changing their economic incentives. Nudges are not mandates. The most frequently mentioned nudge is the setting of defaults, which are pre-set courses of action that take effect if nothing is specified by the decision-maker. This type of nudge, which works with a human tendency for inaction, appears to be particularly successful, as people may stick with a choice for many years. Like most e-commerce sites and apps, Nike's mobile apps and website include both default settings and nudges once enough data about the customer has been collected, as well as the previously discussed progress cues and social connections mentioned in Chapter 5 describing Strategy 3: Strengthen customer commitment by providing choice and control.

- Peak-end rule: We covered this in the very first strategy as demonstrated by Lemonade. According to the peak-end rule, our memory of past experience (pleasant or unpleasant) does not correspond to an average level of positive or negative feelings, but to the most extreme point and the end of the episode.[28]

Customer testimonials like the ones below speak to an immersive experience that is highly memorable:[29]

- "Love this brand and website. You can customize your favorite cleats and other types of athletic shoes. Shipping is fast and they offer lots of sales, specials, and the chance to earn bonus dollars."—Bobby of Weatherford, TX

- "I love the Nike brand, but I have to say they scored a huge deal by signing Michael Jordan to the Nike brand. That is the most wonderful thing that ever happened in sports!"—Amancio of Vega Alta, PR

- "I love my Lebron X. Its Airmax 360 cushioning is perfect for someone who plays under the basket (like me). No knee pain for me :) and it's stylish too."—Juan Paolo of Quezon City

- "This is a professional store, well stocked, great customer service representatives, ready to answer your questions or help you find something, courteous and well mannered, and a pleasure to be around. If the store has it in stock, they will find it for you."—Ray of Milwaukee, WI

- "I've always been a fan of Nike. I love my Frees, Air Max and Roshes because my feet are most comfortable when I wear them. Recently, we've been to Japan and I was able to chance upon these Nike Huaraches at a very affordable price. My husband and I decided to buy them, and it was the best decision we made that time! They were the most comfortable shoes we've ever worn."—Elisa of Quezon City

Results

Has it paid off? In FY22, digital sales represented approximately 24 percent of Nike brand revenue, which has more than doubled from approximately 10 percent in FY19, driven by consumer-direct acceleration strategy. Like every retailer, the pandemic tested Nike as well. For the first nine months of FY20, Nike reported strong financial performance, then with the lockdowns, retail stores closed, first in China and then the rest of the world. In the fourth quarter, revenue declined 38 percent to $6.3 billion. However, digital sales increased 75 percent in the fourth quarter and accounted for approximately 30 percent of total revenue.

Summary

Writing this chapter itself felt like an immersive experience. As I emphasized at the outset, if you don't work for a $46.7 billion company, don't be disheartened, there is a lot to take away from studying Nike's approach to designing immersive experiences. One thing to pay attention to, beyond all the technology and advanced design, is how intentional Nike is at aligning its mission and values into the physical and digital experiences it delivers.

2022 represented the company's 50th anniversary in business, and in a video introducing their "2021 Breaking Barriers—Impact Report," John Donahoe commented, "What I love about Nike is that we are a brand of action. We don't just say we want to create positive change in the world, we set out to just do it."

This report is worth reading for any company interested in reaching not only its bottom line but its higher purpose as well. Creating an experience that immerses your customers in your products and services is one thing, but immersing them in your brand and what it stands for is another thing altogether.

And that is a short story of Nike.

Key insights

- Immersion can be thought of as "the sensation of being surrounded by a completely other reality that takes over all of our attention and our whole perceptual apparatus."

- Cross-channel integration positively affects customer retention, and blending digital and physical touchpoints drives customer empowerment and retention.

- Delivering a powerful immersive experience begins with a profound understanding of individual customer segments and what they value.

- When it comes to personalizing immersive experiences, ensure that back-end systems like inventory management and fulfillment are synchronized to front-end platforms that predict demand against inventory. (Avoid the sizzle without the steak.)

- Amplify brand authenticity by looking for ways to embed your brand signature at points in immersive experiences that would add value to the customer and reinforce your brand promise.

- Consider extending your physical/digital experience into the metaverse to participate in the emerging Web3 marketplace.

What's next?

As I said at the outset, the Nike example really is a careful assembly of human, physical, and digital assets that are hard to match. But just in case you are worried that we may have peaked too early—do not fear. If you have ever waited in a grocery line so long you thought you might miss your kid's high school graduation, we are about to explore the solution to that. Welcome to Amazon Retail!

09

Design Strategy 7: Link digital assets to leverage value over cost

"Innovation is messy, it's nonlinear. But if there's one thing that I would say that helps this process, it is our organizational DNA… We sweat the details on behalf of the customer, patiently and diligently over many years with this long-term focus. That to me is the thing that is essential to bringing invention to life."[1]

DILIP KUMAR, VICE PRESIDENT, AMAZON WEB SERVICES (AWS)
APPLICATIONS

As we discussed earlier, the reason Blockbuster found it impossible to catch up to Netflix was the fact that Netflix had built a value network that would have taken Blockbuster years to copy and with their capital structure so invested in stores, it was just never going catch up. This last design strategy, linking digital assets that create significant value over cost, is perhaps the most impactful because if successful, the competitive advantage it can produce can be challenging for any competitor to win against.

The concept of leveraging value over cost was introduced to me by my colleagues at the Harvard Business School: James Heskett, Earl Sasser Jr., and Leonard Schlesinger. The idea is that for every dollar invested in operating expense, not only should it generate greater value in terms of income, but these operating platforms, technologies, or standards should reinforce each other to achieve even greater leverage. For example, as we learned in the previous chapter, a well-designed mobile app, that is powered by an advanced machine learning algorithm along with computer vision technology that can personalize an in-store purchase in real-time during the shopping experience, may sound futuristic, but you could become immersed in such an activity today at Nike's House of Innovation on Fifth Avenue in New York City. *That* is leveraging value over cost. Individually, each of these elements adds value, but connected, they amplify the value of the others tenfold.

In fact, many of our best practice case studies are examples of this final design strategy to a great degree:

- Lemonade's combination of a powerful, friendly, intuitively designed mobile app connected to machine learning algorithms which provide real-time risk-adjusted pricing connected to a unique business model with incredibly low operational overhead.

- Spotify's proprietary recommendation engine linked to individual preferences drawing on large data sets of behavioral data and collaborative filtering that generates a personalization flywheel between listeners and artists.

- CEMEX Go's touchless mobile-first ordering and fulfillment experience connected to truck telematics, customer service, and automated notifications all updated in real-time to accounting, billing, and HR systems.

- Starbucks' omni-channel store, app, website, payment, and rewards experience with backend integration to their supply chain to inform demand forecasting and pricing strategy as well as store staffing and inventory replenishment.

- Nike's extraordinary integration of several apps, with their store experience, immersive technologies, and product co-creation platforms connected to the Nike member community.

In some cases, like in our Lemonade example, these assets were part of a vertically integrated digital platform from day one. As Shai Wininger, Lemonade's co-founder, once put it, "Lemonade is a tech company doing insurance, not an insurer doing an app."[2]

CEMEX, meanwhile, was an established business with a strong customer base, and though they contracted with some external technology firms to provide additional capabilities, they built the CEMEX Go platform on their existing infrastructure. But note, having achieved so much in connecting the front-end customer experience with their back-office fulfillment systems, the next logical step CEMEX has taken is to join the OpenBuilt collaboration of companies as part of a digital ecosystem whose mission is to reinvent the entire global construction industry.

Digital ecosystems

What is a digital ecosystem? There is a litany of definitions. Tata Consulting Services defines it as "a complex network of stakeholders that connect online and interact digitally in ways that create value for all."[3] That seems a tad academic. I tend to favor the description given by Benjamin Talin, CEO and founder of MoreThanDigital:

> Focusing on bringing extra value to customers by optimizing data and workflows from different internal departments, tools, systems, as well as customers, suppliers, and external partners.[4]

This definition seems more straightforward, and helps make the point that the result of doing an excellent job from linking digital assets is to create greater value for customers from operations. It may be that a natural extension of this activity leads to opening up your capabilities to external partners.

A framework by scholars at Boston College and Boston University[5] provides a helpful way to think about digital ecosystems. They suggest the highest form of competitive advantage in the design of a digital ecosystem is demonstrated by the following conditions:

- aggregate multiple sources of product-in-use information (often through data connection via real-time sensors);
- a propensity to control the hub of a digital ecosystem network;
- relevance in many overlapping ecosystems;
- domination of ecosystems through control over multiple sources of product-in-use information.

Now, this too might seem like a mouthful, but the key points these researchers are making is that where a company positions itself within such a configuration of ecosystem participants matters in terms of achieving a sustainable competitive advantage. Hence, in selecting a best practice company to serve as an example of this design strategy in action, we turned to Amazon, given they have created perhaps the largest digital ecosystem in the world.

The challenge of choosing Amazon, however, is that they are so large, we could get overwhelmed by the enormity of their business model, so we will limit our focus to Amazon's physical retail strategy, starting with their grocery business.

Let's begin by addressing some of the criticism Amazon have received about their performance to date in the grocery sector. In a recent CNBC article entitled "Amazon's sprawling grocery business has become an 'expensive hobby' with a cloudy future," business reporter Annie Palmer wrote:

> Amazon has introduced a dizzying array of services—Prime Now, Fresh, Go and others—in its effort to become a giant in the $750 billion US grocery market… Still, it's just a niche player in the industry. As of mid-December, Amazon.com and Whole Foods accounted for a combined 2.4% of the grocery market over the past 12 months, while Walmart controlled 18%, according to research firm Numerator.[6]

Fair criticism, for which she is not alone in pointing out the remarkably slow traction to gain share, especially after paying over $13 billion to acquire Whole Foods in 2017.

But like many things in life, your conclusions about something are naturally biased by the lens you view it through, and any industry analyst weighing the considerable investments and marginal returns by a company as formidable as Amazon, might come to the very same one.

However, for the next few pages, I invite you look at this through a different lens. Because the reason we selected Amazon as the best practice example of this design strategy is that like all of our other case studies, Amazon takes this idea of linking digital assets to an entirely different standard. Like Nike, Amazon is unique, so it may be challenging to imagine how you might apply their approach to your business, but the value in going deep into how Amazon thinks about entering and eventually growing share in a market by linking its digital assets together is well worth the investment. As a result, I suspect you will see Amazon's physical retail strategy through a very different lens, and perhaps your own business along with it. This view isn't just about linking digital assets to favor a cost advantage but describes a process for shaping a value proposition and value network that create significant competitive advantage.

Before we get started, let's level-set the core tenets Amazon considers when thinking about entering any market. This begins by asking three simple questions that provide a filter for deciding if an opportunity is worth the investment:[7]

> " Like many things in life, your conclusions about something are naturally biased by the lens you view it through.

- Is the opportunity big enough? Is it something that has the potential to be a significant business to warrant the investment it may require to win?

- Is there a tangible customer need driving whatever problem it is that could be solved? Amazon has always focused on exceeding customer expectations on three attributes: selection, price, and convenience. Not only because they are important to customers, but because they are durable. People will always want a relevant selection of products to choose from, to pay a fair price for that product or service, and crave experiences that are as convenient and as frictionless as possible. Selection, price, and convenience. Highlight those three words as we proceed forward in this chapter.

- Finally, does Amazon have a differentiated way of providing the service that actually addresses the need, and do they have the skills inhouse to meet it? If not, can the skills needed be acquired in order to be able to offer this differentiated service?

Honestly, that is about it. If the opportunity gets past these three filters, the company will create a long-term vision of how to win, create the business case with clear milestones, and start the innovation process.

Let's now turn to the Amazon retail experience to see an example of linking digital assets that not only leverages value over costs but creates a powerful competitive advantage through what Prof. David Rogers describes as delivering both a superior value proposition and value network.

The experience—Amazon Go: solving a chronic problem

Over the years, our project teams have spent a lot of time with retail and grocery clients working on how to reduce checkout time and improve the experience. Everything from "line-busting" that included providing sales staff with payment-enabled tablets to allow customers to pre-pay prior to checkout, to the implementation of self-checkout technology. In fact, a 2017 study of self-checkout solutions concluded:

> There is evidence that self-checkout attributes positively impact user perceptions of service quality. Speed of using the service and perceived ease-of-use emerged as important determinants of customers' evaluation of self-checkout quality. Interestingly, reliability was considered the most important determinant of self-service quality. According to Meuter et al. (2000), this could be explained by the

novelty of the technology, which makes performing ("doing its job") accurately a source of satisfaction. Perceived control and fun/enjoyment were viewed as less important factors.[8]

Fun? Enjoyment? Really? Hindsight being a perfect science, we have to keep these findings in context of what self-checkout was trying to solve. Cashier-based checkout lines that could stretch all the way back to the dairy freezer. Neither fun nor enjoyable.

While every other grocery company in the world was reading studies like the one referenced above and asking "How can we improve the checkout experience?", the Amazon Go team was asking a different question: "Why do customers have to check out?" As the then Amazon Go Project Manager, Gianna Puerini, said at the time, "They probably have something they'd rather be doing."[9]

In terms of origins, Amazon Go launched to the public in Seattle in 2018 and there are currently more than 25 store locations in the United States. They vary in size from 450 square feet to 3,250 square feet front of house and offer hot breakfast, ready-to-eat lunch options, cold beverages, coffee and espresso drinks, food items from local bakeries and kitchens, and every-day essentials.

Amazon Fresh launched in the UK in March of 2021 and as of September 2022, there were 19 store locations. Amazon Fresh stores offer everything you'd want from your local convenience grocery store, including fresh meat, poultry and fish, dairy, fruit and veg, and bakery.

Store arrival

When you arrive at the store all you need is an Amazon account, the free Amazon Shopping app (Amazon discontinued the original Amazon Go app in December 2021), and your smartphone. You open the app, tap "In-Store Code," and scan in with the QR code presented. At select Amazon Go store locations, you can also enter the store by using a credit card linked to your Amazon account or by using Amazon One, a new contactless way for people to use their palm to enter and pay for items purchased at Amazon Go. Once you have entered, you just shop for something tasty or find some staples you need to add to your pantry or freezer, and put them into your bag. Changed your mind about that bag of brownie bites? No worries, just put them back. Your virtual shopping cart will be updated in real time. No other scanning required. Once you have everything, off you go. Leave, skedaddle, scram, exit, no lines, no waiting because there is no checkout. Now, if you miss the friendly repartee you may have had with a cashier, you may stop to ask an Amazon Go employee for a wine recommendation to pair with that meal kit, or ask them about some of the local food brands the store features, but that is it. Once you're done shopping, you're on your way. You just go.

Behind the scenes

It really does seem like magic the first time you experience it. Dilip Kumar, Vice President AWS Applications, explained the technology behind the curtain: "When you come into the store, you should be immersed in shopping. We don't want technology to be a barrier. We want it to be part and parcel of something that just exists so you can be doing whatever it is that you came to the store to do. Our job is to make sure that the technology disappears."[10] Amazon's Just Walk Out™ technology uses computer vision, sensor fusion, and deep learning algorithms to automatically detect when products are taken from, or returned to, the shelves and keeps track of them in a virtual shopping cart.

> " It really does seem like magic the first time you experience it.

CRACKING AN INDUSTRY-WIDE PAIN POINT—WAITING IN LINE

Solving the challenge of not having to wait in line required getting into some technical "heavy lifting." These are the six problems that had to be solved to get Amazon Go from the lab into the market:

- Sensor fusion: Aggregate signals across different sensors (or cameras because this was solved using nothing but computer vision).
- Calibration: Have each camera know its location in the store very accurately.
- Person detection: Continuously identify and track each person in the store.
- Object recognition: Distinguish the different items being sold.
- Pose estimation: Detect what exactly each person near a shelf is doing with their arms.
- Activity analysis: Determine whether a person has picked up vs. returned an item.

The question "Who took what?" could not be solved as a series of independent picks. Amazon had to track each person the whole time they were in the store, from the moment they walked in until they had left. Among the problems that had to be solved by the locator component were:

- the occlusion, where a person is blocked from view by something in the store;

- the tangled state, where people are very close to each other.

The next task was to ensure the labels were preserved across frames in the video, moving from locating to tracking the customers in the store. The problems experienced in this phase included disambiguating tangled states. When people get very close together, this lowers the confidence of who's who. The Go store technology handles this by marking these customers as low confidence, so they get scheduled to be re-identified over time. There is a follow-up phase for distinguishing Amazon associates, who likely demonstrate different behavior than customers (for example, they would likely put items on shelves rather than taking them off). The Amazon team took on the ambitious project to generate synthetic activity data using simulators. Within these simulators, they needed to create virtual customers (including variations in clothing, hair, build, height, etc.), cameras, lighting and shadows, and simulate the same camera hardware limitations.

SOURCE Sections reproduced from Rohit Kumar, Salwa Shaikh, Automated cashier stores: Amazon Go technology, *International Research Journal of Modernization in Engineering Technology and Science*, 4(6), June 2022.

Finishing strong

Though there are no cashiers, laws were passed in several US states concerned that customers without the means to carry a smartphone were being discriminated against, that all Amazon Go stores must accept cash payments. So, though there aren't cashiers as you would see in a typical convenience store, there are (and have been since the first Amazon Go store opened) employees in each of these stores, stacking selves and greeting customers, and helping new customers understand how it all works. "I probably say it 25 times a day... I love saying 'just walk out,' it brings a smile to my face."[11] Right, just walk out. Your virtual shopping cart is available to you on your Amazon app along with all your other Amazon purchases. In some locations you can even return Amazon purchases made online to an Amazon Go store.

Leveraging value over costs

Data analytics firm Brick Meets Click estimated that the Amazon Go flagship store in Seattle generates $2,700 in annual sales per square foot of selling space, with an average of 50 inventory turns per year.[12] This sort of performance would be matched by only a handful of retailers while also reducing traditional operating expenses like the cost of checkout personnel and equipment. However, some retail analysts have questioned whether the cost of deploying the technology for a typically low-margin industry is worth it. Some cashier-less tech suppliers say costs to set up and maintain the systems can easily reach into the millions. But from its launch, Amazon went for years without turning a profit and it has never been afraid to enter a new market or be willing to take the brunt of losses before finally turning a profit. As former CEO Jeff Bezos has said in the past:

> If everything you do needs to work on a three-year time horizon, then you're competing against a lot of people. But if you're willing to invest on a seven-year time horizon, you're now competing against a fraction of those people, because very few companies are willing to do that.[13]

And very few companies see the opportunity through the lens of creating both a superior value proposition and a hard-to-imitate value network.

Expanding to grocery

In February of 2020, Amazon opened Amazon Go Grocery (since rebranded to Amazon Fresh), a smaller-format grocery store, in Seattle's Capitol Hill neighborhood. The first full-size Amazon Fresh store opened in Woodland Hills, California in September 2020 and brought the same technology from a 1,800 square foot convenience store in to a full-size, 35,000+ square foot grocery store, with two recent store openings in New York and Illinois measuring at 50,000 square feet each.[14] Mr. Kumar explains: "There's no real upper bound. It could be five times as big. It could be 10 times as big."[15] The Amazon Fresh store provides "a wide assortment of national brands and high-quality produce, meat, and seafood; plus, our culinary team offers customers a range of delicious, prepared foods made fresh in store, every day."[16] Mr. Kumar shared the development process in a recent interview. "We tried to go department by department to be able to say, 'What do people really look for in a neighborhood grocery store?' We felt like the just-walk-out shopping experience in a residential neighborhood, in a residential grocery store, would resonate very well."[17] Besides Just Walk Out™ technology, the new Amazon Fresh Stores introduce some additional features.

The Amazon Dash Cart enables the customer to skip the checkout line, but also provides a whole new shopping experience. The cart uses a combination of computer vision algorithms and sensor fusion to identify items put into the cart and knows where the customer is in the store, and hence can make recommendations for nearby products and serve up promotions based on the items you are adding to your cart. It even weighs produce for you, so if you had asked Alexa to add bananas to your virtual shopping cart while at home the day before, that item appears on the cart after you have scanned a QR code generated by the Amazon Shopping app when you start using the cart.

Frustrated with trying to find a store associate to help you find an item? No more; there are "Ask Alexa" devices placed through the store so you can just ask Alexa where to find those bananas you had added to your list. After passing through the Dash Cart lane, you can take the cart to your car to unload your purchases and off you go. Just drive off.

Amazon has introduced this newer version of the Dash Cart to a Whole Foods store in Westford, Massachusetts, to be followed by a few additional Whole Foods Market stores and many Amazon Fresh stores in the US. Whole Foods Chief Technology Officer Leandro Balbinot commented: "As many of our customers return to their in-store grocery shopping routines, it's exciting to introduce new and unique ways for them to shop our stores."[18]

Just Walk Out™ technology licensing

In a recent Forbes article entitled "5 reasons why Amazon Go is already the greatest retail innovation of the next 30 years," senior contributor Chris Walton commented:

> ❝ The Amazon Dash Cart enables the customer to skip the checkout line, but also provides a whole new shopping experience.

Amazon bets on universal truths, and the idea that no one wants to spend any time waiting in line to pay is about as universal as it gets... Don't agree? Try it. And then ask yourself, if you had the same experience at your favorite grocery store, say at a Tesco, an Aldi, or even at a Circle K (the companies on the forefront of deploying Amazon-like tech themselves), and all else being equal, wouldn't you choose the ability to walk out without standing in line every time? You damn well know you would and are lying to yourself if you think otherwise.[19]

You know you are onto something when your competitors start copying you. Ahold Delhaize USA launched a small pilot store called Lunchbox in Quincy, Massachusetts that offers "frictionless checkout." Paul Scorza, Ahold's CIO for Retail Business, stated, "Our philosophy on innovation is to be what we call a 'fast follower.'"[20] They are experimenting with their version of Just Walk Out™ technology and believe they can do it for a much lower cost.

On March 9, 2020, Reuters reported that Amazon would offer their Just Walk Out™ technology to other retailers[21] and indeed, the company launched a website to describe the service and invite inquiries. Much like Amazon Go, the customer scans or taps a credit card to enter the store, selects or puts back the items they want, and then (don't make me say it) they just go. Early customers include Hudson Travel Convenience Stores, the Climate Pledge Arena in Seattle, and the TD Garden in Boston whose President Amy Latimer was quoted as saying, "We are always looking to leverage technology to bring fast, easy, and touch-free amenities to our guests, and we are excited to collaborate with Amazon to use their Just Walk Out™ technology in these MRKT stores."[22] The fact that Amazon has begun to license this technology isn't surprising. What is most interesting to note, however, is that in November of 2021, *Charged: Retail Tech News* reported that Amazon reduced the pricing to customers dramatically, getting the operating cost of a 1,000 square foot, cashier-less location down to just $159,000 per store annually.[23] But even more interesting, this news outlet was quoted as saying:

The costs are spread out through the fees for using Amazon Web Services (AWS) cloud technology and hiring remote employees to manually verify the accuracy of the checkouts in stores, as well as other tasks.[24]

Now this is a salient point. First, Amazon linked three digital assets (computer vision, sensor fusion, and deep learning algorithms) to create Just Walk Out™ technology for their own Amazon Go stores. Now, as they begin to license it, they are linking their digital platforms to deliver a robust set of technologies and services which, over time, will leverage greater value over costs for their customers and position them at the center of the emerging digital ecosystem. A tipping point of customer adoption begins. Dilip Kumar explained this to us in my interview with him:

> Our core tenet for creating these suites of services is not just our first-party stores, but also for third-party stores. The world is full of very interesting retailers selling all kinds diverse and interesting shopping experiences… so how can we take the best of what they do and marry that with what we're good at? That's where I see our retail technologies going over the next five years.

Link digital assets to establish a value network: logistics, smart home, and AWS

Recall that Amazon started in the grocery industry in the delivery business, so it should be no surprise that Amazon Logistics would emerge as an obvious partner to start linking digital assets to establish a formidable value network.

Amazon Logistics

Say hello to Scout. Amazon Scout is a six-wheeled autonomous robot used to deliver packages, that debuted on January 23, 2019, in Snohomish County, Washington. Amazon Scouts are about the size of a large cooler and move on sidewalks at a walking pace. In July 2020, the service expanded into Atlanta, Georgia, and Franklin, Tennessee, and in 2021 Amazon announced plans to open a Scout Development Center in Finland to work on developing 3D technology to improve the robots' safety.

Amazon has registered a host of new patents recently, including one for "mobile fulfillment centers with intermodal carriers and unmanned aerial vehicles," which describes a system for combining drone delivery and automated fulfillment. Amazon is spending significant amounts of money to expand its existing logistics infrastructure.[25] In fact, the volume of patents coming out of Amazon designed to expand their ability to link digital technologies is impressive. For example, a patent granted on September 3, 2019,

> ❝ *A tipping point of customer adoption begins.*

was for "aerial vehicle delivery on items available through an e-commerce shopping site." It describes "an unmanned aerial vehicle (UAV) configured to autonomously deliver items of inventory to various destinations." The patent description includes the following details:

> In addition to selecting a delivery method, the user may choose a delivery location. With the implementations described herein, a user now has the ability to choose "Bring It to Me." With this option, the actual location of the user is determined, and the UAV delivers the items to the current location of the user. The current location of the user may be based on, for example, a determined location of a portable device (e.g. mobile phone) associated with the user.[26]

Add to this that on August 31, 2020, Amazon received federal approval to operate its fleet of Prime Air delivery drones,[27] a milestone that allows the company to expand unmanned package delivery. Amazon said it would use the approval to conduct rigorous testing. It is perhaps relevant to note that despite their struggle to advance this technology introduced on a *60 Minutes* episode back in 2013 by Jeff Bezos, Google's parent company Alphabet has had success in Australia conducting suburban drone deliveries with their subsidiary Wing. These drones have delivered over 10,000 cups of coffee, 1,000 loaves of bread and 1,200 roasted chickens without facing a single issue.[28]

Alexa Smart Home

As Stuart Patterson suggested in Chapter 1, the future is around ambient technologies that facilitate personalized, proactive voice interactions. Alexa Smart Home's vision is centered on just that concept. It is there when you need it and fades into the background when you don't. Alexa AI Senior Vice President and Head Scientist Rohit Prasad said in a recent interview:

> Ambient intelligence is the science that makes it possible for the disparate devices, sensors, and technologies in your environment to seamlessly work together to assist and delight you at every moment. This intelligence is there when you need it—it even anticipates your needs—but it disappears into the background when it is not needed. With functionalities like Routines and Hunches that help Alexa anticipate your needs and automate your day, Alexa is, at the core, what Amazon is doing with ambient intelligence.[29]

But if you thought Scout was cute, wait until you meet Astro, Amazon's new home robot. Astro is a "new and different kind of robot, one that's designed to help customers with a range of tasks like home monitoring and keeping in touch with family. It brings together new advancements in artificial intelligence, computer vision, sensor technology, and voice and edge computing in a package that's designed to be helpful and convenient."[30] Astro can be used to check that your home is safe and secure and integrates with Ring Pro Protect. It can help with elder care and bring Alexa to every part of your house. So, if you are in the sunroom reading a book, you can ask Astro to add those bananas to your virtual shopping list. Astro was available in 2022 for $1,449.99, but as part of the Day 1 Editions program it was on offer for an introductory price of $999.99 with a six-month trial of the Ring Protect Pro subscription included.[31]

A clear picture emerges. As one legendary innovator once said, "The best way to predict the future is to invent it."[32] Consider the digital assets and platforms Amazon is connecting:

- Just Walk Out™ technology, now being licensed at a significantly discounted operating cost, you might conclude to achieve a disproportionate share of the market, first-mover advantage, and to create demand for cashier-less checkout.

- AWS to host the Just Walk Out™ technology deployment across all of their locations and with the opportunity to provide additional security and application services—from analytics to robotics and even call center solutions as needed.

- Dash Cart, expanding beyond Amazon Fresh at least to a handful of Whole Foods locations today, but you might expect many more in the future, delivering both cashier-less checkout and a better, more efficient, convenient, and faster in-store experience.

- Alexa, quickly evolving with ambient capabilities, located before you arrive in your home, in the Astro home robot, and located throughout the Amazon Fresh (and eventually) Whole Foods stores.

- Free home delivery—and eventually Amazon Logistics services to drive down costs even further.

- AWS-hosted big data analytics understanding all of this behavior to drive new levels of personalization, customer insight, and supply chain management.

It is not like Amazon doesn't have competitors. Start-ups like Grabango, AiFi, and Zippin are offering cashier-less solutions. But if you were the management team of a large grocery chain, who would you buy from when Amazon's solution begins in the consumer's home through Alexa and continues when the consumer visits the store or, better yet, selects home delivery? You might argue that surely these other competitors are building APIs to the Google Assistant and Alexa themselves… perhaps they are, but at what cost? How much greater convenience? And once the customer has engrained their order-ing habit as a habit, maybe even a ritual, how easy is it going to be to unseat Amazon from those customers? This is the definition of a value network.

Scale the value network: Whole Foods

Now the game gets serious, and we start to understand why Amazon paid what was widely acknowledged as a premium to acquire Whole Foods. With 500+ stores located in neighborhoods with households quite likely to have an Alexa device, in urban areas with sidewalks and garages for autonomous robots like Scout to arrive at or a friendly drone to land, Amazon's customer segmentation strategy appears to align with the value network they are investing in. Now if these 500+ Whole Foods stores could also be used as online ordering fulfillment centers, Amazon takes leveraging value over costs all the way to the margin. A CB Insights report sheds some light on this:

> Some analysts claimed Amazon's purchase of the retailer was short-sighted, and that Whole Foods' reputation as a premium retailer—with prices to match—was at odds with Amazon's low-price, high-volume model. However, this analysis overlooked a key source of value for Amazon's acquisition: namely, the potential to use Whole Foods stores as ready-made distribution centers. With Whole Foods' 500+ locations across the US, Amazon gained quick access into the highly competitive grocery retail market. Even without its inventory, equipment, and storage facilities, Whole Foods' physical locations were valuable. Moreover, many Whole Foods stores are located in affluent urban areas and typically attract higher-income consumers with a preference for high-end grocery products—a similar demographic to that most likely to shop for groceries online, according to a Gallup survey.[33]

> ❝ *Now the game gets serious, and we start to understand why Amazon paid what was widely acknowledged as a premium to acquire Whole Foods.*

Now the opportunity for scaling is clear. It would not be surprising to see Amazon expand in the UK market as well as Spain, Italy, and Germany in the coming years.

As Amazon has done with other services, they often improve margin by decreasing costs through these scaled efficiencies. Whole Foods now delivers a much more competitive price level compared to before the acquisition in line with Amazon's strategy, and given that last-mile delivery accounts for 53 percent of total shipping costs,[34] if things like closer fulfillment centers (Whole Foods), Amazon Scout, and drone-based delivery can shrink those costs even further, Amazon can find even more savings to share with customers and shareholders. With each digital asset linked to form a highly differentiated value network, it's time to talk about the icing on all this cake: data.

Generate data insights: retail store analytics service

Listen, this chapter may be the hardest one to keep up with. I am finding it tough going and I am writing it! But now just consider the level of data Amazon will collect from all of this "product-in-use information." Data from Amazon One, your general online purchase information from Prime, the path you take and the items you purchase (and put back) from Dash Cart through an Amazon Fresh store—the list is significant and all stored on AWS cloud infrastructure.

Not surprisingly, Amazon recently introduced a new physical retail analytics service called Store Analytics that offers brands "data-driven insights about the performance of their products, promotions, and ad campaigns."[35] The platform aggregates and anonymizes the data so no individual personal information is shared; however, brands will have access to how their products are "discovered, considered, and purchased in applicable stores to help them inform decisions related to selection, promotions, and ad campaigns."[36] Though any customer can opt out of having their individual data included, as cited earlier, from previous research only those among us most adamant about issues of personal privacy typically do. In terms of retailers, Mr. Kumar reinforced Amazon's privacy policy when he said, "We prohibit the use of Just Walk Out™ technology data for anything other than supporting Just Walk Out™ retailers."

Exploit nearby adjacencies: Amazon Style

To make the case for how this can scale to close adjacencies, consider that Amazon recently opened their first 30,000 square foot Amazon Style fashion store in Los Angeles. In this store, customers using the Amazon Shopping app can send items to a fitting room, where they can use a touchscreen to browse more options, rate items, and request more sizes or styles that are delivered directly to their fitting room closet within minutes using "on-site operations, with advanced technologies and processes used in Amazon fulfillment centers."[37] This is quite different, obviously, from a grocery store or convenience store trip where the customer may generally know what they are there to purchase. The fashion shopper may be looking to be inspired, to have their fashion tastes expanded, and hence the Amazon Style store—in true Amazon "fashion"—brings selection, price, and convenience, their three most durable value attributes, to a retail fashion experience, enabling consumers to discover as well as shop.

The details

This description of the experience has covered a lot of details, but let's drill a bit deeper into some of the AWS technology that could be linked to serve a variety of Amazon's businesses. Remember these two conditions cited by those Boston researchers around creating a competitive advantage from digital ecosystems:

- a propensity to control the hub of a digital ecosystem network;
- relevance in many overlapping ecosystems.

Amazon Rekognition is a good example. This product allows the user to integrate picture and video analysis to an application using deep learning technology. It helps in identifying various objects. For example, you can find your products on store aisles by recognizing the logos. In addition, to ensure their position to "control the hub," AWS services like AWS Lambda (virtual compute capability) easily integrate with Amazon S3 (for cloud storage). Dilip Kumar explains the role of AWS in Amazon's Retail Strategy: "If you think about any of these technologies, since day one we have used AWS services behind the scenes. As a result, we can offer Just Walk Out™ technology as part of an entire application to retailers. Take Amazon One. We give them the device and they plug it in, then they can start taking orders with very little effort. For Just Walk Out™ and Amazon One, we offer these services at an application level vs. an infrastructure services level as our customers are store operator vs. developers."

A visit to the AWS website describes a long series of technologies available to developers to build from and this suite of retail technologies is no different.

The heart of the matter

From a design standpoint, there are several reasons why linking digital assets is important. For retailers, Amazon's Just Walk Out™ technology has some clear implications. Early customers like Hudson Group cited earlier, which operates over 1,000 retail locations that sell a variety of essential travel products and snacks, have seen improvement in both transactions and basket size.[38] It makes sense. If you are a rushed traveler with little interest in waiting in line to make your flight, just walking out may translate to actually rushing out. But the increase in items per transaction is interesting, and may be due in part to the reassignment of cashiers to customer support roles.[39]

Secondly, a study completed in 2021 looked into the effect of AI-enabled checkouts on consumers' purchase intent and evaluations of the retailing environment. They found that AI-enabled checkouts led to a higher level of arousal, which in turn yielded more favorable store atmosphere evaluations and higher purchase intent.[40] This is relevant because a previous study that centered on the reasons for purchase abandonment in retail stores concluded that:

> ... in more stressful shopping environments, task-oriented shoppers' purchase abandonment is more than four times that of recreation-oriented customers.[41]

However, as always, adoption of new technologies globally can vary widely. One study considering AI-enabled checkout in Saudi Arabia found customer anxieties actually rose as they worried about data privacy as well as how to use the new technology, especially older consumers.[42]

From a behavioral science perspective, conditions like ambiguity aversion (the tendency to favor the known over the unknown) or cognitive dissonance (just walking out may conflict with my self-image of not being seen as a shoplifter) may come into play as these solutions are introduced.

> ❝ AI-enabled checkouts led to a higher level of arousal, which in turn yielded more favorable store atmosphere evaluations and higher purchase intent.

Just Walk Out™ technology and Dash Carts do provide the company with ample opportunity to apply other powerful behavioral science tactics, including attribute framing (fresh meat described as 95 percent lean versus 5 percent fat free), incentives linked to your Amazon Prime account, and nudges (the ability for an individual to maintain freedom of choice and to feel in control of the decisions they make but to "nudge" them toward healthier choices), which could appear on your Dash Cart screen.

In terms of the broader design challenge of how you might link digital assets for your company, this is harder to comment on as every business is different. The way you might pursue this will depend on the needs of your customers and the connected digital assets that would create additional value for them.

But all of our clients' experience in applying this design strategy to their business suggests the "view has always been worth the climb." The chapter describing the design accelerator will provide a clear set of steps to help you chart your path forward.

Results

Amazon ended fiscal year 2021 with revenues of $469.8 billion, a growth of 22 percent over the previous year. In 2021, gross profit reached $197.5 billion, delivering $38.2 billion in pretax income after spending $56 billion on technology and content.[43] On May 12, 2021, *The New York Times* reported that during the COVID-19 pandemic, Amazon's profit soared 220 percent, Y/Y growth in Q1 2021[44] as consumers turned to online ordering. It went on to report that 200 million people pay for Prime memberships, and that households with Prime memberships typically spend twice that of non-members. We didn't talk of the important role that Prime plays in their business model, but perhaps the sheer numbers speak for themselves. But as with our other best practice case studies, we like the customers to have the final word:

- "Love the concept just grab and go! I have seen the Amazon Go video and really want to visit. How they detect what I pick is amazing. Very convenient. I love this place in terms of no queue, don't have to wait for the long lines when you want just a bag of Doritos or sandwich or one can of Coke :) All you have to do before you enter is download the Amazon Go app and register.—Naphat S., Bangkok[45]

- Six stars out of five: after having experienced Amazon Go, I only want to shop at Amazon Go. The selection is nicely curated, all products are high quality, and its super-fast and smooth. No checkout needed, just walk out the door with your stuff!!!—Matin, Evanston[46]

Amazon's ecosystem includes 200 million Echo devices, 572 physical stores, a digital ad business, 400 private label brands (from Basics to Presto to Solimo), 43 subsidiaries, an e-sports business, a cloud business, blockchain and IoT services, healthcare initiatives (Care), and several startup funds.[47] We chose to focus on just the physical retail business for a reason: no one would buy a 5,000-page business book.

Summary

Iterate.ai co-founder Jon Nordmark suggests that "Amazon's strategists ignore traditional boundaries and borders. The focus: add services, digitize, link everything together, and speed up. The Amazon flywheel fuels a circular, data-driven ecosystem that's bolstered by open innovation."[48] Before you leave this chapter, reflect on how your company might connect the digital technologies or platforms you currently have to better leverage value over cost to create a value network that would be hard for any competitor to copy.

Key insights

- Focusing on value attributes that are both relevant and durable for target customers can provide long-term financial success.
- Linking digital assets has the potential to leverage greater value for customers over operating costs.
- Linking digital assets presents the opportunity to participate in a broader digital ecosystem.
- Best practice companies focus on controlling the hub of the digital ecosystems they participate in, forming both a superior value proposition and value network.

- The data collected from linking digital assets provides opportunities for adding greater value over time.

- A broader set of behavioral science tactics may emerge as large data sets generate more insight into consumer behavior.

What's next?

Now we need to discuss how to take these 7 Design Strategies and apply them. How is that highlighter of yours holding up? If it has met the end of its useful life, unwrap another—I think you may need it as we begin sorting how to separate the "signals from the noise" so you are solving the right problems that will turn your customers into advocates.

10

The 7 Design Strategies summary

"Strategy only exists in the behavior of leaders."[1]
LEONARD SCHLESINGER, BAKER FOUNDATION PROFESSOR AT HARVARD
BUSINESS SCHOOL

We covered a lot of insights and best practices through these seven cases and summarized the key ones at the end of each chapter. Here is a list of the insights we felt were worth noting, as well as five that are worthy of further exploration.

Ten important case study insights

1 Empathy is not only delivered by humans: This was so well articulated in our Lemonade example, but it could have been described in many of the other cases. The idea that empathy is solely the domain of humans is just not true and will become even more exploited over time as ambient, proactive, conversational AI-based user interfaces converge with the other technologies described, creating frictionless, empathetic experiences.

2 A digital-first experience can enable a powerful "flywheel" in business performance: You read the word "flywheel" in Spotify, Starbucks, Amazon, Lemonade, and CEMEX. That should be a clue that this is something to pay attention to. It isn't a new idea, but if it exists in your business, a digital-first focus can turn it faster, and with greater reach.

3 When it comes to a digital-first experience, the back office IS the front office: My longtime colleague Jeanne Bliss often says: "Everybody wants

self-service until they don't." It's a great point and one I suspect we can all relate to. The Starbucks story probably highlights the peril associated with this the most, but they have responded boldly and at scale. Take a page out of the CEMEX and Nike examples and understand the operating processes and technologies that need to be in place to meet the demand your digital-first experience will need to fulfill.

4 Embedding machine learning in your business model rather than your marketing stack takes personalization to a new level: This to me is a big insight. It is most obvious in the Spotify, Nike, and Lemonade examples, but relevant to every company that has considered personalization as something limited to the marketing team and all about increasing conversions. Push your thinking to apply machine learning to your entire business model. The results could be extraordinary.

5 Consider how you test a minimal lovable experience over a minimal viable product: This insight from CEMEX is a favorite, as for a long time I had planned to write an article about "the myth of the minimal viable product," but CEMEX beat me to the punch. When applying Agile methods, be sure to engage customers with prototypes that don't just meet their needs, but against those touchpoints that really matter, exceed them to create loyalty and even greater willingness to pay.

6 The transition from the attention economy to the value economy signals a new era in UX/UI design: This is highlighted in the Spotify case and all readers should pay attention, especially those obsessed with extending screen time on their apps and websites. The core idea is that what will drive greater lifetime value isn't the number of clicks but the quality of those clicks and the value they deliver to the user "over a healthy content diet." Every web and mobile app developer take note—there is a new metric heading your way.

7 Digital assets that are linked can deliver a superior value proposition as well as a value network that can be hard to imitate: This was highlighted in literally every example, though we focused this design strategy with Amazon Retail given the extent of their leadership on the topic. Visit cxdigital.ai to explore this concept further and consider purchasing my colleague David Rogers' excellent book *The Digital Transformation Playbook* for more information on this.

8 The metaverse isn't coming, it's here: These things don't creep up anymore. One minute you hear about this idea of streaming music instead of downloading songs and then boom: you look at your phone

and you have three subscription services! The metaverse could have just that effect as it is scaling so quickly, as enabled by the five technologies described in the 3Cs. Put a team on it—go deep into it and see if you emerge with something meaningful to your employees and your customers. Who knows, you may even find the potential for a ritual in the metaverse.

9   There is a new, more powerful way to calculate customer lifetime value: We only referred to this in the Spotify and Lemonade cases, but the way digital-first companies are calculating customer lifetime value and combining it with predictive analytics is taking the traditional approach to a whole new level. In a digital-first world, CLV goes from being a lagging to a leading indicator, from being static to dynamic, and potentially becomes a core metric guiding investment and strategy decisions. For more information on new research we are pursuing on this topic, visit our website: cxdigital.ai.

10   Put your best customers to work: This is a reference to a chapter we wrote in *The Ownership Quotient*[2] but is so well exemplified by VMware and how they have so expertly fostered a customer community that achieves so much in terms of both customer co-creation and HR development in their industry. Sometimes in this business you just must salute and say, "Well done. How do *we* do get some of that?"

Five worth further exploration

1   Overachieving ESG targets for best practice companies is the norm: We did make some reference to this in the CEMEX and Nike examples, but we could have written an entire book on the commitment and seriousness that each of these companies has made to not just meeting their ESG targets but exceeding them.

2   Aggressively embracing diversity: Again, we could have written chapters about the way Lemonade, Spotify, Starbucks, literally every exemplar company featured have always and continue to make inclusiveness and diversity central to their strategies for success.

3   Deeply understanding the intersection of technology and human-centered design: It may appear that a company like Amazon, Lemonade, or Spotify is wholly consumed with technology, but drill in deeper and you discover a deep understanding of how technology and humans interact to produce loyalty-building experiences.

4 The all-important role of leadership: Again, something we did not touch on, but I hope it made itself obvious based on the various leaders we quoted and referenced. Visit cxdigital.ai for greater detail around the leadership competencies required to lead a successful CX/Digital implementation.

5 The Service Profit Chain—as relevant as ever: When you look at Starbucks, Nike, Lemonade—all of our best practice examples are models of linking employees, customers, and profits—it appears that the core service profit chain tenets have survived the test of time and are as important today as they were when they were introduced those many years ago.

That is it: ten key insights and five we didn't want to overlook. I hope you found them helpful, but this is not a rest period. It's time to get busy as from here, we are diving deep into Part 3: The Playbook to bring all of these and other best practices to life!

11

Part 3: The playbook

"I don't think you should run from a legacy, or run from pressure or run from expectations. I think you should run toward it."[1]

DOC RIVERS, NATIONAL BASKETBALL ASSOCIATION COACH

Full disclosure, the first version of this book started with this section and introduced the 7 Design Strategies midway. There is a justification for this, but in the end, it seemed to make more sense to take you right into these seven best practice companies to build the rationale for following a proven process for avoiding the potential perils of digital-first experience design and realize its promise.

What follows are four chapters that our consultants at CX/Digital apply with our clients to help them navigate the many options available to them. The quote I chose at the beginning of this introduction reveals a premise to the work we will review. Improving or in some cases redesigning all or major parts of the customer journey will take you into the heart of the matter of your own company. There is just no avoiding it. Your IT group, finance, HR, marketing, etc. all will be at the table, even for something as simple as replacing an out-of-date IVR system. That's a good thing; you want them engaged right from the beginning as any good Agile approach would dictate. But with it will come some expectations, some required commitments, and some pressure to perform. Although this book doesn't speak to some of the leadership competencies required to bring a digital-first strategy to life, visit our website at cxdigital.ai and you will find resources that you might find helpful.

FIGURE 11.1 CX/Digital definition

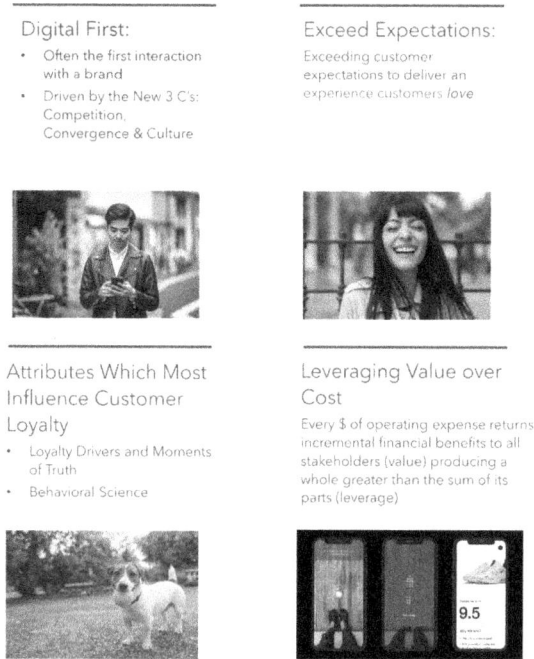

Digital First:
- Often the first interaction with a brand
- Driven by the New 3 C's: Competition, Convergence & Culture

Exceed Expectations:
Exceeding customer expectations to deliver an experience customers *love*

Attributes Which Most Influence Customer Loyalty
- Loyalty Drivers and Moments of Truth
- Behavioral Science

Leveraging Value over Cost
Every $ of operating expense returns incremental financial benefits to all stakeholders (value) producing a whole greater than the sum of its parts (leverage)

Digital-First definition

Perhaps a good place to begin is to suggest a definition for a digital-first experience that achieves competitively superior results. We define this as:

> Delivery of a digital-first experience that exceeds expectations on those attributes which most influence customer loyalty, while leveraging value over cost.

The next four chapters will provide detailed understanding of each of these elements, but you may want to bookmark Figure 11.1 for future reference.

The playbook

The playbook is divided into four somewhat sequential sections, though you find yourself iterating between them depending on the extent of your organization's redesign efforts.

Start by solving the right problems

As so well described in the CEMEX Go case study, this chapter walks you through what is required to ensure that any enhancement you choose to invest in solves real customer problems and ensures wide-spread adoption if delivered through a "minimal lovable experience." You will learn how to identify those key loyal drivers and moments of truth that are central for driving loyalty and growing market share.

Build your business case

This chapter builds on the data you have collected and guides you through the steps required to develop a business case for your project that will ensure your initiative is funded based on the incremental revenue and gross margin dollars it will generate.

FIGURE 11.2 Playbook elements

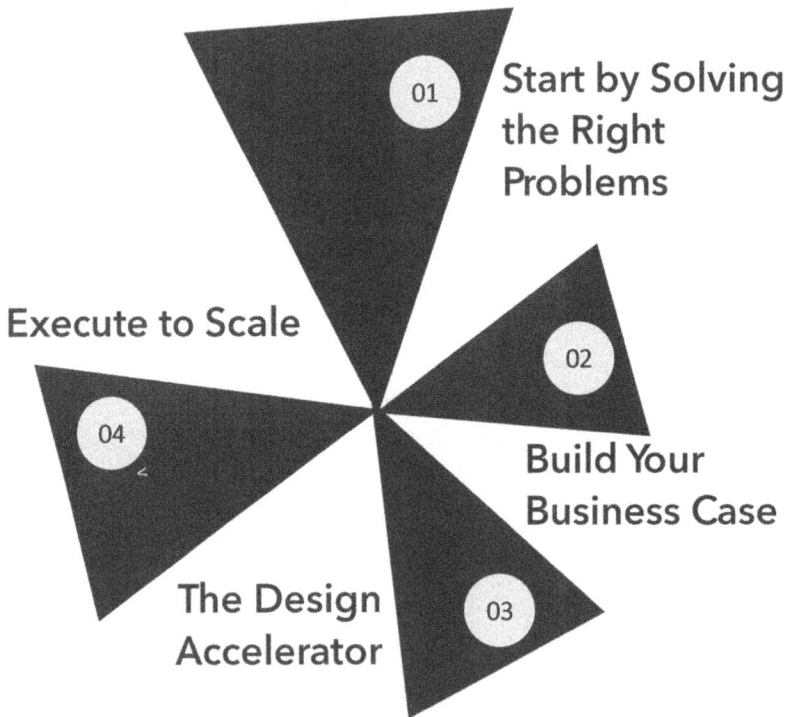

The design process

This chapter takes you through an Agile-based process for going from insights to solutions that can be tested and validated to deliver a digital-first experience that will both produce a superior value proposition and set you on the path toward shaping a powerful value network as described in the Chapter 9.

Execute to scale

Finally, with a validated new digital-first customer experience, it's time to go from pilot to production. We use a fictional case study, assembled from several different client projects to protect confidentiality, to provide you with a solid grounding in the steps and tools necessary to broaden your pilot success to your various regions and markets.

Anatomy of a customer experience

To level-set our taxonomy on what we mean by things like customer experience and moments of truth, the next few pages will unpack the key elements of how we think about understanding the experience of the customer and create greater context for the insights to come.

When Shaun Smith and I co-authored *Managing the Customer Experience*,[2] we introduced the concept of a Branded Customer Experience®.

Shaun and I defined a Branded Customer Experience® as one that was:

- consistent—in terms of delivering that experience over time and location;
- intentional—in terms of delivering a customer experience to support the brand;
- differentiated—from competing brands;
- valuable—in terms of offering a customer proposition which meets target customer needs.

Obviously delivering a Branded Customer Experience® is easier to write about than actually do. When we consider the work of delivering an experience that exceeds customer expectations on those interactions that really matter, it helps to break it down into parts to see where the opportunities are for improvement. This includes five key elements.

> " Obviously delivering a Branded Customer
> Experience® is easier to write about than
> actually do.

The customer journey map: stages, touchpoints, and interactions

Customer journey mapping has become quite popular of late. The way to think about it is to break the journey into three foundational elements: stages, touchpoints, and interactions.

- Stages: Stages in your customer journey are the highest-level descriptor of touchpoints and interactions your customers experience. Think of each stage as a major phase along the path of the customer journey.

- Touchpoints: These are the functional activities that occur within each stage. They can be linear, non-linear, or even time based. Touchpoints are the places where a customer intersects with the brand. For example, a customer might learn about your company's services through different touchpoints such as word-of-mouth, advertising, a sales meeting, or a social media post. There are usually many interactions associated with any given touchpoint.

FIGURE 11.3 Branded Customer Experience®

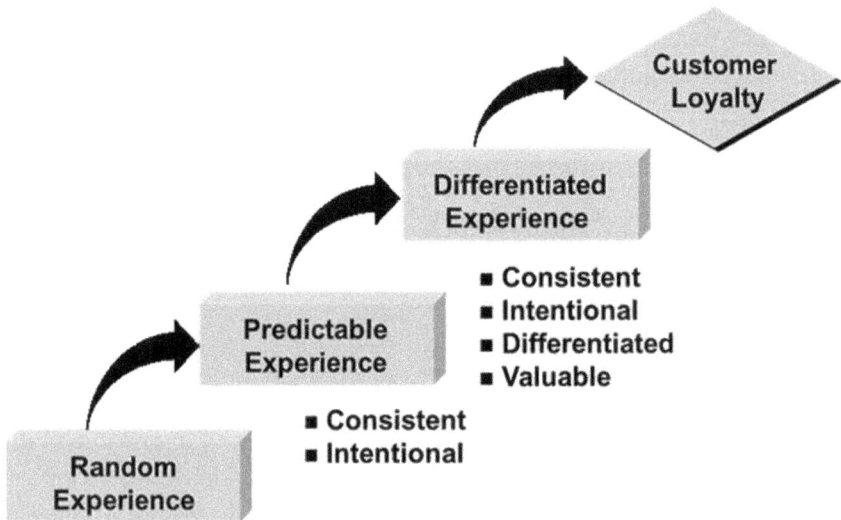

- Interactions: These are the specific, granular "first-person" interactions customers are either doing, thinking or feeling within each touchpoint. Generally, interactions will fall into any channel and would include one of three categories:
  - Sensory: These appeal to all of our senses. For example, Krispy Kreme pipes the smell of hot donuts into the street, appealing to your sense of smell. Often when you enter, a frontline employee is standing there greeting you with a tray of donut samples that came right out of the donut maker minutes earlier.
  - Functional: This is about the steps the customer needs to take to complete the transaction associated with the touchpoint. Withdrawing money from an ATM, registering my name and social insurance number, waiting in line to check out. These are the functional steps required to complete the experience.
  - People: At some point in most experiences (though not all) a customer will interact with an employee. The greeter you meet when you visit Walmart, the account manager that calls on your company selling copiers, or the call center rep that settles your billing dispute are all human interactions that take place across the experience.

Brand signature

What is a brand signature? It is something an organization does that reinforces its brand promise and at the extreme, creates notoriety. For example, the Tiffany Blue Box with its distinctive color or Westin Hotels and Resorts Heavenly Bed are both embodiments of those companies' respective brand personalities.

Moments of truth

Moments of truth is another overused term. The way we think of it is that throughout the experience, there are interactions (ideally embedded with your brand signature) that demonstrate a strong influence on your customer loyalty drivers (see below), especially those interactions that happen frequently. For example, a retailer may find that "associate availability" is a strong loyalty driver and a moment of truth occurs when the search for such an associate begins. Exceeding customer expectations around a specific moment of truth should have a clear line of sight to positively impacting one or more loyalty drivers, which in turn produce greater retention, advocacy, or spending. Be sure to "finish strong" when designing experiences that engender loyalty.

Loyalty drivers

These are the "stars of the show" because you will use them in developing your business case. There are usually no more than 4–6 key drivers that have the greatest impact on customer retention, advocacy, and spending, and it is critical, as indicated above, to understand which moments of truth have the greatest influence over scoring you high on any of these drivers. When it comes to loyalty drivers we want to understand:

- Which loyalty drivers (sometimes called value attributes) have the strongest relationship with overall satisfaction and loyalty?
- What level of performance is required to achieve "top box" satisfaction or likelihood to recommend performance, but overperforming would not drive more loyalty?
- How are we performing on these key drivers relative to competitors?
- What moments of truth most influence the key loyalty drivers?

It is important to be thorough in identifying loyalty drivers and consider what statisticians call the "butterfly chart." It takes the same rank order loyalty drivers identified but considers the degree to which each provides a penalty versus a reward. For example, a retailer may learn that associate availability may indeed be the most important loyalty driver, ranking far higher than speed of checkout, but if you perform poorly on speed of checkout, it may have a greater "penalty" and drive greater attrition than the same performance on associate availability. Improving speed of checkout may not create the same level of loyalty as associate availability, but it may be more damaging if you don't achieve a baseline level of performance. That is when approaches such as zones of tolerance research (described later) can provide rich insight.

The emotion curve

Finally, management experts Chase and Dasu[3] teach us that three forces strongly influence how customers feel about a service encounter:

- Sequence: People prefer service encounters that improve quickly over time and that end on a positive note. An unpleasant ending dominates the memory of the entire experience.

- Duration: People judge time differently:
  - When mentally engaged, they don't notice time passing.
  - The greater the number of segments in a pleasant encounter, the longer—and more enjoyable—the encounter feels.
- Rationalization: When an encounter sours, people:
  - look for a single cause;
  - conclude that deviations from rituals caused the problem;
  - blame individuals, not systems—unless they feel empowered.

As I referenced earlier, when you take the time to research and map the customer experience, one of the things you generate is the customer emotion curve.[4] The hotel example in Figure 11.4 is a simple illustration of the emotion curve.

As a customer interacts with your company across different touch-points, positive, neutral, or negative emotions are triggered. There are some critical points to understand about the emotion curve that we will discuss later, so bookmark this page as we will come back to it. The most important thing to keep in mind is that customers tend to remember either the peak of an experience (either a high or a low) or what happens at the end of the experience. In behavioral science, this is referred to as the "peak/end rule." So, as with Richard Chase and Sriram Dasu's advice to experience designers, be sure to "finish strong" when designing experiences that engender loyalty.

Key insights

- We define Digital-First as "delivery of a digital-first experience that exceeds expectations on those attributes which most influence customer loyalty, while leveraging value over cost."
- Four elements form a playbook for implementation: 1) separating the signals from the noise, 2) building your business case, 3) the design process, and 4) executing to scale.
- A Branded Customer Experience® is defined as being consistent, intentional, differentiated, and valuable to target customers.

FIGURE 11.4 Emotion curve—hotel example

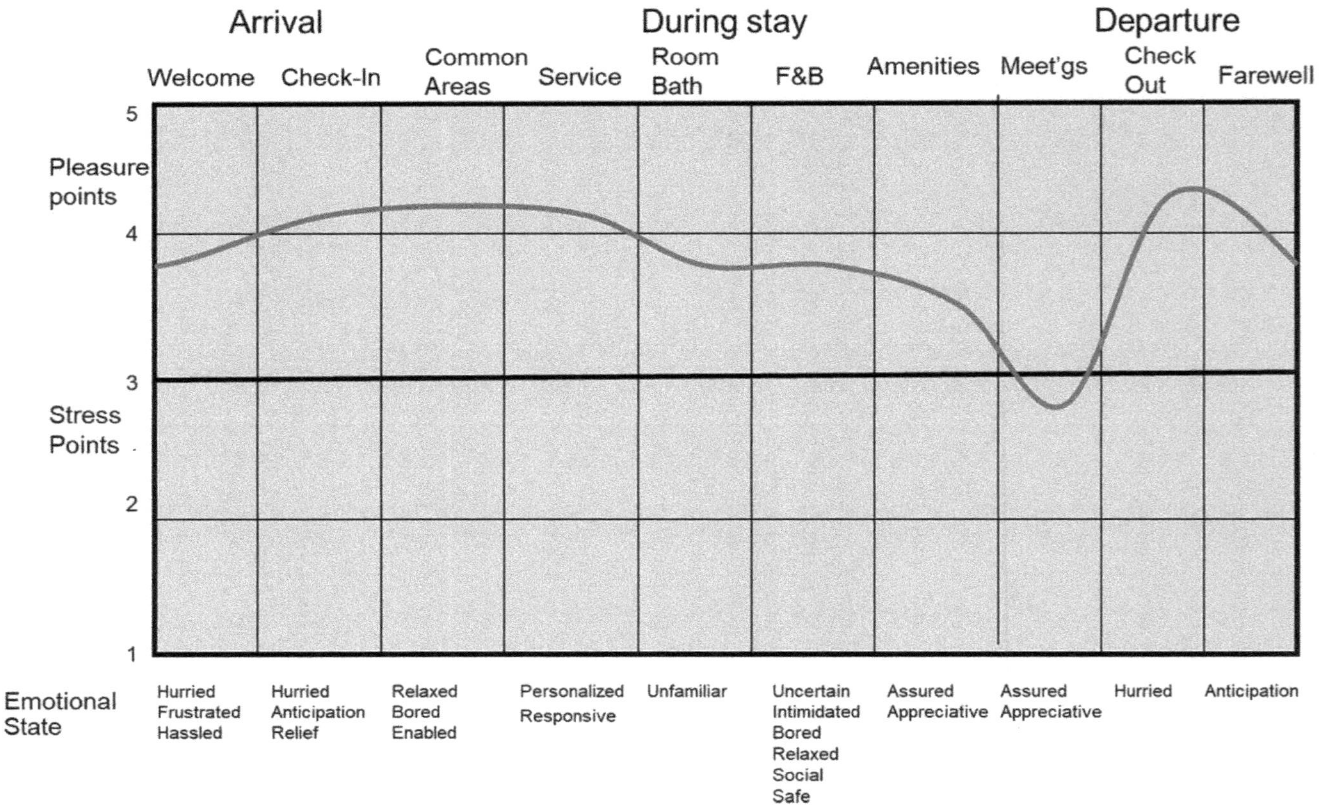

	Arrival		During stay				Departure	
	Welcome	Check-In	Common Areas	Service	Room Bath	F&B	Amenities	Meet'gs	Check Out	Farewell

Pleasure points: 5, 4

Stress Points: 3, 2, 1

| Emotional State | Hurried Frustrated Hassled | Hurried Anticipation Relief | Relaxed Bored Enabled | Personalized Responsive | Unfamiliar | Uncertain Intimidated Bored Relaxed Social Safe | Assured Appreciative | Assured Appreciative | Hurried | Anticipation |

- Five elements make up the "anatomy of a customer experience": journey mapping, brand signature, moments of truth, loyalty drivers, and the emotion curve.

Summary

Having a common language to describe customer experience design lets everyone understand what is required and what is at stake. With this foundation we welcome you to dive right into the CX/Digital playbook! Go *toward* the pressure… it will only make your efforts more rewarding!

12

Start by solving the right problems

"If you don't know where you're going, any road will take you there."

A few years ago, we had a client in the vacation cruise business that was very committed to guest experience. They had made a significant investment in reducing the amount of time it took for guests to get on board the ship but saw no meaningful improvements to guest satisfaction or incremental onboard spending. If you have never taken a cruise, you should know that the line to get on board can be like nothing you have ever seen before, and if it is a particularly hot day, that Miami sun can be brutal. Getting 3,000–4,000 guests and crew on board efficiently and safely is quite the task.

Here's the rub. It turned out that while the cruise line defined the beginning of the "embarkation" journey from when the guest arrived at the port, the guest defined it as the second they awoke in their hometown at about 4:09 a.m. to get their 15-year-old kid out of bed. The overriding emotion that most guests experienced when they actually joined the line wasn't frustration with the wait to get on board, it was relief that they had actually made it (if this is starting to sound a bit personal, well, I will let you speculate as you wish). As a result, reducing the waiting time to board by 20 or 25 minutes simply wasn't a material enough change to garner any influence on satisfaction or spending.

This sort of thing goes on in organizations every day. The problem isn't that you are wrong, the problem is you are right. It's just not the most important problem that deserves time and resources to fix.

Getting started on this journey begins with a profound understanding of customer needs, expectations, and preferences—effectively separating the "signals from the noise" to isolate those changes that would make a meaningful difference—solving the right problems. There are three things we need to keep in mind:

- First and foremost, we need to see the journey both functionally and emotionally, through what the customer experiences holistically (not just where and when their interactions with your company begin and end).

- Always remember that what customers are trying to achieve is a result rather than the consumption or use of your products or services. It's fine to be proud of your products and services, but they aren't the endgame. The endgame is the outcome they create for your client. Even if you were selling the Mona Lisa, the point isn't in the painting, it is in the pleasure it would provide to its owner. Your product or service is a "means" rather than the "ends."

- Before you increase a dollar of operating costs to improve the experience (assuming it isn't required for regulatory or safety reasons), you need to ensure it will deliver an incremental financial benefit to shareholders that the customer is willing to pay for and ideally improves the employee experience in some measurable way.

Five steps for separating the "signals from the noise"

There are five steps required to focus on the right problems. However, this isn't a one-time exercise, as later during the design effort you will be connecting and interacting with customers through rapid experimentation. But you need to begin by completing an initial "deep dive" to develop a profound understanding of how you are performing relative to competitors.

The five steps are:

1 Enroll the core team, key stakeholders, and a guiding coalition.
2 Map the "as is" customer and employee journey.
3 Summarize and share qualitative insights.
4 Mystery shop competitors and study benchmark best practice companies.
5 Validate qualitative insights with quantitative methods.

Let's take them one at a time.

Step 1 Enroll the core team, key stakeholders, and a guiding coalition

A client we worked with years ago had a saying that holds true today: "People support what they help build." When getting started on this journey, it can be tempting to proceed by yourself or with a couple of other "believers." But at this point you don't know what you don't know. Think broadly in terms of your core team membership to include representation from operations, marketing, technology, call center ops, e-commerce, HR, etc. Their individual involvement and contribution will change as the project goes through its natural phases. Enrolling a diverse team from the beginning ensures you will move along faster in the long run.

Secondly, a study conducted by The Forum Corporation looked into what distinguished the best project leaders. It turned out that effective project leaders were organized, set clear review processes, and communicated well, but what distinguished the very best was that they got, and sustained, the buy-in and involvement of key stakeholders. Just getting sign-off and approval for the budget is good, but it's the first step. You have to build a plan on how you will keep your key executive sponsors and other stakeholders connected and engaged in the effort throughout the life of the project.

Finally, even though this group will get larger down the road, you can begin to form relationships that will eventually form your guiding coalition of leaders that will evangelize and help lead the implementation plan that will follow.

Step 2 Map the "as is" customer and employee journey

Your overall goal in this step is to get as clear a view of the current customer and employee journey as you can. Remember, the employee view is as important as the customer view as they are two sides of the same coin. There are several sub-steps to consider.

GO TO GEMBA
Gemba literally means "the real place" in Japanese. It suggests that to really understand something, you can't just review a dashboard of trend data, you

> *What distinguished the very best was that they got, and sustained, the buy-in and involvement of key stakeholders.*

must physically go to the place where the issue is happening, talk to the employees, and understand the process. We learned about this years ago during a benchmarking visit to Toyota. It falls under the category of developing what our hosts described as "profound knowledge" of the customer and employee experience.

As a result, when we start working with a new client we work very hard to develop "profound knowledge" by going to Gemba. We spend a lot of time with frontline employees, job shadowing them during peak and non-peak periods. On one such occasion our consultant spent a day with a home services technician filling cracks in attics in heat of over 100 degrees, navigating around a customer who opened her front door carrying a half dozen snakes (I mean, you simply can't make this stuff up), and getting firsthand understanding of the current experience for both customers and employees.

HIGH PERFORMER STUDY AND PERFORMANCE FACTOR ANALYSIS
If your current customer experience involves a lot of human interaction, such as in retail or hospitality, or in after-sales call center support, then a key step is to conduct a study of what distinguishes high performers in your most critical customer-facing roles. Especially if one of your goals is to increase customer interactions via digital channels going forward.

There is real science associated with identifying what distinguishes high performers from moderate performers, but the pay-off is significant if you can understand which frontline behaviors, delivered at an "Exceeds expectations" level, mean that other interactions can perform at a "Meets expectations" or even "Below expectations" performance level but still achieve an overall top box customer satisfaction score. We describe these behaviors as being able to "carry the top box score."

To identify the factors that help, we apply a model which analyzes the work environment factors that impact human performance.

We always conduct several role-specific interviews before finalizing the broader survey, so that we are asking questions that are relevant to each role. The insights this reveals into the degree to which an organization's frontline staff are being set up for success or not, and where the biggest gaps are to be closed, are invaluable when you go from design of the improved experience to execution.

FIGURE 12.1 Sample partial employee survey results (anonymized)

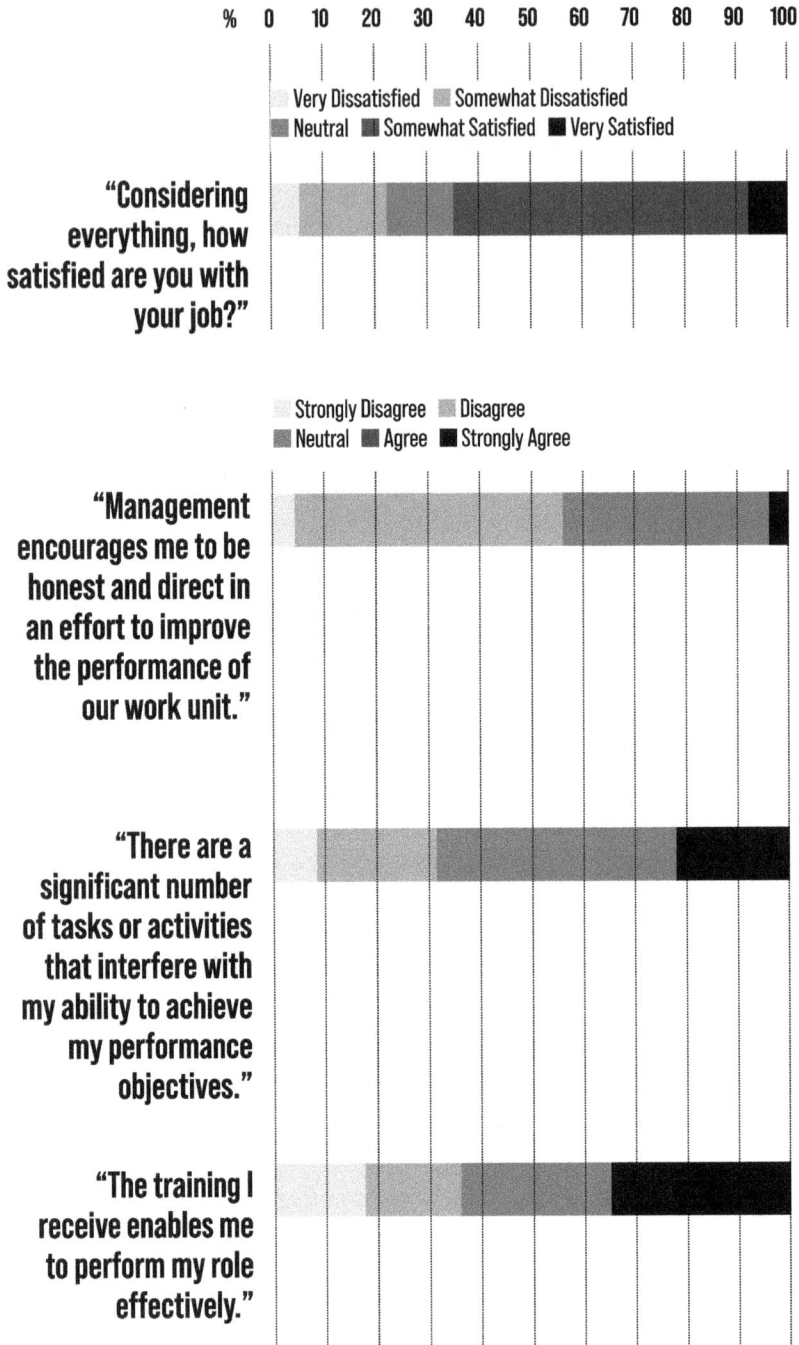

WALK A MILE IN YOUR CUSTOMERS' SHOES

With the keen insights generated from being in the field across your different channels, now it is time to observe customers as they navigate through your store, use your website, your mobile apps/bots/virtual assistants, attend one of your client conferences, and talk or chat with your salespeople and call center representatives. When you do this, it is helpful as you observe customers to make note of human, functional, or digital interactions that produce positive, negative, or neutral experiences. Later you will worry about the degree to which these interactions reinforce your brand promise and ensure customers are achieving their goals or not, but for now, just be a good amateur ethnographer and make note of what works well, what doesn't, and, if possible, how frequently it appears to happen.

INTERVIEWS, FOCUS GROUPS, AND ETHNOGRAPHY

You are now in a far better position to conduct interviews and/or focus groups with customers. The good news is that companies make it easy to capture this data virtually. Through video-based interviews and focus groups, customers can be invited to share their view of the experience, what works, what could be improved. Which touchpoints and interactions are most valuable to them? Which are least valuable? How do you rate relative to your competitors? You can even recruit them to shop your firm and a competitor in advance and capture their experience with a mobile app to share during the discussion. An experienced facilitator can ensure you capture important insights that you will use during the next few steps.

CREATE A MAP OF THE AS IS CUSTOMER AND EMPLOYEE JOURNEYS

We talked about the elements of the customer journey in the previous chapter so now is the time to generate a map of what that journey entails. In terms of creating one, we have found the following steps to be both the most efficient and the most accurate:

1 Select a journey template to use. There are several but select one that ensures it can represent the omni-channel visualization of the experience and that can codify the emotional highs and lows as well as the moments of truth that have the greatest influence over your loyalty drivers.

2 Pick a customer segment/persona and work with two or three product/ service managers to create a very high-level—holistic—view of the customer and the employee journey. This can all be done virtually via Teams or Zoom.

3 Next, assemble a group of high-performing frontline staff to review the draft journey map(s) and make changes, adding their ratings to identify their view of chronic problems and opportunities to delight, as well as their view of the emotional highs and lows for both employees and customers. (Refer to our review of the components of a customer journey map in Chapter 11.) You may even want to plot a preliminary emotional curve to test with customers.

4 With a well-documented internal view of the customer and employee experience, create a simple PowerPoint presentation of the journey map (as well as having the map itself available online) and run a series of live or virtual focus groups with 6–8 customers, representative of your target customer base. The data you collect should inform a qualitative but accurate view of the customer journey.

You may also go right from step 2 to step 4 and use your strawman journey map to meet with customers—there is an argument that this eliminates any potential bias that may come from conducting step 3. The benefit of following the four steps described, however, is that it provides greater insight into the experience prior to your customer focus groups, and helps you avoid spending time with customers uncovering things you could have learned from internal resources.

SERVICE BLUEPRINTING

A second tool we use is called service blueprinting. It documents the operating processes that support the delivery (consistent or otherwise) of customer interactions that are below the "line of invisibility," for example to document the service processes and behaviors that are contributing to both strong and poor customer satisfaction performance. It is a powerful data-collection framework when you spend time with operations, customer service, marketing, sales, and HR—to collect data on what processes are contributing to both the good and bad experiences identified from the customer journey map. As you read in Chapter 5, CEMEX uses customer journey maps and service blueprints extensively.[1]

NON-VALUE-ADDED ANALYSIS

Another tool to help you go even deeper is a non-value-added (NVA) analysis that is used for reducing process time and eliminating waste. Waste is defined as any activity that does not add value to the product as defined by the customer. In Lean Six Sigma, every activity is categorized as either a value-added (VA) or non-value-added activity. However, some NVA activities may be necessary for regulatory or other reasons and are called essential non-value-added (ENVA) activities.

HIGHLIGHT THE EMOTIONAL AND COGNITIVE PROCESSES THAT EXIST

There are as many forms of ethnography as you can imagine, from the "follow me home" techniques used by companies like Intuit to video ethnography that we have used to probe beyond stated consumer behavior into their motivations, emotions, and thinking about a particular topic or brand. A must-read for anyone doing this work is *How Customers Think* by Gerald Zaltman.[2] In fact, the deep metaphor elicitation technique, called ZMET, introduced by Olson Zaltman, is particularly effective.

ISOLATE OPPORTUNITIES FOR CHANNEL OPTIMIZATION

In a world where I can buy property insurance from Lemonade in about 90 seconds from a mobile app, understanding the digital and physical channel behavior of customers is crucial, especially if any part of your business case involves savings by migrating interactions currently delivered live via an agent or store employee to a digital channel.

In fact, if most of your customer interactions are through digital channels, this may be an excellent way to start developing "profound knowledge." The customer will "tell us" exactly how they feel about the experience if we just pay attention to their behaviors and extract the insight their paths through our digital and physical channels provide. There are excellent tools on the market today that allow you to track and attribute customer behaviors to identify the touchpoints that are either enablers or inhibitors to customers trying to achieve a goal.

> ❝ *Understanding the digital and physical channel behavior of customers is crucial.*

DECODING THE CUSTOMER EXPERIENCE WITH DATA

In 2017, a large telecommunications company faced compounding challenges of low customer satisfaction, low digital and self-service adoption, as well as high call-in volumes driving up overall cost-to-serve. As the organization kicked off high-profile digital transformation and CX improvement initiatives to address these challenges, it quickly realized that it had no scalable way to find, size, and monitor the cross-channel friction points that were driving poor outcomes. Web and mobile data sat in one place; IVR and agent interaction data in another; and more modern service channels like voice and chat bots were just getting off the ground. In response, they deployed customer journey analytics, aggregating customer interaction and sentiment data from across channels and systems, linking it all at the customer level.

This became the cornerstone of a data-driven, continuous-improvement process where channel teams could find cross-channel friction points (e.g. web and mobile pages driving high call-in rates), prioritize and make the business case for improvements based on satisfaction and cost impact, and monitor efficacy of improvements in real-time as they were deployed. Over the next five years, this approach enabled the company to increase digital and self-service containment by more than 30 percent, decrease overall call volume by the same magnitude, and increase their net promoter score by double digits.

SOURCE Pointillist by Genesys

In one client project, our goal was two-fold:

1 to determine which path through their cross-channel experience had the greatest influence on the customer becoming an "advocate"; and

2 calculate the average cost-to-serve by customer segment.

The "heat map" y-axis describes the individual number of customer transactions by contact reason. The x-axis aligns those volumes to the specific channels used for each of these contact reasons. Analyzing these transactions for each customer segment allowed us to estimate cost-to-serve transaction costs by channel and by segment.

Although there are multiple ways to study cross-channel behavior, a combination of ethnography and transactional data is of most value. The latter provides insights into how your customer is interacting with your company, the former reveals the why.

Ethnographic techniques that capture the customer's activities on camera have proven particularly useful for communicating later with other internal teams. We've used video-based surveys we call "missions" to allow a customer to use their mobile phone to upload a video or audio file as they respond to questions as they go through an experience and include this media directly into the AS IS customer journey map.

FIGURE 12.2 Contact reason by channel heat map

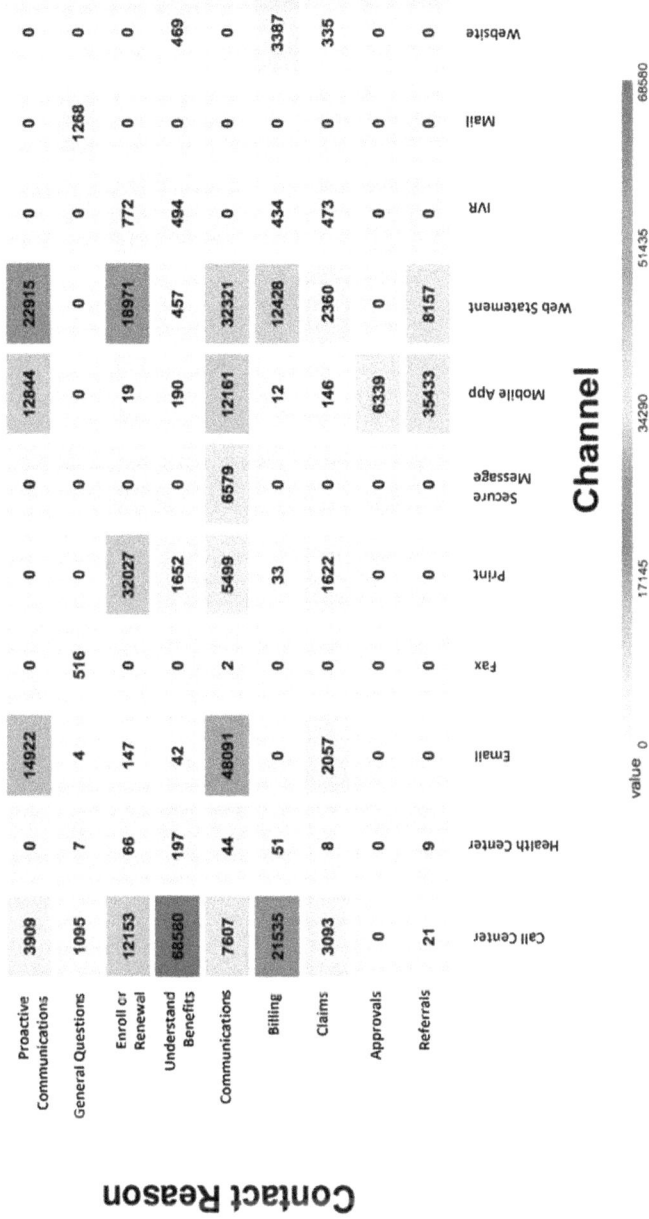

I will come back to this in the next chapter when we drill down into building your preliminary business case because understanding how to increase digital versus live-interaction channels to reduce cost-to-serve isn't a bad idea, it just needs to balance operating costs with what drives spending and customer engagement. For now, we just need to understand, for each customer segment:

- In what channels do customers tend to start their interaction?
- What channels do they tend to default to if they are not successful in completing their contact reason?
- Where do these various paths lead?
- What final (if any) satisfactory resolution do they achieve?

Step 3 Summarize and share qualitative insights

The result of step 2 should allow you to produce some key artifacts that will be required before moving to steps 4 and 5. These include:

- a visualization of the customer and employee experience in the form of both an AS IS journey map and an AS IS service blueprint;
- a qualitative view into chronic problems and opportunities to delight that exist in the current customer journey;
- the emotional and cognitive state of the customer;
- an analysis of the potential opportunities to optimize your delivery channels to better serve customers and reduce cost-to-serve;
- the key enablers and inhibitors facing frontline employees in serving customers and the behaviors that distinguish high performers in key frontline roles;
- finally, your hypothesis on the loyalty drivers and the moments of truth you believe have the greatest influence over them.

The result of this data collection produces three very important deliverables:

- A web portal that the core team and key stakeholders can access to drill into any of the details of what has been discovered. The degree to which you have captured customer comments with video will increase visits to this site. Be sure to add some form of discussion board to begin the conversation about what is being learned.

- A report detailing the qualitative technical analysis of the current customer and employee experience that is being delivered today.
- A 10–15-page executive summary presentation of these findings and their implications.

The end of this step includes sharing what you have learned with your executive sponsors, guiding coalition, and other key managers that might be interested in what you have discovered. A word of warning. These insights are still qualitative. As soon as you put this on paper, no doubt someone will want to start acting on what was captured. On one such occasion, the CEO of our client, convinced that pricing was the key loyalty driver, was ready to launch a price war after our detractor analysis of qualitative data. We were able to convince him to wait until we completed the quantitative validation, and sure enough, pricing fell far down the ranked attribute list, and rose to the top only when the highest-ranking loyalty drivers were performed poorly.

Step 4 Mystery shop competitors and study benchmark best practice companies

Although it is just a few data points, it is a good idea to mystery shop two or three of your top competitors. Your marketing or strategy team may provide you with some form of SWOT analysis, but some firsthand experience as a potential customer can prove invaluable.

Once this phase of your research is complete, it's time to summarize what you have learned and from the themes that have emerged, target some best practice firms to study, especially those outside of your industry, to see how they have solved similar problems (not necessarily the same problem) to provide a new lens into your customers' current experience and "take a page" out of someone else's playbook. One of the most powerful case studies we use with management teams is the CEMEX case that proceeded their digital transformation reviewed earlier. Back then, CEMEX wanted to improve how they could schedule and navigate their cement trucks through an urban center as complex as Mexico City. To accomplish this, they didn't benchmark other cement companies, they studied leading US taxi and courier companies to see how they managed capacity and fleet scheduling.

Over the years we have taken leadership and design teams to visit different best practice firms, from the Ritz-Carlton Hotel to FedEx. It is hard to duplicate the impact an actual site visit can have in terms of not just generating insight but, as important, creating motivation for a leadership team to take action to improve their business in significant, measurable ways.

In the absence of being able to be there physically, we have had good success with structuring virtual visits and even developed video-based benchmarking modules (20-minute self-paced small-group sessions) to help a design team pull out the relevant best practices that could have implications for improving their customer experience.

At the end of the day, you are looking to challenge your own organization's assumptions about the experience you are delivering, what is possible, and what the benefits could be if you achieved it.

At the end of step 4, you can add to your data set:

- a list of relevant innovations or best practices from your external benchmarking activities of one or more world-class companies;
- a list of your top 1–3 competitors' overall strengths and weaknesses when it comes to delivering a competitively superior experience;
- a list of your top 1–3 competitors' specific performance (better, worse, or same) on your key loyalty drivers.

Step 5 Validate qualitative insights with quantitative methods

As in qualitative research, there are a few ways to go about approaching quantitative validation. However, to have the data you need to generate a business case that your CFO will take seriously, you need to have statistically significant evidence to support your claim in terms of the estimated revenue and operating margin the data suggests can be achieved.

Although survey research is a typical way to conduct quantitative studies, new quantitative focus group technologies provide accelerated ways to validate qualitative insights and even elicit further improvements in real-time from hundreds and even thousands of customers.

Text analytics solutions from a myriad software companies that apply artificial intelligence and natural language processing using regular expression classifiers or classifiers developed from client code books represent a

> ❝ At the end of the day, you are looking to challenge your own organization's assumptions about the experience you are delivering.

powerful way to isolate potential loyalty drivers and their associated moments of truth.

On several client projects we have used all three of the above toolsets. For example, we collected and coded unstructured data into themes that were additive to our qualitative research. We then tested our new hypothesis with 150+ customers using a quantitative focus group platform. With these key learnings in hand, we constructed a survey to validate our hypothesis with a survey platform. Again, the right quantitative method and tools are determined by your goals and the data that is available.

"INTERROGATE THE FACTS UNTIL THEY CONFESS"
The CEO of one of our customers had a saying that I have never forgotten. I think he adapted it from a similar comment made by British mathematician I. J. Good in an address to the Institute of Mathematical Statistics:[3]

Interrogate the facts until they confess.

I cannot tell you exactly why I like that statement so much, other than that in some quirky way, it reflects the level of rigor I have learned is required to make improvements to the customer experience that you will be able to build a legitimate business case around.

So, besides understanding your customer loyalty drivers and which moments of truth have the greatest influence over them, depending on your business, you may want to consider one other technique that we have found helpful in ensuring you get those facts to "confess." It is called zones of tolerance research.

ZONES OF TOLERANCE
You need to capture enough data to create a statistically accurate, representative picture of what is possible in order to "size the prize" for investing in the customer experience.

A zones of tolerance study not only prioritizes the customer's loyalty drivers (or value attributes) in terms of importance to the customer, it also asks them to define the desired versus acceptable performance levels.

It builds off of the service quality expectations gap model,[4] but in this case, the tolerance gap is the difference between desired service and the level of service considered adequate. The larger that gap, the more likely it is that the customer will be dissatisfied.

FIGURE 12.3 Zones of tolerance: relation between importance and expectations

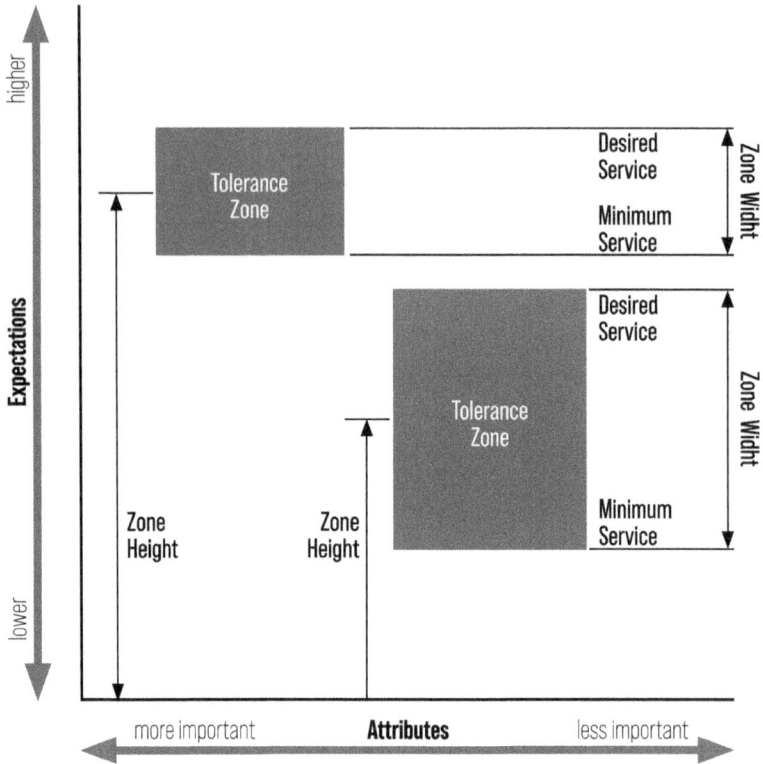

This type of analysis does require the assistance of a professional survey design and statistician. Although you can find a YouTube tutorial on just about anything, this is not something to include in that search field. However, the investment can be worth it as it provides a more granular view of expectations and answers additional questions such as: 1) Why do customers seem to be retained despite being dissatisfied? 2) How do we perform against our best competitors on the key tolerance gaps?[5]

As long as a comprehensive qualitative process has been conducted to select the loyalty drivers or value attributes to be used in the follow-up zones of tolerance survey, the results can be a key input to the business case we will discuss in the next chapter.

Summary

Every company's needs are different so don't be intimidated by the list below. What matters is having the right data, not necessarily this entire ideal list. Also, although we have suggested a sequence from qualitative to quantitative, it doesn't always work that way. Sometimes you may begin with the results of a significant survey project and work from that data set to reveal the loyalty drivers.

Some of these data items will be more relevant than others. Here we go.

TABLE 12.1 Top 10 list—ideal data set

Item	Questions
Loyalty drivers	What are the key loyalty drivers or value attributes that are most important (in weighted rank order) to your most loyal and profitable customers?
Expectations and emotions	How do you perform in terms of meeting, exceeding, or not meeting expectations on these key loyalty drivers relative to your best competitor(s)? What positive, neutral, and negative emotions do customers feel as they traverse the journey, especially across channels?
Moments of truth (MoTs)	Which MoTs in the current experience have the greatest influence on any or all of the key loyalty drivers and how consistently do you deliver at an "exceeds" level on these important MoTs?
Employee behavior	For businesses with a significant volume of frontline human interactions: • What are employee behaviors that could "carry a top box" score if other attributes are just "meeting expectations" or reaching a "minimum" zone of tolerance level? • What are major organization or process barriers getting in the way of frontline employees serving customers in delivering on your brand promise?
Unmet needs	What additional needs do your customers have that you may not be meeting, especially if a competitor is advancing solutions to address these needs?
Non-value-added activities (NVA)	What non-value activities could be eliminated or reduced to create more value and improve the experience?

(continued)

TABLE 12.1 (Continued)

Item	Questions
Channel behavior	How are customers currently engaging with your organization? What channels have the highest/lowest volumes? At what touchpoints and channels do customers complete the transaction, appear to get stuck, or even abandon the journey? Is there an opportunity to migrate costly customer interactions that would be better delivered via digital channels without diluting your brand promise while actually making the experience better?
Best practices	What best practices were relevant for your organization from benchmarking world-class firms that are delivering a superior customer experience on similar loyalty drivers?
Data	Is there data you collect today that could be of value to customers, especially if combined with other open-source or licensed data sets?
Innovation	What innovations could you consider introducing that your customers would find significant value in, including investment in a set of linked digital assets that would provide a competitive advantage today and in the future?

What's next?

Once we have unshakeable facts of what creates spending, retention, and advocacy in the current experience, as well as the causes of churn and customer dissatisfaction, we have to prove that improvements would generate incremental revenue, gross margin dollars, and/or reduce operating expenses. We need to build a business case that will make the argument that investing in the customer experience is a better use of capital than probably a half dozen other projects competing for those dollars, including things like stock buy-backs, new product introductions, or strategic partnerships.

Said more simply, you need to create a business case that makes it clear that investing in the customer experience is a superior use of capital than the worthy alternatives that exist.

So, let's get started.

13

Build your business case

"It's an unfortunate reality that many companies, despite the rise of CCO and CX work, still are not entirely clear how to value customers."[1]

JEANNE BLISS, AUTHOR, CHIEF CUSTOMER OFFICER

You may have heard a statistic that says "seven out of ten customer experience initiatives fail." I hope you treat this assertion with a healthy skepticism as it certainly isn't consistent with our experience. When things do go sideways with a CX project, however, one of the reasons we observe isn't that the initiative missed its business case objectives—most of the time, it simply never had them in the first place.

Frankly, if you can't create an argument that investing in the customer experience isn't a stronger use of capital than its worthy alternatives, then why are you pursuing it? With that mindset, the next few pages are going to break down how you go about creating a business case that your CFO will not only take seriously, she or he will wonder why you aren't working in their department.

There are actually three forms that this business case will take. The first version is the preliminary business case. This is a fact-based business case used on all of the customer behavioral data, collected with an estimate of the project costs to generate incremental revenue, gross margin dollars, and operating expense savings. The second version is the final business case, which is an updated version of the preliminary case with more precise estimates of program costs and cost-to-serve improvements. The third version is the quarterly update. This uses the final version of the case as a baseline but updates it on a frequent basis, reporting the degree to which the original financial targets have been achieved or not—and if not, how the implementation is being adjusted to get back on track.

Remember, what distinguishes high-performing project leaders is that they get and sustain key stakeholder buy-in and involvement. As a result, your business case isn't a point in time, it is a commitment to what your team believes, based on data, can be delivered to shareholders by investing in changes to the customer experience.

We will review two examples of preliminary business cases (edited to protect client confidentiality and proprietary information), *the value of a promoter*, and *quantifying the financial benefits of a digital-first experience*. I suspect you will find them both valuable as you could combine elements of each to produce one single business case.

Before we begin, we need to pay attention to Jeanne Bliss's advice at the top of the page and address something that is required for either of these two examples: the calculation of customer lifetime value.

Customer lifetime value

There are several ways to calculate customer lifetime value, including a method that can incorporate the value of social media.[2] For our purposes, the one that we applied to this first example is quite straightforward:

- Average purchase value—the value of all customer purchases over a particular timeframe (a year is usually easiest), divided by the number of purchases in that period.

- Average purchase frequency—divide the number of purchases in that same time period by the number of individual customers who made a transaction over the same period.

- Customer value—the average purchase frequency multiplied by the average purchase value.

- Average customer lifespan—the average length of time a customer continues buying from you.

There are things missing from this formula such as the cost of acquisition and the average cost-to-serve over the customer lifespan, but they can be added later.

Five steps for building your business case

Of course, there are several ways to create a business case, but the hope is these two examples will speak to what makes building a customer experience effort somewhat unique. Though they include different elements, they each track to the following five steps:

1 Validate the incremental value of consistently exceeding customer expectations on key loyalty drivers.

2 Attribute incremental spending to the contribution of each key (weighted) loyalty driver.

3 Conduct sensitivity analysis to estimate incremental satisfaction and spending generated from improvement to moments of truth which have the most influence over key loyalty drivers.

4 Identify costs savings from improving the experience by eliminating NVA activities and migration of interactions to lower-cost channels that improve the customer and employee experience.

5 Estimate all program costs and net incremental revenue, gross margin dollars, and operating margin improvements generated by the improved experience.

Again, the business case relies on the job you did as detailed in the previous chapter at isolating those moments of truth and loyalty drivers that create customer loyalty and generate incremental spending, so if you skipped that chapter, scroll back and read it through. We won't go anywhere.

The value of a promoter

In working with this client in the home services industry, we followed the process described in the previous chapter and validated through qualitative focus groups followed by a representative survey received from over 1,790 customers. We generated the data we needed to prepare the preliminary business case:

The top loyalty drivers in rank order were:

1 Ontime arrival (9.75 influence)

2 Responsiveness (9.56)

3 Customer service (9.33)

4 Professional technicians (8.41)

5 Product quality (8.20)

6 Price/Value (8.04)

The key to success was the technician arriving on time. When expectations for arrival were clearly communicated and met, customers became promoters. When they arrived late, or not until the next day, they were more likely to become detractors and then price became the leading value attribute or loyalty driver.

The "receive service" touchpoint was revealed to be the key moment of truth and several specific interactions reinforced the perception that the client had made a good decision hiring the company:

- The technician set clear expectations on what he/she would accomplish during the service call.
- The technician demonstrated thorough knowledge of their products and services.
- The technician was quick and efficient while onsite in addressing my needs.

The employee behaviors where our client scored lowest on performance were also the top three employee behaviors by importance:

- Provides options that will meet my needs.
- Shows empathy for my situation.
- Practices respectful listening when communicating.

The most innovative idea customers found most attractive was: "I was consistently updated via SMS messaging to confirm the technician's expected arrival time."

This data revealed some clear implications for the customer experience:

1 Well-defined competencies that describe superior technician behaviors.
2 Improving actual on-time scheduling performance as well as establishing company-wide service standards associated with appointment expectations setting and communications.
3 National expansion of the SMS-based communications system for managing customer expectations around on-time arrival.
4 National expansion of service standards.
5 Development of a more robust digital ordering, tracking, and monitoring system.

But to start working on these implications we would have to demonstrate how such improvements would generate incremental economic impact.

The good news was that because we were able to isolate the historical spending of all customers that completed the quantitative survey with their detractor, passive, promoter groupings, we learned that a promoter spent annually an additional 20 percent over non-promoters and based on each group's retention rate, we were able to determine the customer lifetime value of each.

The model in Figure 13.1 allowed us to predict the revenue impact of increasing any of the moments of truth that positively impacted one or more of the loyalty drivers and then it automatically generated the incremental revenue impact from these improvements given our data suggested this would grow the base of promoters.

The business case

Now that we had a predictive model, we could take the various initiatives generated out of our design sessions that formed the new customer and employee experience and build financial lift targets based on this data to create our preliminary business case. Here is an example charter from one of six initiatives.

FIGURE 13.1 Predictive model business case simulator

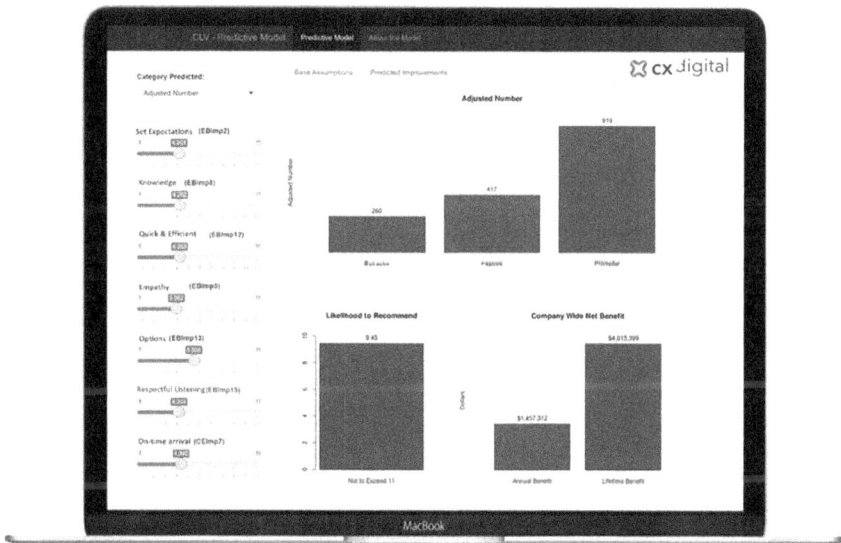

INITIATIVE: FRONTLINE BEHAVIORS

Problem/Opportunity statement

Recent research highlighted specific touchpoints in the experience related to product knowledge, respectful listening, and demonstrating empathy, which represent opportunities for us to differentiate from competitors, improve our net promoter® score[1] (NPS®) performance, and increase average sales transaction per customer. Improving NPS® by increasing our performance on these key attributes will have a direct impact on our financial performance.

Business case

Our research has established that on average a promoter spends over their lifetime 20 percent more than non-promoter customers. Further, the result of our quantitative study validates that product knowledge, respectful listening, and demonstrating empathy explain 13.5 percent of what contributes to creating a promoter. Improving on these three attributes by just 5 percent over a 12-month period should increase our percentage of promoters by 1.7 percent. An annual increase of promoters by 1.7 percent would have an annual increase on incremental revenue of $904,979 in transactional spending.

The total of these six initiatives amounted to almost $7.2 million in incremental revenue against program costs of approximately $2.6 million—a tidy return on investment. We typically categorize these projects in one of three time-horizon buckets we call the "three-lane highway."

LANE 1—FIX IT

These are 90-day or less projects, often lower-cost, less complex solutions that address short-term problems that are actually producing dissatisfied customers. In our example, new uniforms and national service standards would fit into lane 1.

> **66** *The total of these six initiatives amounted to almost $7.2 million in incremental revenue.*

FIGURE 13.2   Final business case: $7.2 million incremental revenue

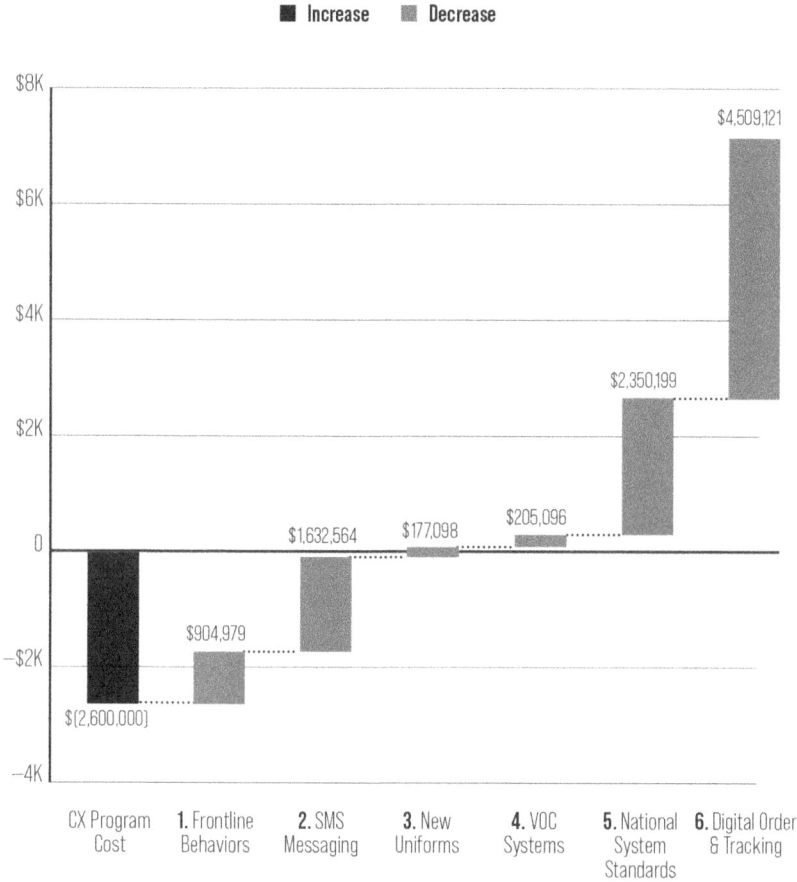

LANE 2—IMPROVE IT

These are slightly longer term, 6–9-month projects involving multiple func
tions and product teams that will provide measurable benefits to two or
more stakeholders. Most organizations have the capacity for 3–5 of these
initiatives over a calendar year. In our example, frontline behaviors and SMS
messaging would fall into lane 2.

LANE 3—TRANSFORM IT

This is the longest time horizon, 1–3 years, and usually involves the upgrade
or implementation of a new system to create a step-change level of innovation

to the customer experience. In our example, VoC system and digital ordering, tracking and monitoring system would fall into lane 3.

This preliminary business case became final once all of the detailed program costs were itemized through the implementation planning work. It generated a set of KPIs to report on program variance to the goals set out for each of the six initiatives as well as other overall KPIs, including NPS®, average contract value, conversation rates, call center volumes, and first-call resolution.

Quantifying the financial benefits of a digital-first experience

This project was referenced in the previous chapter, and it may be relevant to those of you with significant call center operations. Digital first is forcing lots of organizations to rethink how they leverage more digital channels to interact with customers. At first, this tended to be an exercise in cost savings as having a customer learn about their membership information on a website or mobile app obviously is a lot lower cost than talking or chatting with a live agent.

But progressive organizations like CEMEX are leveraging digital channels not just because they are less costly but because they deliver a customer experience that their target customers value, increasing personalization and exceeding their expectations.

In this preliminary business case example, we began with qualitative research, visiting the client's various call centers, meeting with call center support representatives along with their supervisors to learn about the goals and metrics of each. We then worked with our client to pull a sample of approximately 17,000 clients who represented over 1 million transactions over a timeframe of 12 months. To track the customers' engagement across channels, we grouped the interactions by reason and created a ticket, which was a combination of the client ID and their reason for calling. This ticket was then used to map the channel usage for a particular client ID by reason for calling over the time frame of the sample. This provided us with customer journeys (or tickets) for each of 15 customer sub-segments and for each contact reason.

Our client had already calculated the customer lifetime value for each segment, so our task was to determine the cost-to-serve for each of these

FIGURE 13.3 Call reason by segment

Per Segment and Reason

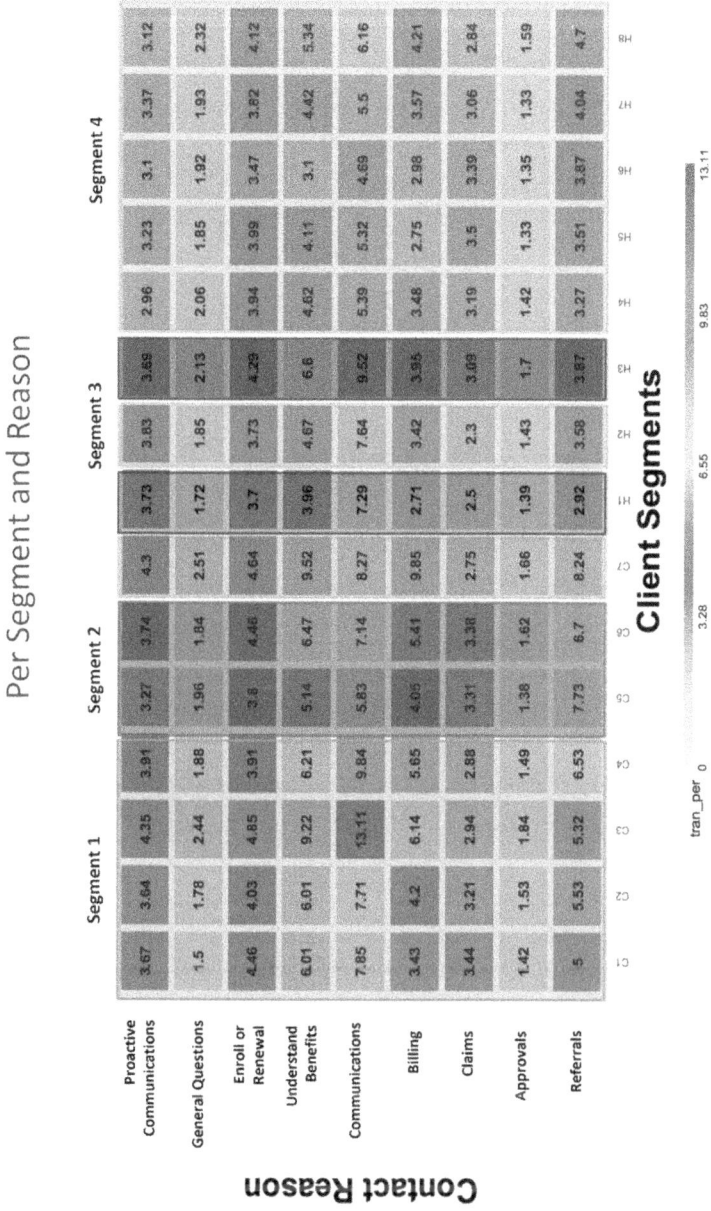

segments and estimate what the financial benefits would be if a certain level of call transactions could be migrated to digital channels. Here is how this is calculated at a high level:

1 Create a matrix listing representative sample volumes of transaction channels and reason codes.

2 Determine channels with costs that are not differentiated by reason (e.g. web channel costs are likely the same regardless of the reason for the web transaction, whereas call costs may be different for different reason codes due to length of calls required to resolve more complex call reasons).

3 Populate the same matrix with cost/transaction data.

4 For each customer segment, calculate cost-to-serve by multiplying transaction volumes by the respective cost/transactions and adding across all transactions executed during the sample period, allocating operating expenses by contact reason and channel, then dividing by the total number of customers in the segment.

5 Enterprise cost-to-serve can then be calculated by summing cost-to-serve across each segment. This then allows you to run scenarios of the costs savings that can be projected by migrating contact reasons from the call center to digital channels, many of which could be fully handled (to the customers' delight) within the channel itself.

To be clear, this is just one approach to addressing this issue. We have had other clients with journey management and optimization software that can generate these sorts of results in real-time using very powerful reporting dashboards. Some solutions include AI features that can predict the root causes of customer containment "leakage" (why x percent of customers didn't complete a transaction in a specific channel), and even identify customers at risk of "soft churn"—an analysis of behavioral customer state changes that could signal a strong probability of losing them to a competitor.

The business case

The results were significant. The biggest opportunity in terms of optimizing the customer experience with the channel mix came from migrating "transactional" interactions away from the call center, toward lower-cost channels, and reducing wait time, eliminating call-backs and call transfers, and dramatically increasing satisfaction.

FIGURE 13.4 Migration volume estimates

Call Migration / Migration Volumes

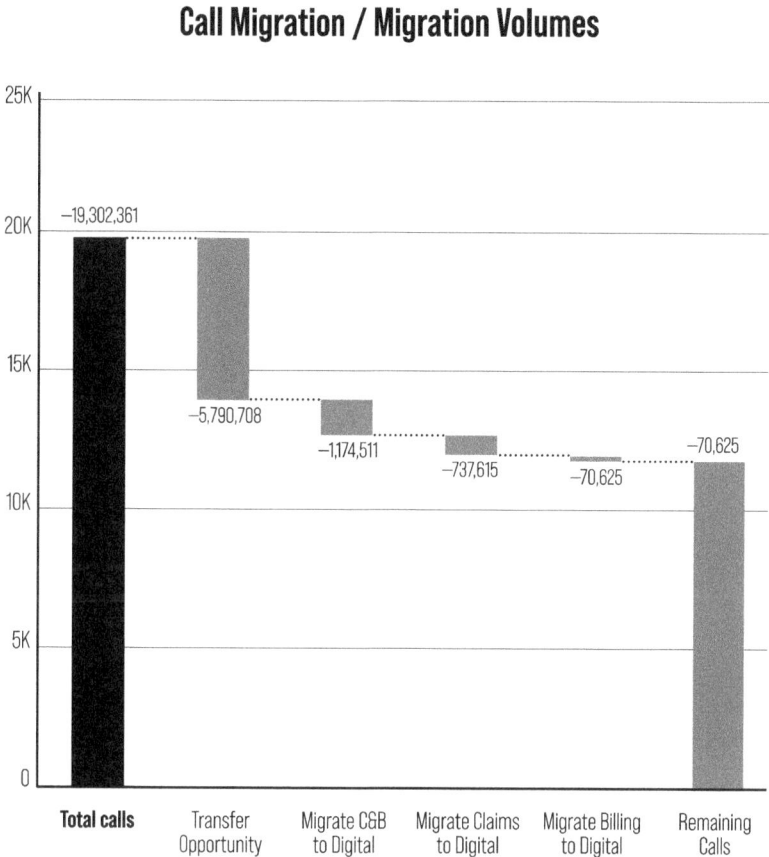

The biggest opportunity in terms of optimizing the customer experience with the channel mix came from migrating "transactional" interactions away from the call center.

FIGURE 13.5 Financial opportunity

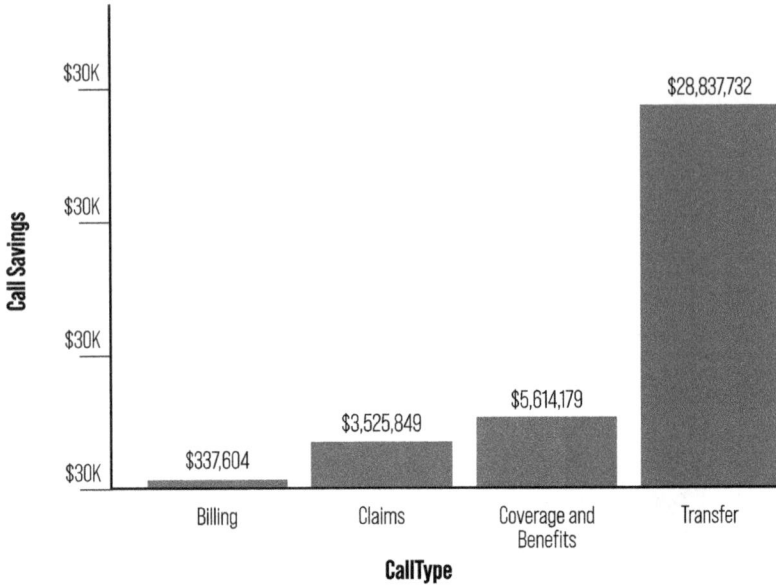

The project estimates in Figure 13.4 show future state volumes from migrating calls by 15 percent for C&B, 30 percent for claims, 20 percent for billing to other digital channels—total of 1.9 million calls migrate to some other digital channel, saving $4.73/contact.

The costliest NVA activity within the call centers occurred when the member was transferred. This activity costs the company approximately $28.8 million per year. 1.9 million call center calls were transactional in nature and good candidates for migrating to lower-cost digital channels, with potential savings of $9.5 million per year.

Summary

Building a business case requires some rigor and the support of research and financial professionals. You may invest some budget in this, but if you do it well, it will be worth every penny. For every customer experience, there is a set of loyalty drivers and critical moments of truth that influence them, that drive specific behaviors which positively impact revenue and margin performance. And though you will use tools to stay connected to customers as you go into the design phase, starting with a quantitatively validated data set, that isolates the most critical changes that will drive behavior change for your most valuable customer segments, is crucial for separating "the signals from the noise" and prioritizing the right problems to solve.

What's next?

With a fact-based business case in hand, it's time to consider how you will deliver on the financial upside you know exists, and to design improvements to the experience that will achieve (and even exceed) your final business case projections.

14

The design process

CHARLOTTE BEERS, CHAIRMAN EMERITUS, OGILVIE

I have probably referenced this quote by Charlotte Beers a thousand times or more. What you are ultimately trying to achieve is the "emotional involvement" of your customers. They have to care that your company is part of their life and that they can't imagine a substitute. That is what makes a brand that customers love.

In this chapter we are going to walk through all seven steps of the design process. At the highest level, the major steps in this approach are summarized in Figure 14.1.

Some steps will be reviewed more briefly than others as much of their content will have been covered already. Also, this process applies Agile project management principles that have been widely written about and we will reference a few Agile tools as we proceed.

For those readers interested in learning how CX/Digital works with our clients to apply AI tools and journey orchestration and optimization software to accelerate the process described in this chapter ever further, turn to Appendix 2: The CX/Digital Design Accelerator.™

1 Understand the current customer experience

We have talked so much about the data you need to collect to complete this step in the process. Ideally, we want to include all of those data items and

FIGURE 14.1 Design process

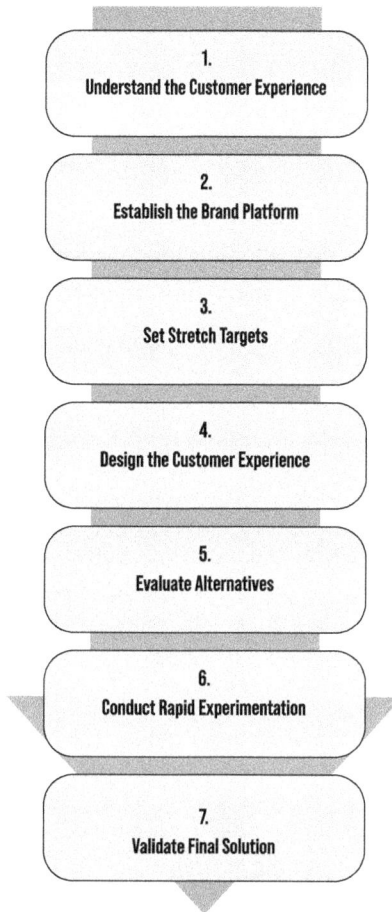

1.
Understand the Customer Experience

2.
Establish the Brand Platform

3.
Set Stretch Targets

4.
Design the Customer Experience

5.
Evaluate Alternatives

6.
Conduct Rapid Experimentation

7.
Validate Final Solution

artifacts, such as the AS IS journey maps and AS IS service blueprints, ending in a summary of the validated loyalty drivers in rank order, the moments of truth that have the greatest influence over them, and other data relevant to your business such as channel usage, high-performer behaviors, etc. There are as many ways to share this data with your core team and key stakeholders as there are data to share. When you are planning your first design session, if you are meeting physically, it is always important to post as much of this content on the walls as you can, as journey maps and service blueprints are easier to understand in large formats rather than PPT presentations.

Included in this step is your preliminary business case as this will inform both your stretch design targets and the improvements you choose to prioritize during the design phase.

2 Establish the brand platform

Every improvement strategy needs to be anchored in your firm's brand platform. This includes three elements, shown in Figure 14.2.

Your brand positioning statement should describe your target customer, the market you are playing in, what you are promising in terms of emotional and rational benefits, and the facts that prove why you are a better choice than your competitors. At the core of what we mean by brand position is what you stand for. Target is a popular, well-known American example. Its brand position is *Style on a budget*.

Now let's chat about your brand promise. Once a customer has moved through the path to purchase, what have you promised him or her in terms of tangible value? Did you measure up? Did the experience he or she received match the promise you made? Even more important, is your brand promise

FIGURE 14.2 The brand platform

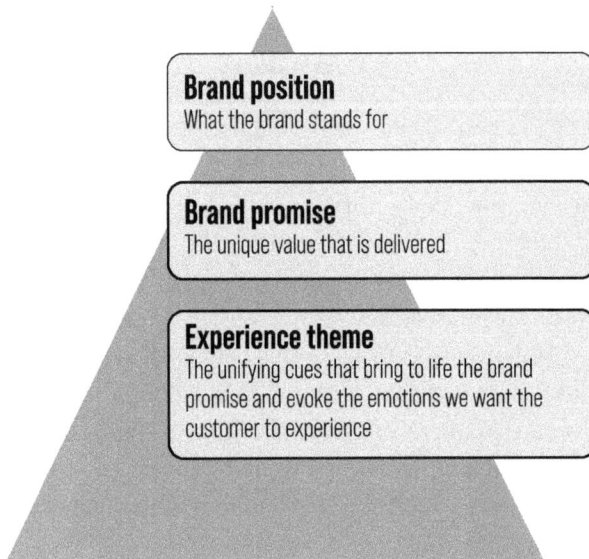

Brand position
What the brand stands for

Brand promise
The unique value that is delivered

Experience theme
The unifying cues that bring to life the brand promise and evoke the emotions we want the customer to experience

consistent with your company's brand position? If you are known in the market for reliability or safety, is the promise you're communicating consistent with the way your customers think about you in the first place?

Sometimes the brand promise is an external expression of the value your company has committed to deliver. To continue our example from above, for Target, its brand promise is: *Expect more. Pay less.*

In our book *Managing the Customer Experience*: *Turning Customers into Advocates*, Shaun Smith and I defined the brand promise as "an articulation of what target customers can expect from their experience with an organization."[2] It describes the proposition and the value that this represents to the customer. We shared some examples:

- Carphone Warehouse: Simple—impartial—advice.
- First Direct Bank: A bank designed around you, which doesn't expect you to fit around it.

Each of these statements represents a clear articulation of the value you should expect if you choose to buy from these companies. They are, quite simply, promises. And a promise needs to be kept or else it's not a promise, it's a lie.

Here are some criteria from *Managing the Customer Experience* that can help you evaluate your brand promise:

- Value: It should be of value to target customers: Richard Branson believes the Virgin brand is based on five key factors: value for money, quality, reliability, innovation, and a sense of fun.

- Need: It should speak to Maslow's hierarchy of needs. For example, Harley-Davidson promises "We fulfill dreams," which directly targets those seeking self-actualization.

- Action: It must be achievable. A private banking group translated its brand promise into standards for each client interaction.

- Focus: It must be the focus and anchor for the organization. It serves as the promise made to customers, what the brand represents to customers and employees, and the internal values required to deliver it.

> " And a promise needs to be kept or else it's not a promise, it's a lie.

- Deliver: Finally, the promise cannot be made lightly, it has to be delivered. In the words of Steve Jones from Galton University, "The good opinion of the public will become increasingly important to big brand owners. If you've got a message, it has to have some truth to it, or you'll be found out."[3]

The experience theme is what we use to align the experience we will design to the brand promise. As stated in the graphic, it is the unifying cues that bring to life the brand promise and evoke the emotions we want the customer to experience. Take a look at your empathy map and:

- determine the emotions that have to be generated or enhanced;
- determine the emotions that have to be mitigated.

Remember:

- Emotions influence what we remember.
- Emotional memories are distinct.
- Emotions influence what we perceive... and how we behave.
- The emotional tone you want to engender is based on the attributes that the firm wants to associate with the brand. Examples:

  o Caesars Entertainment: Feeling of luck
  o Joie de Vivre hotel chain:
    – Edgy (Phoenix Hotel—Rolling Stone magazine)
    – Serene (Hotel Vitale—Country Living).

For a convenience retailer we worked with years ago, their brand platform was:

- brand position: Fresh, clean, friendly
- brand promise: We make your life easier and simpler
- experience theme: Full, full service.

To develop the experience theme, we typically work with a small core group of 3–5 leaders who develop options for the broader core team to consider.

3 Set stretch design targets

Setting design targets helps your team stay on track to design improvements that matter to target customers. They should be developed based on what you learned from your research efforts. There are three parts to this step:

- human-centered design principles and tools;
- benchmarking world-class companies;
- goals and needs by stage: the TO BE customer journey map.

Human-centered design

The Interaction Design Foundation describes the four principles of human-centered design as:[4]

1 People-centered: Focus on people and their context in order to create things that are appropriate for them.
2 Understand and solve the right problems, the root problems: Understand and solve the right problem, the root causes, the underlying fundamental issues. Otherwise, the symptoms will just keep returning.
3 Everything is a system: Think of everything as a system of interconnected parts.
4 Small and simple interventions: Do iterative work and don't rush to a solution. Try small, simple interventions and learn from them one by one, and slowly your results will get bigger and better. Continually prototype, test, and refine your proposals to make sure that your small solutions truly meet the needs of the people you focus on.[5]

This is good advice, and these principles are embedded in the design process. Two tools that you will find useful that help with the first and second principles are personas and empathy maps. Personas are a tool widely used in design thinking to help you more robustly describe your target customer segment as a fictional character that summarizes the needs, preferences, attributes, behaviors, and common activities of the segment. The Interaction Design Foundation does a nice job of describing four types of personas on their website:[6]

- goal-directed personas;
- role-based personas;

- engaging personas;
- fictional personas.

They also take you through ten steps to creating your personas that are quite helpful.

An empathy map is defined by the folks at Adobe as:

> A visualization tool used to articulate what a product team knows about a user. This tool helps product teams build a broader understanding of the "why" aspect behind user needs and wants. This tool forces product teams to practice empathic design, which shifts the focus from the product they want to build to the people who will use this product. As a team identifies what they know about the user and places this information on a chart, they gain a more holistic view of the user's world and his or her problems, or opportunity space.[7]

It is helpful to do this exercise prior to setting goals or targets, as it forces your team to stay grounded in the customer's needs rather than your product or service goals.

Benchmark best practice companies

With your personas well defined and an empathy map for each completed, review the best practice companies you benchmarked in your research phase to consider any innovations that you learned about that could inform the goals you may send in the next step. For example, one of our clients learned how 1-800-Got-Junk will often call a customer that they know is moving before they arrive to ask them if they want them to bring the customer a coffee, given they assume they may have packed their coffee maker. A small gesture, but it obviously communicates something much more about the brand (brand authenticity).

Goals and needs by stage

Now as you consider your AS IS customer journey map, start to create your TO BE customer experience map, starting with refining (if you need to) the name of each stage to reflect the customer's goals rather than your services. For example, customer experience thought leader Jeanne Bliss, the founder of Customer Bliss, during a recent podcast recounted the story of a client she worked with in the aviation business who redefined part of the customer journey from the "parts and service experience" to the "keep me flying experience."[8] Once you feel you have a "customer back" set of stages, then as a team, build out the customer's goals for each stage.

Finally, for each moment of truth (and typically there should be no more than 4–6 of these) set an initial stretch design target. For example, if one of your MoTs is about on-time delivery, consider your zones of tolerance results if you have them and what you may have learned about how best practice firms perform in a similar industry, and set a stretch design target that will outperform your best competitor and exceed customer expectations (consistently).

4 Design the customer experience

Every organization is different, so it is hard to be prescriptive on the best approach. We suggest structuring the design process based on:

- the business context—incremental versus transformational;
- narrow product/service scope or broad;
- domestic or international;
- the level of aggressiveness dictated by the stretch design targets;
- what the data says is important to customers;
- the level of capability of the organization in terms of sales, marketing, HR, operations, IT, and distribution.

Once the core team is in place, we recruit a guiding coalition of leaders from all levels and functions in the organization. It is helpful to bring this group together physically for 1–3 design sessions, but much can be accomplished via Zoom or WebEx virtual platforms.

Besides the core team and guiding coalition, I have found it helpful to invite external resources at different points in the design process, including customers, subject matter experts, and industry thought leaders. Regardless of the structure, the design process between face-to-face and virtual working sessions, and individual assignments, the set of activities tends to be consistent. They include the following.

Contracting

The first step includes the project leader meeting with the executive sponsor(s) and confirming their support and involvement in the project. You have the preliminary business case to work from, but your goal is to contract with your executive sponsors around scope as well as the broader context you are going to be working in. For example, we were about to launch a significant redesign project with a client until in another meeting we learned they were about to embark on a major change to their POS system. It made no sense to proceed until that was at least through its pilot implementation. Secondly, from a budget standpoint, you need to know what dollars are available and if there are any other sales, marketing, product, or HR changes in the works that you may need to be aware of as appropriate.

Team selection

Assuming you have already recruited the core team to work through the research phase, it's time to extend out to invite a guiding coalition of leaders to be part of the design process. Remember, you want to invite high performers from all parts of the company, not just customer-facing representatives and not just supervisors. Some of the best ideas we have ever witnessed have come from truck drivers, installers, call center agents, and billing representatives. Always remember, this may just be another meeting for you, but for others it might be the first time they ever got on a plane to participate in something like this, so use your good judgment and company standards to create an environment of inclusiveness and respect.

Preparation

If you quickly do the math of the fully loaded cost of getting a group of 12–30 people together, you really don't want to burn too many minutes reviewing content everyone could have read before arriving. Create a "data room"—basically a secure website like Dropbox where all attendees can get access to the data collected from the research phase in advance following your legal team's guidelines around data-sharing confidentiality. Your email invitation to all attendees needs to emphasize the specific documents you require them to review and any assignments you may ask them to complete prior to the first design session.

> ❝ You have the preliminary business case to work from, but your goal is to contract with your executive sponsors around scope as well as the broader context you are going to be working in.

Launch meeting

The launch meeting is typically conducted virtually and represents a final chance for participants who aren't fully committed to self-select out during or, if more comfortable, after the meeting. During the meeting, you describe the process you have designed, what is expected from everyone, the time commitment involved, and the ground rules for when you are together and apart. This is a big deal. Better to weed out participants who were nominated and accepted because they saw it as a perk or career opportunity from the ones who see it for what it really is, a chance to have a tangible impact to improve the business and eliminate barriers to greater success. You want people that see the bigger picture and want to be part of something important.

Design activities

These are always split up into two or three sessions The first time you meet, you will typically cover the project scope, themes and insights from the data collected, the AS customer and employee journey map, personas, empathy maps, etc. We usually assign work in sub-teams before reconvening for the next one or two design sessions where we start redesigning the experience. During these sessions we apply various design thinking tools as well as the 7 Design Strategies to develop improvements or changes that increase the company's competitive performance on attributes that matter but that they should not overdeliver on—as well as improvements that deliver differentiated performance which the data suggests will increase retention, spending, and advocacy. The result is an ideal customer storyboard that will guide your development work going forward.

That was a brief walk-through of the sequence of activities and tools. There are some additional design strategies specific to digital-first improvements to keep in mind.

A "NUDGE" ON NUDGE THEORY

As mentioned in Chapter 2, the current research is not conclusive if consumers will pay a premium for greener products. However, in their book, *Nudge: Improving Decisions about Health, Wealth, and Happiness*,[9] Richard Thaler and Cass Sunstein make the case for how nudge theory can be applied to design experiences that help consumers make healthier decisions, for themselves and, by extension, for the planet. It is based upon the idea that by shaping the choice architecture, one can influence the likelihood that individuals will choose one option over another. As we referenced earlier in several of our case studies, a key factor of nudge theory is the ability for an individual to maintain freedom of choice and to feel in control of the decisions they make. An example of this theory in action includes the grocery chain Pay and Save. They designed their store with green arrows on the floor leading to fruit and vegetable aisles. They discovered that shoppers followed the arrows nine out of ten times and their sales of fresh produce went through the roof.[10]

Additional digital strategies

There are five additional topics that are important to include when designing digital-first experiences.

1 GOOGLE'S MOMENTS THAT MATTER

If you google the phrase "winning the moments that matter" you will be able to download a PDF by the same name that summarizes Google's research into one aspect of the consumer experience:

> In the past three years alone, multi-screen media consumption has increased by 500%, with 90% of web users moving between devices to complete a task, whether it's to shop, plan a trip or browse content... Now there are ever more intent and passion driven moments where consumers are looking for inspiration or information, discovering new things, or making decisions—we refer to these as "moments that matter." These are the "I want-to-watch moments," "I want-to-do moments," "I need-to-find moments," and "I need-to-buy moments." These moments matter to brands because they are where decisions are being made and preferences are being shaped—lean-in moments when we expect our needs and wants to be fulfilled instantly.[11]

The initial version of this document focused on the mobile experience in which the data revealed that:[12]

- 91 percent of smartphone users turn to their phones for ideas while doing a task;
- 82 percent of smartphone users consult their phones while in a store deciding what to buy;
- there was a 2× increase in "near me" search interest in the past year;

- 53 percent of people will leave a mobile site if it takes more than three seconds to load;
- for every one-second delay in site load time, conversions fall by 12 percent.

What's the message? Simply put, consider the moments of truth in your customer experience and compare them to Google's research. As you design additional digital interactions, besides understanding the four types of moments their research uncovered, your digital solutions need to perform with acceptable speeds and load times or you will quicky become irrelevant.

2 CUSTOMER NETWORK STRATEGY

David L. Rogers' ground-breaking best seller *The Digital Transformation Playbook: Rethink Your Business for the Digital Age* provides a wealth of helpful advice and tools. He makes the point that today's consumers are networked with each other and companies must rethink how they engage with them through the purchase funnel and retain them over time. Prof. Rogers identified five core behaviors of customer networks:[13]

1 Accessing digital data and interaction, quickly, easily, and constantly.
2 Engaging with digital content that is sensory, interactive, and relevant.
3 Customizing our digital experiences to suit our own particular interests and needs.
4 Connecting with each other, by sharing ideas and opinions.
5 Collaborating on shared projects and goals.

If your company's digital interaction with your customers has been limited to your website, a mobile app, and a Twitter feed, you may want to dig into these insights during your design process as it forces an important discussion around what would be of value to your customers, especially when seen through the lens of these five customer network strategies.

3 DATA ARCHITECTURE

No matter what improvement you choose to focus on, underlying all of it needs to be a robust data architecture. Much has been written on this topic, especially over the past three years, and getting into the details of what that should entail for any single organization is beyond the scope of this book. We worked with one large insurance client with which, given the enormity of the time and cost to align their internal legacy systems, it made more sense to take the redesigned experience and set it up as a completely separate subsidiary given the speed and cost effectiveness that cloud-based infrastructure from AWS and others could provide. Clearly part of this data strategy includes governance processes around privacy as well as security compliance, depending on what countries your data is hosted in, but generally speaking, your IT DevOps team will manage those requirements.

Having said that, there are low-code application development platforms to solve some of these challenges through innovative front-end platforms with APIs that can eliminate or reduce the programming required to deliver a seamless omni-channel experience. Every company is different and the steepness of the challenge from a data standpoint can't be answered in this chapter. Professor Rogers does provide an additional tool called the data value generator that can help your team frame the opportunity for leveraging data in the experience. It follows a five-step process for generating new strategic ideas for data.[14]

- Define area impact and KPIs.
- Value template selection:
  - *Insight*—Understanding customers' psychology, their behaviors, and the impact of business actions.
  - *Targeting*—Narrowing your audience, knowing who to reach, and using advanced segmentation.
  - *Personalization*—Treating different customers differently to increase relevance and results.
  - *Context*—Relating one customer's data to the data of a larger population.
- Concept generation.
- Data audit.
- Execution plan.

Prof. Rogers' tool is a good starting point to consider how data that you may have never thought of as an asset before can be applied and perhaps combined with open-source or other data to deliver on one or all of the previously mentioned customer network strategies.

> ❝ No matter what improvement you choose to focus on, underlying all of it needs to be a robust data architecture.

4 A/B TESTING AND CHANNEL ADOPTION ANALYSIS

If there is one thing I am sure this book has got you thinking about it is the way you approach the concept of choice architecture, because in a digital-first experience, in some ways, it is the underlying set of assumptions below the entire experience. The specific customer behaviors you encourage are reflected in this strategy and representative of all of our best practice companies from Lemonade to Amazon. The power of digital is that with the right journey management and optimization platform, you can conduct low-cost A/B tests and using this technology, observe the degree to which customers default to your new choice architecture or drop out of it. Remember our first design strategy—*design multiple emotional peaks and finish strong*. A lot of your design improvements can be prototyped, tested, and analyzed with automated tools and the results reported in real-time.

5 PLATFORM BUSINESS MODEL

The seventh design strategy—*Link digital assets to leverage value over cost*—is a powerful concept and may naturally lead you into considering a full-fledged platform business model. If it does, recognize there is a whole other set of tools and business model questions to be answered before going too deeply. We have partnered with Geoff Parker and Marshall Van Alstyne, co-authors of the best-seller *Platform Revolution*,[15] and have developed both business cases and platform business models for clients that have helped them concept and design these businesses prior to launch. More information on this approach can be found on our website: cxdigital.ai.

Final advice

Having designed and led so many of these projects over the years, I would summarize this section with the following suggestions.

ERR ON INCLUSIVENESS IN TEAM MEMBERSHIP

We have already mentioned this, but it is worth emphasizing again. We have facilitated quite large design teams and for big organizations such as in healthcare, those teams are going to be large given the number of products, services, and channels. With additional facilitators and a strong design, this can be managed, and you want to have the people that need to be in the room, in the room.

BREAK THE ELEPHANT UP INTO PARTS BEFORE YOU PUT IT BACK TOGETHER AGAIN

When you begin this process, there quite honestly is a point early on when all of the data you collected may be overwhelming and the size of the task ahead may seem insurmountable. If you find yourself in this position, excellent—you know for sure you are on the right path. We always break up our design teams into cross-discipline stage/touchpoint sub-teams, often rotating then across the journey, to work on improving specific stages/touchpoints based on the data collected, the persona's empathy maps, and the loyalty drivers/moments of truth that need to be improved. Not every strategy will be relevant to every touchpoint, but many will and in those cases they prove invaluable. You just have to have some faith that even though you need to break the experience down to improve it, it will come back together in the end to form one seamless, incredibly powerful customer experience.

IF CONFLICT EMERGES, DON'T AVOID IT, HARNESS IT

This is easier to write in a book than actually do, but if you have recruited a great team, there will be disagreements and, ideally, passionate ones. Avoid the temptation to calm these debates or default to compromise. Practice your systems thinking: skillful discussion skills and hold the tension through to resolution and I promise you, it will produce dividends like you could never have imagined.

ITERATE, ITERATE, ITERATE

Whatever your design for facilitation, leave room for several rounds of iteration, moving team members from one stage/touchpoint to build off the work of another. Throw out more sticky notes than you keep and carry on working it until you literally sense the change in the room. This is not abstract, this really happens. At some point, you will have created a set of options for redesign that your whole team will align behind. That is when you are ready to start storyboarding two or three alternatives and get ready for some feedback from customers.

5 Evaluate alternatives

Once the team has developed the newly designed experience, represented in the form of a customer storyboard(s) or storyboard (with options), we complete three activities before the team departs.

Apply the 7 Design Strategies criteria rating

As referenced earlier this is super simple but effective. We take the 7 Design Strategies and rate on a 1–10 scale: how effective the team believes they were at applying each to the customer storyboard representation of the new experience. They also rate the degree to which the new experience will achieve your stretch design targets and positively impact your key moments of truth.

Draft final ideal customer storyboard(s), project charters, and the three-lane highway

The last step from the design process is to create a final ideal customer storyboard(s) and for the key improvements defined, to use a template to describe each initiative, its scope, and its potential impact on delivering the preliminary business case.

These projects or initiatives are then categorized using the three-lane highway model described previously:

- Lane 1—Fix it: These are 90-day or less projects, often lower-cost, less complex solutions that address short-term problems that are actually producing dissatisfied customers.

- Lane 2—Improve it: These are slightly longer term—6–9-month projects involving multiple functions and product teams that will provide measurable benefits to two or more stakeholders. Most organizations have the capacity for 3–5 of these initiatives over a calendar year.

- Lane 3—Transform it: This is the longest time horizon, 1–3 years, and usually involves the upgrade or implementation of a new system to create a step-change level of innovation to the customer experience.

6 Conduct rapid experimentation

Now that you have completed what you believe will be changes that will achieve your preliminary business case it is time to build some prototypes to test your solution(s) with the target customer base to ensure it will work.

TABLE 14.1 Convergent and divergent experiments

Convergent Experiments	Divergent Experiments
Scientific experimental design (e.g. A/B testing)	Informal experimental design (e.g. testing prototypes with customers)
Asks a precise question or finite set	Poses an unknown set of questions
Seeks to provide an answer—needs a statistically valid sample; test and control groups	May provide an answer, or raise more questions—sample size may vary
Confirmatory—focused on direct causality	Exploratory—focused on gestalt effects, such as loyalty
Useful for optimization	Useful for idea generation
Common in late stages of an innovation	Common in early stages of an innovation
Tests the thing itself	Tests as a rough a prototype as possible (good enough)

SOURCE *The Digital Transformation Playbook*, David L. Rogers

Adopting the discipline of rapid experimentation will ensure you avoid falling in love with your solution rather than the problem you are attempting to solve for your target customer.

There are two types of experimentation, shown in Table 14.3.

A great example of a team that applied experimentation to a successful new product launch comes from an emerging markets team at Intuit tasked with developing a product for India's farmers, who make up the bulk of the economy.[16] The team began by immersing themselves into the farmers' environment and learning about their challenges and needs. Selling their perishable crops was fraught with both a lack of pricing transparency and a limitation on the number of markets a particular farmer could afford to reach.

The team's initial idea of an eBay-like marketplace proved technically and culturally untenable, as did their second creative solution. But they persisted, and using very low-cost prototyping methods, their third idea emerged and looked promising: an SMS notification service that would inform farmers of the prices being offered at various markets before they actually left their farms. At the end of the test, they found that both buyers and sellers had adopted it, and that the farmers' incomes were raised by 20 percent—double their original goal. That impact continued as the final product, now called Fasal, was developed and rolled out as an automated service providing customized text messages to more than 1 million participating farmers.

There are five lessons to learn from this example:

1 The Intuit team didn't just try to understand the customers' needs, they got their hands dirty—in this case literally—in order to acquire more profound knowledge of the situation, the key stakeholders, and both the obvious and sometimes more subtle cultural dynamics at work.

2 They developed multiple solutions and kept iterating to understand what worked and what didn't work until they landed on a solution that actually gained measurable traction.

3 They didn't over-build any of the potential solutions. Even the eventual winner was tested with an Intuit employee in an office with multiple phones, sending and receiving messages to and from the farmers via SMS messaging.

4 At the outset, they set a goal: Develop a product that will help farmers raise their income from crop sales by 10 percent. What is interesting about this goal is that it wasn't about gaining advantages for Intuit, at least initially. They didn't strive to "grow Intuit sales in the agriculture segment by 10 percent." They kept their focus on the outcome first, knowing their own benefits would come if they solved a real customer problem.

5 Finally, they didn't declare success until they saw a change in actual customer behavior. Rather than distributing surveys to gauge interest in the new service, they were able to actually see their pilot participants start using it.[17]

Once the options you designed have been fully tested, you are ready to launch your changes. The next chapter will detail how you go from your ideal customer storyboard to scaling it across the enterprise, but once the solution has been in market, it is important to complete one last step.

7 Validate final solution

As stated earlier, it is critical that the preliminary business case is not a static artifact, never to be thought of again. As a result of the previous step, you are ready to complete your final business case and begin quarterly updates because you have real data around adoption rates, spending, and increases in things like NPS® or customer effort scores, that should inform the assumptions set in the preliminary business case. Ideally, you will create a dashboard that tracks these changes on a quarterly basis through some form of structured and unstructured data collection.

Summary

The power of the design process is that by using new AI and collaborative platforms, we can design solutions in less than half the time we would have as recently as three or four years ago. I hope this walk-through of the process was enough to get your synapses pulsing with ways to adapt it to your company.

What's next?

Last but not least, it is time to take that ideal customer experience storyboard and successful pilot or proof-of-concept results and turn it into a scaled solution that customers will see and feel. Get ready to execute to scale.

15

Execute to scale

"Whatever your goal is, you will never succeed unless you let go of your fears and fly."[1]

RICHARD BRANSON, CEO AND FOUNDER, VIRGIN GROUP

The final mile in our journey concerns how you scale what you have piloted into a full production capability that is phased in over a carefully coordinated release plan. This will include dependencies, communications requirements, and capacity-to-demand considerations. To help this come alive, we present a fictional case study, adapted from several real-life clients to illustrate how you go from storyboard to execution. We will start with the final ideal customer storyboard developed by the CX design team at a fictional company: Tenix Polymers and follow it right through to the seven levels of execution required to scale their final, validated solution.

Welcome to Tenix Polymers

Tenix Polymers is a chemical manufacturer and an emerging leader in the high-tech polymer materials market serving the automotive, construction, healthcare, energy, and cosmetics industries.

The design team for Tenix spent the past several weeks understanding the needs and expectations of their customers in the automotive industry that use their polyurethane, plastics, and high-performance coatings products where their biggest competitor, DBR Global, has had few challengers to their significant global market share. The team applied qualitative and quantitative tools to identify the loyalty drivers and moments of truth and

FIGURE 15.1 Illustrative ideal customer storyboard

TENIX IDEAL CUSTOMER
EXPERIENCE STORYBARD

TENIX POLYMERS: STRETCH DESIGN TARGETS

1. Deliver an experience that earns a price premium as an innovation leader.
2. Reduce our cost-to-serve by the smart application of digital technology that delivers on the most important LOYALTY DRIVERS, while integrating human interactions (VALUE Behaviors) that ensure we become our customers' TRUSTED PARTNER.
3. Drive significant growth in market share.

MOMENTS OF TRUTH TO CONSISTENTLY EXCEED CUSTOMER EXPECTATIONS

- First Plant Visit
- New Customer Onboarding
- First Product Delivery
- Real-time Digital Twinning
- Automated Ordering and Billing
- Issue Resolution

BRAND PROMISE:

Tenix Polymers delivers innovative chemical solutions:

- We FOCUS on your needs.
- We EMPOWER our people to exceed your expectations.
- We are INNOVATORS, applying technology to enable our customers to deliver even greater value in the products they produce using our award-winning compounds and polymers.

Tenix Polymers Tagline:
Driving Innovation

HEARD ABOUT...

Trimmler Motors counts on Tenix for all of its polymer, specialty plastics and coating needs, to keep their factories running at full capacity. Tenix is an up and comer in the industry, as they have started to challenge the global leader, DBR Global one satisfied customer at a time. Steve Remington, Trimmler's Director of Manufacturing started to research Tenix after their current provider, DBR, missed an important delivery just before a really busy production schedule. That was when Steve went online and discovered the Tenix website.

He had heard about Tenix from a colleague of his at a trade show but was skeptical that what his friend claimed could be true. A service guarantee that backed up their delivery window commitment? A dedicated support team connected to each plant through digital twinning technology? Touchless ordering with full delivery transparency through...(more)

HELP ME DECIDE

The first time Steve visited the Tenix website it was clear this company made understanding his needs a priority. Their easy-to-use tools allowed him to compare Tenix's total value proposition to that of DBR's. By submitting just a minimum amount of information, the website provided him with a pricing analysis, pro-forma financial scorecard, and their recommendations on the most effective products for his needs including information about their new PCR and PIR polycarbonates derived from mechanical recycling which...(more)

MAKE IT EASY FOR ME TO BUY

The first meeting with Nicole was as impressive as the website experience. Nicole took the time to really learn about his business and Steve gave her a tour of the plant, the manufacturing cells in which their products would be used including the three large coating platforms...(more)

benchmarked several world-class companies including Lemonade, CEMEX, and BMW. After two intense design sessions they developed a powerful ideal customer storyboard.

Tenix Polymers: stretch design targets

Our goals include:

1   Deliver an experience that earns a price premium as an innovation leader.

2   Reduce our cost-to-serve by the smart application of digital technology that delivers on the most important loyalty drivers, while integrating human interactions (value behaviors) that ensure we become our customers' trusted partner.

3   Drive significant growth in market share.

Moments of truth to consistently exceed customer expectations

- First plant visit.
- New customer onboarding.
- First product delivery.
- Real-time digital twinning.
- Automated ordering and billing.
- Issue resolution.

Brand promise

Tenix Polymers delivers innovative chemical solutions:

- We FOCUS on your needs.
- We EMPOWER our people to exceed your expectations.
- We are INNOVATORS, applying technology to enable our customers to deliver even greater value in the products they produce using our award-winning compounds and polymers.

Tenix Polymer's tagline: *Driving Innovation.*

Ideal customer experience storyboard

HEARD ABOUT...

Trimmler Motors counts on Tenix for all of its polymer, specialty plastics, and coating needs, to keep their factories running at full capacity. Tenix is an up and comer in the industry as they have started to challenge the global leader, DBR Global, one satisfied customer at a time. Steve Remington, Trimmler's Director of Manufacturing, started to research Tenix after their current provider, DBR, missed an important delivery just before a really busy production schedule. That was when Steve went online and discovered the Tenix website. He had heard about Tenix from a colleague at a trade show but was skeptical that what his friend claimed could be true. A service guarantee that backed up their delivery window commitment? A dedicated support team connected to each plant through digital twinning technology? Touchless ordering with full delivery transparency through their customer portal or mobile app? Invoicing that isn't just 100 percent accurate to the bill of lading (BOL), it even provides tips on how to save money through better-timed advanced purchases to lock in the best possible price when there is volatility in the chemicals market? Given how much polymer costs contribute to the costs of goods sold, even incremental savings on a unit basis can make a big difference when ordering larger volumes.

HELP ME DECIDE

The first time Steve visited the Tenix website it was clear this company made understanding his needs a priority. Their easy-to-use tools allowed him to compare Tenix's total value proposition to that of DBR. By submitting just a minimum amount of information, the website provided him with a pricing analysis, pro-forma financial scorecard, and their recommendations on the most effective products for his needs, including information about their new PCR and PIR polycarbonates derived from mechanical recycling which would help Trimmler's GHG metrics both in terms of using lower-carbon products and improving their end-of-life metrics as part of new mandatory ESG disclosures.

Steve was also able to quickly apply for an extended credit line and after completing a simple form and uploading some documents, his approval and credit limit were provided instantaneously. He was able to read about the account team that would be dedicated to his account and schedule an appointment to meet with his account manager. Her name was Nicole Bartlett—interestingly, she had been to the same college as Steve, though he had graduated several years before her. He sent her a quick text message and heard back from her almost immediately through Slack. He asked if she could bring along a sample of a Tenix contract and she sent it to him directly from the Tenix CRM system. When he selected the appointment from her available appointment blocks, the confirmation message thanked him and automatically sent a calendar invitation to his inbox for him to accept. This company understood what it meant to work in "Trimmler time," as they liked to say. Not every supplier did, so this was a welcome change.

MAKE IT EASY FOR ME TO BUY

The first meeting with Nicole was as impressive as the website experience. Nicole took the time to really learn about his business and Steve gave her a tour of the plant and the manufacturing cells in which their products would be used, including the three large coating platforms. During the meeting, Nicole used her tablet to capture additional information about Steve's requirements and the ways Trimmler Motors tried to differentiate itself from its competitors. She also asked him some very detailed questions to better understand their manufacturing process and delivery requirements, including customized delivery instructions (time of day and gate code sign-in protocol). Nicole explained Tenix's safety standards and shared a safety briefing to ensure safe deliveries for both Trimmler Motors and Tenix employees since some of their products carried hazardous materials certifications. This company's values were front and center.

The resulting proposal Nicole presented a few days later was tremendous. Not only did it recommend a unique set of products that all met Trimmler's specifications, but Steve was also provided with options to choose from their "green," lower-carbon alternatives that included a larger percentage of biomass-derived CO_2 that would help Trimmler improve their ESG performance. DRB had never suggested these sorts of solutions.

Nicole also video-conferenced in the support team on her tablet so Steve could meet them "face-to-face" while they walked through their digital twinning platform, which meant all of Trimmler's cells that used Tenix's products were also mirrored virtually through their digital platform, so both his and their team were able to virtually monitor every aspect of their product use and performance in real-time. This took quality assurance and performance optimization to another level.

Nicole then demonstrated how Steve or any of his authorized purchasing managers could automate all of his scheduled deliveries through the customer portal and set alerts through their preferred channels and frequency as to when deliveries would be arriving. The sensors that were included in their solution and replicated virtually would take the worry out of knowing when to place an order so Steve and his team could focus on more important things, like ensuring their production line was operating at full capacity to demand. Every manufacturing manager's dream.

Contracting was easy. It was all done on Nicole's tablet using DocuSign and the SAP online ordering system. Even Steve's contracts manager was impressed with how they were able to handle some last-minute contract changes and that Nicole was able to approve some simple edits to the contract herself. With a sufficient line of credit established, Nicole also took the time to walk Steve and his purchasing managers through what their first invoice would look like and then Jeff, his Tenix customer support representative, described the steps he could take for auto renewal as well as how to adjust his order should demand spike or fall off. It was as simple as turning a virtual dial on his laptop or speaking to the application on his smartphone or tablet. Once he verified his authority level with a password, or in the case of the mobile device his voiceprint or thumbprint, all of the affected systems from scheduling to billing would adjust in real time and notify Steve of the changes through his preferred channel.

KEEP MY BUSINESS RUNNING

Every evening before there is a delivery, Steve or his assigned purchasing manager on the order receives a message through their preferred channel with a visual rendering of each cell's inventory levels, prompting them to choose which delivery window they want to receive product this week. They can confirm the schedule right from their mobile device or laptop. Once they select the delivery window that is most convenient, a photo of the driver who will make the delivery is immediately sent along with a message from the dispatcher confirming the security code the driver should use to gain access to the plant. Steve makes a point of meeting the Tenix driver and although they are often different drivers, they all seem to have knowledge of Steve's orders and the types of products they use, and the driver always thanks Steve for his business and asks if there is anything else Tenix could be doing to help his business. The very first time he asked that question, Steve said "Yes!" He asked the driver to be sure to tell the dispatcher to confirm the security code before each delivery. The driver responded, "We're on it!" and since that time they always check.

After every delivery, Steve and his team receive an SMS, email, or in-app message asking about their satisfaction with the delivery and if they would recommend them to a friend or colleague. When Steve replied with a 10 out of 10, he was redirected to a mobile web service that thanked him for his positive response and introduced the "3 for 3" program. Tenix offered him a 3 percent discount on his next delivery if he would refer Tenix to three prospective new customers. Each of them would receive a 3 percent discount on their first order. Why not share his positive experience with others, like his brother-in-law who is a materials manager for a large cosmetics manufacturer, another market Tenix competes in.

MAKE IT EASY FOR ME TO PAY

Perhaps the best thing about Tenix is how they handle billing. Not only is it immediate but it provides Steve with three things that no other competitor ever provided:

- Steve can go online and see each transaction, completed or in process, with status and documentation for every order.
- It provides an update on pricing volatility in the polymers base product market and suggests pre-ordering options to lock in preferred pricing.
- It describes a month-by-month and year-to-date view of Trimmler Motors' total spending and communicates how much they saved each quarter by bundling all of their polymer and coating spending with Tenix.

This data is available on the customer portal dashboard, but it is helpful to Steve to link to it from the automated billing process. The dashboard also alerts Steve if Tenix forecasts greater demand in the market for any of his specific products that could increase prices. With this information, it may be a good time for Steve to increase his inventory while prices are stable. No other supplier in the industry provides this sort of real-time, cost-saving information.

SOMETHING WENT WRONG

As good as Tenix is around on-time delivery, they aren't perfect. On two occasions Tenix missed the delivery window by over an hour. Once, it was due to a flood that forced all traffic to detour around the reservoir, and the other time the Tenix truck blew a tire. But true to their word, it was easy for Steve to contact support and redeem their guarantee of 3 percent off of the current order that was late. Support with Tenix is different than with any other company. The CSR did not have to check with her supervisor before granting the refund, she went ahead and updated the current invoice in real time and his invoice was adjusted on his very first call. What was wonderful about the interaction with the CSR was how they greeted Steve and seemed to know so much about his business. They respected his time and always thanked him for being a customer. Although he is delighted his support team is available, he hardly ever needs to contact them as literally all of his questions are handled by interactive notifications, their online chatbot, and a mobile-first dashboard that tracks and reports all of his transactions with Tenix.

HELP ME GROW EVEN MORE

Reordering with Tenix is about as easy as 1-2-3. Steve always receives a notification before the renewal to confirm there are no adjustments. If he forgets to respond, the regular order auto renews and the dispatcher confirms the driver security code—without fail—before each delivery that Steve can validate from his mobile device. One of the things that enables efficiency for Tenix and adds value for Trimmler Motors is the algorithms and artificial intelligence that improve demand prediction for all of Trimmler's chemical product needs with efficient just-in-time scheduling. This proprietary system from Tenix works in real-time to minimize inventory while securing optimum volume pricing for a majority of chemical products (including Tenix's) that Trimmler uses. Given the volatility of the chemicals market, this system drops significant savings right to the bottom line.

Once a year, Steve receives an email survey from Tenix to consider their performance over the past 12 months and on a 0 to 10 scale, asks if he would recommend them. Just for fun, he rated them a "0" to see what would happen and within 30 minutes he received a call from the regional manager who told Steve it was their practice to follow up on any customer rating under a 6 within one hour of receiving their response. The manager was clearly relieved to hear it was a false alarm and he invited Steve to join their quarterly customer user group meeting that was being held at the local Marriott hotel in town. He was encouraged to bring up to three business associates he thought might be good potential Tenix customers. At the meeting there would be some of Tenix's suppliers who were sponsoring the event talking about new products that might be of interest to Steve and his associates, as well as other Tenix customers who were part of the customer user group community, sharing some ideas on manufacturing best practices. Steve asked the manager to send the invites to him right away and he would confirm his attendance through the customer portal.

"On it!" the manager said and sure enough the four invites appeared in his inbox a moment later.

On it is right! Steve liked the sound of that. Tenix wasn't just his polymer supplier—they were his trusted partner. Was it worth the slight premium he paid? You bet, because of what it saved him in terms of reliable delivery, optimized inventory, and overall lower cost of ownership from their ESG product performance. Steve knows that Tenix will always be there for him so he can worry less about having enough of the right product and more about keeping his production line up and running and quality levels higher than ever before.

The purpose of the customer experience storyboard is to describe the ideal experience. Let us rate it against the seven strategies in Table 15.1.

TABLE 15.1   7 Design Strategies criteria rating

Design Strategy	Rating	Example
1. Achieve emotional peaks across channels, finishing strong	8	Tenix designed several digital and human interactions that delivered emotional peaks, including the immediate credit approval to the first virtual "face-to-face" meeting with the account team.
2. Create a personalization flywheel that grows customer engagement	8	The storyboard cited ways that Tenix applied AI to forecast what Steve's demand was going to be, married with ways for him to hedge his purchases to get the best price. Over time, as Steve received benefits from this Tenix-specific hedging solution, this could produce a virtuous flywheel, especially if markets became more volatile.
3. Strengthen customer commitment by providing choice and control	9	Through the design, Steve was provided with notifications and options that gave him and his team control over their purchasing and scheduling activities.
4. Foster ownership through customer community and co-creation	4	The lowest score. Though Steve did get invited to join the Tenix User Group, their score on co-creation is low. However, the digital twinning capability does engage Trimmler in terms of collaborating with Tenix.
5. Inspire rituals that create shared meaning	6	Unlike a B2C business, creating rituals can be more difficult, though their well-crafted personalized communications and regular delivery updates could be argued to constitute a form of ritual since they speak to the customer's emotions and goals, and the social connection to the Tenix account team.

(continued)

TABLE 15.1 (Continued)

Design Strategy	Rating	Example
6. Empower customers through immersive experiences	8	Digital twinning is being embraced by many manufacturers, especially in the automotive industry, and the virtual, synchronized shared digital configuration of Trimmler's factory floor cells using the Tenix product provided significant benefits that clearly led to customer empowerment in spades.
7. Link digital assets to leverage value over cost	9	The digital assets that Tenix was investing in were outpacing their larger, less nimble competitor. These included 1) the digital twinning technology to optimize product/machine performance, 2) touchless ordering, renewal, and monitoring, 3) AI-based demand forecasting with suggested hedging to provide greater cost savings across the majority of their chemical products, 4) innovative "greener" products than competitors that reduced the total product cost for their customer, 5) customer user groups for sharing best practices, 6) a service guarantee for on-time delivery with "no-hassle" redemption, and 7) simple referral and rewards programs. All components reinforced each other and formed a "whole greater than the sum of their parts."

Finally, how well did the Tenix design team deliver on the firm's brand promise and moments of truth? Did you feel that this experience was driving innovation?

- Were they FOCUSED on Trimmler's needs?
- Were their people EMPOWERED?
- Did the company demonstrate INNOVATION by applying technology to enable Trimmler Motors to deliver even greater value?

Let's assume that from here, the team went on to apply rapid experimentation and prototype enough of their solution to confirm the impact it would have to achieving the preliminary business case. The question becomes, how does it scale? How do we go from this compelling ideal customer storyboard that represents a significant competitive advantage to actually delivering such an experience?

The three-lane highway and staged releases

As mentioned earlier, the "three-lane highway" is a time-horizon categorization that provides a helpful way to stage initiatives or projects that over time will deliver on the storyboard with each release. It is helpful to think about the entire implementation the way a software development team builds software using Agile project management, especially if most of your improvements are digital.

Once each project has been carefully defined and linked to the preliminary business case, the framework for execution has seven levels to it:

1 The ideal customer experience storyboard: This is a key document because in a few simple narrative pages, it describes to the entire organization what the customer's holistic experience includes as well as what it doesn't include.

2 TO BE service blueprint (and/or process maps/journey orchestration modeling/flowcharts): From the ideal customer experience storyboard, projects or initiatives are launched, some in sequence and some in parallel depending on their interdependencies. The TO BE service blueprint draws a clear line from each key moment of truth to the supporting standards and measures behaviors, processes, and technologies required to deliver on it consistently. A TO BE journey orchestration model details the ideal channel behavior of customers, embedding automated triggers to respond proactively to customer needs. For example, a customer who just had a bad experience with your support center might be automatically removed from promotional messaging until an outreach treatment can be launched to remediate the problem.

3 TO BE playbooks: Drilling in even deeper, the TO BE playbook documents the specific steps, handoffs, data inputs/outputs, accountabilities, and other elements to deliver on each activity, ensuring all deliverables are consistent and synchronized.

4 Agile epics and stories: For those interactions that require technology delivery or support, Agile epics and stories are written by the business users to guide the IT team's development effort. If you are new to Agile project management, there is a wealth of information available for you to become familiar with this process.

5 Change management: Overseeing all of this (including the release schedule below) is the change management plan that ensures the organization is prepared to embrace the changes and deliver the experience at a very high level. This plan will typically include but is not limited to:

o internal communications (learning maps, blogs, program portals, etc.);

o stakeholder analysis and engagement plan;

o role-specific training;

o where required, job structuring or reporting changes;

o leadership alignment training;

o new journey-based customer measurement systems;

o enhanced recognition and reward programs and other HR initiatives;

o local implementation teams that deploy all the change management final deliverables ahead of the release schedule (just-in-time).

6 External communications plan: We separate the external communications plan from the internal communications plan above. Clearly, you want to communicate to customers in advance of the changes you will implement, what they can expect, why you are doing it, and provide a channel to collect their feedback and act on their responses.

7 Release schedule: Remember, each element of the final design has already been tested through the rapid experimentation step, so you are now in full production mode. Having said that, you will still phase in increases in functionality in planned releases, and with each release gather customer input in case there are required regional adaptations that may have been missed in your MLE. They call it "agile" for a reason.

We have already reviewed the ideal customer experience storyboard, so let's take each of these one at a time.

TO BE service blueprint

Like many of the tools described in this book, you are just one Google search away from finding more information about them, or visit our website at cxdigital.ai to learn more. So I won't get into the details of how you construct one of these, but this tool is important because it will become the "connecting tissue" between your ideal customer storyboard (or your TO BE customer journey map if you created one) and operations, sales and marketing, and HR organizations. In this one artifact, we take the ideal customer storyboard or TO BE customer journey map and detail out the processes, standards, data collected, and systems etc. connecting onstage activities (things the customer can see, touch, feel, hear, and smell) with offstage activities (things that are behind the scenes, invisible to the customer) for the things they actually experience to work. These include operating standards, data feeds, systems and supporting processes, sometimes from third parties required to deliver the experience. Figure 15.2 is an example of a zoomed-in portion of a TO BE service blueprint from the "Keep my business running" stage of the ideal customer storyboard, connected to an activity in the TO BE service blueprint.

TO BE playbooks

You will note that the yellow box that says *Driver delivery (arrive, confirm delivery, complete delivery)* has code FD17 associated with it. That code refers to a specific code in the playbook that documents what is required to deliver the product to the customer. Remember that the first customer delivery was a moment of truth, so there can be zero mistakes on how this is planned, measured, and managed. You will notice it also captures the "steps of service" that will be included in the change management plan as training for frontline roles, including that truck driver.

Agile epics and stories

Since there are digital interactions required to complete the delivery, that software needs to be either developed or configured and requires an Agile story (an epic is a collection of stories) to be crafted and added to the development team's workload. Figure 15.4 is an example of the story that supports the driver delivery code FD17.

Change management

This topic deserves an entire book in itself, and it may be a sequel to this one. Luckily, many have written on this subject already so we will just touch on it briefly. Depending on how big the changes are that you are implementing, you may need a comprehensive implementation roadmap. Typically, these involve several streams of activities, executed over three phases.

FIGURE 15.2 Ideal customer storyboard to TO BE service blueprint

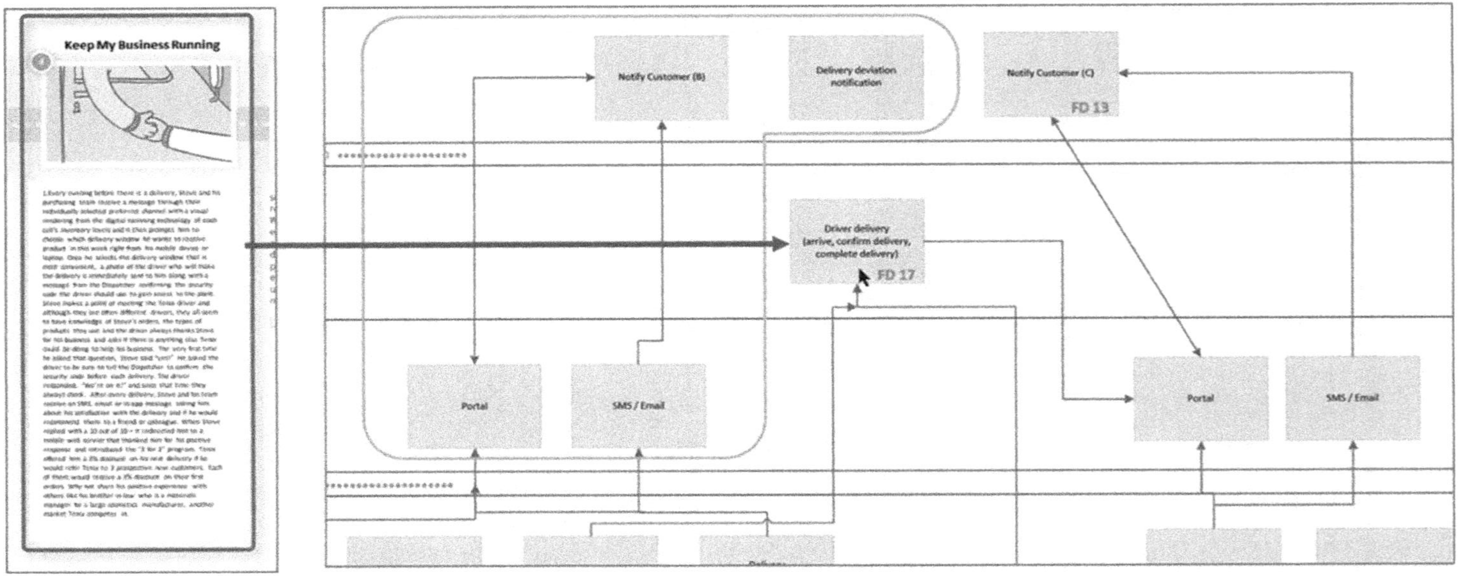

FIGURE 15.3 TO BE service blueprint to TO BE playbook

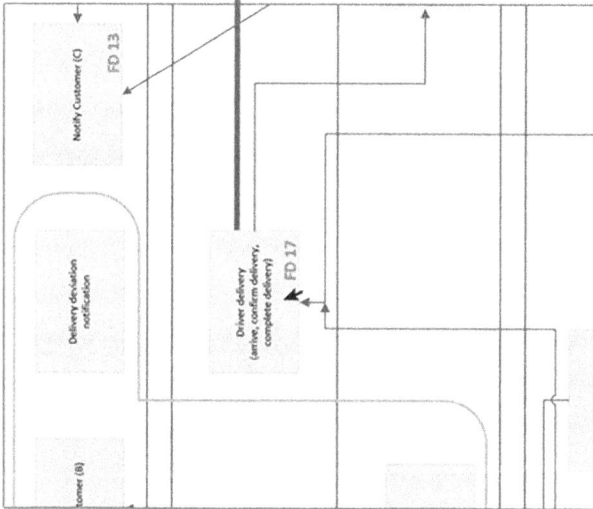

FD17: Driver Delivers Product

		Steps of Service
Process Step ID	FD17	
Step Outbound Arrows to:	FD18, FD21	
Step Inbound Arrows from:	FD15	
Process Step Name	Driver Delivers Polymer Product – TT34 Batch 11	
Process Step Executed By Role:	Driver	
Process Step Description	Driver arrives at the correct site and unloads product into the correct receiving tank	1. Friendly greeting 2. Confirmation of delivery details with security staff 3. Shows appreciation to proceed.
Process Step Specifications (Required Quality, Speed, Lag before next)	Quality – On time arrival at site. Safety procedures followed. Accurate tank stick readings determined. Products unloaded into correct tank(s). Lag – 1 hour	4. Complete tank fill.
Handoffs / Returns within Process Step	Stick reading entries into TVR Inventory device confirming available capacity for drop. Driver delivers Bill of Lading and a delivery ticket to customer. Driver enters delivery details into TVR device.	5. Enter data 6. Provide customer with BOL and Delivery Ticket and enters into system 7. Update system
Process Step Metrics (Quality, Speed)	Products delivered to correct tanks. No safety-related incidents occurred. Customer receives correct copy of BOL and delivery ticket.	8. Thanks customer and asks if there is "anything else I can do for you today?"
Process Step Systems Used	TVR	
Process Step Physical Evidence	BOL and delivery ticket delivered to customer. Post-delivery stick readings align with delivered gallons. Delivery details received	

FIGURE 15.4 TO BE playbook to Agile stories

FD17: Deliver Delivers Product

	Steps of Service
Process Step ID	FD17
Step Outbound Arrows to:	FD1B, FD21
Step Inbound Arrows from:	FD15
Process Step Name	Driver Delivers Polymer Product – ITEM Booth 31
Process Step Executed By Role:	Driver
Process Step Description	Driver arrives at the correct site and unloads product into the correct receiving tank. / 1. Friendly greeting 2. Confirmation of delivery details with security staff 3. Shows appreciation to personnel.
Process Step Specifications (Required Quality, Speed, Log before next)	Quality – On time arrival at site. Safety procedures followed. Accurate tank stick readings determined. Products unloaded into correct tank(s). Lag – 1 hour / 4. Complete tank Bill.
Handoffs / Returns within Process Step	SKS reading entries into TKR inventory device confirming available capacity for drop. Driver delivers Bill of Lading and a delivery ticket to customer. Driver enters delivery details into TKR device. / 5. Enter data 6. Provide customer with BOL and Delivery Ticket and enters into system 7. Update system.
Process Step Metrics (Quality, Speed)	Products delivered to correct tanks. No safety related incidents occurred. Customer receives correct copy of BOL and delivery ticket. / 8. Thanks customer and asks if there is "anything else I can do for you today?"
Process Step Systems Used	TKR
Process Step Physical Evidence	BOL and delivery ticket delivered to customer. Post delivery stick readings align with delivered gallons. Delivery details received

	A Epic	B Story ID	C Story Title	D As "WHO"	E I want "WHAT"	F So that "WHY"	User Story (Who, What, Why)	Process Steps
33	First Delivery		Delivery Deviation Notification	New Customer	receive a notification if there is going to be any deviations from the delivery time that was promised in the scheduling notification	I can make any required adjustments to accommodate the change	As a New Customer, I want to receive a notification if there is going to be any deviation from the delivery time that was promised in the scheduling notification, so that I can make any required adjustments to accommodate the change	FD13
34	First Delivery		Driver Makes Delivery	Tenix Driver	have all required documents and notification that this is the customer's first delivery	I can make the delivery accurately and execute the "first delivery" protocol	As a Tenix Driver, I want to have all required documents and notification that this is the customer's first delivery, so that I can make the delivery accurately and execute the "first delivery" protocol	FD17
35	First Delivery		Customer Receives Delivery	New Customer	receive a timely, accurate delivery that recognizes I am a new customer	I can continue to build trust in my new Tenix relationship	As a New Customer, I want to receive a timely, accurate delivery that recognizes I am a new customer, so that I can continue to build trust in my new Tenix relationship.	FD17
36	First Delivery		First Experience Survey	Tenix leader	send out and receive back a Tenix First experience survey and some result analytics	I can understand the experience new Tenix customers have and make revisions to processes as required	As a Tenix leader, I want to send out and receive back a Tenix First experience survey and some result analytics, so that I can understand the experience new Tenix customers have and make revisions to processes as required	FD32/25
37	First Delivery		Delivery oversight	Tenix leader in Ops or Sales	see accurate, timely reporting on delivery effectiveness	I can take actions to ensure ongoing delivery accuracy and timeliness and address any issues proactively	As a Tenix leader in Ops or Sales, I want to see accurate, timely reporting on delivery effectiveness, so that I can take actions to ensure ongoing delivery accuracy and timeliness and address any issues proactively.	N/A
38	Service Recovery		Customer Reports Service Issue	New Customer	be able to report a service issue rapidly through my channel of choice (phone, sales, web)	any service issues can be addressed timely	As a New Customer, I want to be able to report a service issue rapidly through my channel of choice (phone, sales, web), so that any service issues can be addressed timely.	SR1.1.5/2
39	Service Recovery		Driver Reports Service Issue	Tenix Driver	be able to report a service issue rapidly	any service issues can be addressed timely, possibly prior to causing a customer impact	As a Tenix Driver, I want to be able to report a service issue rapidly, so that any service issues can be addressed timely, possibly prior to causing a customer impact.	SR 3

PHASE 1 PREPARE THE SOIL

Each stream will represent a core set of activities that work together to prepare the organization for the next phase, but none more than Phase 1 as it is about establishing a core implementation governance team, building executive understanding and involvement, and achieving some important early wins, to demonstrate to the organization the considerable impact that can be achieved by focusing on the customer.

PHASE 2 ENROLLING THE ORGANIZATION

In this phase we build on the early wins and innovation initiatives put in place during Phase 1 and extend these efforts to every level of the organization, enrolling teams and functions in a well-thought-out series of events. A regular communications cadence around progress must be established. Broader access and application of tools or systems are embraced, and project goals and results are transparently exposed in the organization, to foster greater collaboration.

PHASE 3 SUSTAINING THE GAINS

This phase builds on previous successes and introduces more advanced capabilities. HR systems are fully aligned and with a full baseline of performance data completed, linking customer experience measures to compensation programs, starting with senior management, and eventually cascading to other levels of management.

Internal communications

When it comes to internal communications, what works well for one firm might fail miserably for another, so there just isn't a proven turnkey solution. But it does help to start with a plan, and then to adjust it as you gather momentum, as doing nothing is just not an option.

There are a few things we have learned about communications that will quickly unwind your implementation roadmap if you are not careful, and others that will help ensure your success:

- Frequency counts: Time without communications and people will tend to rationalize reasons for the lack of contact, based on their own fears or assumptions. Their own subjective conclusions are usually far worse than the actual reality. You might think, "Well, I don't want to tell anyone anything until we get this or that aspect figured out first." Wrong. Be transparent, be clear about what you know and what you don't know, and be willing to ask for help. Err on communicating too frequently rather than not often enough. Worry less about quality and more about quantity.

- Make it about them: A good program by its nature is two-way. Use the opportunity to showcase what is happening in the field as well as in corporate or with the product/service groups. Your investment in creating a guiding coalition will pay off big time now.

- Connect it to milestone achievements: Never miss the opportunity to link your communication efforts to achieving specific plan milestones and celebrating small wins. Enough small wins in a row and you can declare victory!

- The power of learning maps: Every single time we have designed and rolled out learning maps—both physical and digital versions—I am always amazed at the level of discussion and engagement that they produce. I have seen both types work, but if you can afford to use the large, poster-size maps with cards and bring your teams together physically, it is a very powerful experience. The digital versions have some advantage besides avoiding the cost of printing in that they can be delivered virtually and hence a bit faster, and it is easier to track which teams have completed their sessions. But the same cascading strategy where each leader deploys with their teams is a great approach and we have worked with clients where we conducted one learning map at launch, a second one after our pilot results, and a third just before rolling out the whole newly redesigned customer experience.

- Open it up to customers: Obviously, you must walk before you can run, but we have worked with clients that have opened up their communications portal to customers, sometimes via an online customer community or with a private website for customers and employees. There are some great benefits to this, especially if you integrate it into a broader VoC architecture, but it clearly needs to be well timed and led by someone with experience in how to manage these types of programs.

Release schedules

When you start working with Agile development teams you will learn about something called a burndown chart. A burndown chart shows the amount of work that has been completed during a two-week Sprint, and the total work remaining. Burndown charts are used to predict the team's likelihood of completing their work in the time available. I mention this because this is what will inform your release schedule, at least in terms of the digital elements of your improved experience. But here is the lesson I will share with you: *just because a feature or capability is ready for release doesn't mean it should be.* Now, typically, the Dev team doesn't like to hear this because they are working on two-week Sprints that often have interdependencies that the feature they want to push to production (the release schedule) will inform and they don't want to slow that down as they work in a cadence. Hence why there need to be IT members on your core team from the beginning so that the way they plan their development cycles works in lock step with the other aspects of the implementation roadmap such as call center rep training or other system implementations that need to be in place before you layer on top important features like "proactive voice response" or other technologies. In the end, like all things, it tends to be a negotiation but if you plan well and think through the interdependencies and staffing ahead of time, all's well that starts well.

External communications plan

Certainly, the external communications plan is connected to the internal one, but because they often fall under different budget centers, we tend to separate them. And I won't even attempt to suggest a framework for this as every company is different. However, ensuring that you don't overpromise before you deliver is critical. If you want customers to start to experience the new interactions you have designed and start adopting new ways of doing business with your firm, you want to work in lockstep with your external communications team to ensure there are no surprises.

Summary

Going from storyboard to execution is clearly a lot of work, but with a strong core team, a committed guiding coalition, and engaged executive sponsors, you will see it through.

What's next?

You can put that highlighter away finally because we have come to the end of our time together. Let's remember what was promised from the introduction to this book. I said we would:

- introduce you to 7 Design Strategies that research and real-world experience have proven to be invaluable in creating experiences digital-first customers will love;

- share what we have learned about how you separate the "signals from the noise" to start working on problems that if you really solve, customers will reward you for with their loyalty and their spending;

- explain how you take those insights and turn them into a business case that your CFO would find competitively superior to other investment options;

- bring the business case to life by applying an accelerated design process to start making a difference right away;

- walk you through an example of the 7 Design Strategies in action, adapted from several client projects to demonstrate how you go from your redesigned ideal customer storyboard to a blueprint for execution across your organization.

I believe we did all that, and perhaps a bit more. We covered a broad terrain that connected what we know about customer experience with digital transformation, and I believe we have come out the other side better for it. I have done my best to get you "emotionally involved" along the way and to reduce that highlighter of yours down to an empty vessel.

We went to some length to take you through much of the detail on how you focus on the right problems and put those 7 Design Strategies to work to make a difference for customers, employees, and shareholders. But I feel this is easily defensible as in the words of legendary designer Charles Eames:

> The details are not the details. They make the design.[2]

I will leave you with one final insight drawn from a 1950 publication entitled *Computing Machinery and Intelligence*, which included a section authored by famed mathematician and early computer scientist Alan Turing, who ended his chapter with this comment:

> We may hope that machines will eventually compete with men in all purely intellectual fields. But which are the best ones to start with? Even this is a

difficult decision. Many people think that a very abstract activity, like the playing of chess, would be best. It can also be maintained that it is best to provide the machine with the best sense organs that money can buy, and then teach it to understand and speak English. This process could follow the normal teaching of a child. Things would be pointed out and named, etc. Again, I do not know what the right answer is, but I think both approaches should be tried.

We can only see a short distance ahead, but we can see plenty there that needs to be done.[3]

Indeed, there is plenty that needs to be done and little time to waste. Godspeed!

EPILOGUE

It is just over 20 years since Shaun Smith and I published *Managing the Customer Experience: Turning Customers into Advocates*. Today more than ever, understanding where to place your bets to keep turning customers into advocates can be tricky. I hope this book provided you with a practical framework to reduce that risk and make better decisions when it comes to where to invest as you design a digital-first customer experience.

To help gauge where you are in the journey, you can visit our website (cxdigital.ai) and complete a free digital version of the CX/Digital Maturity Assessment found in Appendix 1. This is a first step to evaluate where your organization stands relative to the best practices described in these chapters. There is also a brief survey to capture your feedback on this book. We would so appreciate hearing from you.

Joe Wheeler

Boston, MA

APPENDIX 1

Digital-first maturity assessment

Instructions

To complete a free digital version of the Digital-first Maturity Assessment below, please visit us at cxdigital.ai. After completing the digital survey, you can see how your organization compares to others that have completed the survey.

To use this print version, simply read each best practice and rate your level of agreement using the scale below. Add up your ratings in each section, then divide that total by the number of items (less any N/A ratings) to calculate your average score. Once complete, capture your highest and lowest scoring design strategies at the end of the survey and make a note of your insights using the space provided.

1	2	3	4	5	6	7	N/A
Strongly Disagree	Disagree	Somewhat Disagree	Neither Agree nor Disagree	Somewhat Agree	Agree	Strongly Agree	Not Applicable

TABLE A.1

Design Strategy 1 Best Practices – Achieve Emotional Peaks	Rating
1. Customers can easily pause their interactions in one channel and resume them later in another.	
2. We design emotional peaks at key 'moments of truth' across multiple channels of the customer experience.	
3. We design the customer experience to end on an emotionally positive interaction.	
4. We structure human and digital channels to optimize both cost and the customer experience.	
5. We apply technology to reduce friction in the customer experience.	
6. We apply analytics to detect a customer's emotional state in order to trigger the appropriate digital or human response.	
7. We design interactions that reinforce trust in our brand.	
Total	
Average Score (total divided by 7, less any N/A ratings)	

TABLE A.2

Design Strategy 2 Best Practices – Personalization Flywheel	Rating
8. We make it easy for customers to opt in or out of allowing us to collect data to personalize their experience.	
9. We apply data from third parties to personalize the customer experience.	
10. We employ machine learning and AI tools to personalize the customer experience.	
11. We incorporate customer behaviors, historic preferences, and other factors to train our machine learning algorithms.	
12. We build or acquire technologies that enable us to personalize the customer experience.	
13. Protecting the privacy of our customers' data is a top priority.	
14. The level of personalization we provide improves as customers increase their use of our products or services.	
15. We apply machine learning to continuously increase the value our customers receive from our products or services.	
Total	
Average Score (total divided by 8 less any N/A ratings)	

TABLE A.3

Design Strategy 3 Best Practices – Choice and Control	Rating
16. We provide customers with options to navigate their journey based on their preferences.	
17. We provide progress cues when a customer is completing a defined sequence of interactions.	
18. We provide customers insights into the experience of other customers through social sharing mechanisms like customer reviews or posts.	
19. Customers can choose to complete the whole transaction process (order, payment, delivery, return, etc.) within their preferred channel.	
20. Customers receive consistent product, pricing, and promotion information across all of our channels.	
21. Customers can choose to use the same account to track and maintain all of their stored information from any channel.	
Total	
Average Score (total divided by 6 less any N/A ratings)	

TABLE A.4

Design Strategy 4 Best Practices – Community and Co-Creation	Rating
22. We provide customers with the opportunity to join a customer community.	
23. We celebrate individual community member contributions with various forms of merit and/or recognition.	
24. Our senior executive team actively demonstrates its support for our customer community.	
25. We allocate marketing dollars to grow membership in our customer community.	
26. We rely on our customer community for feedback to improve the customer experience.	
27. Our product development process engages customers to co-create products or services.	
28. We ensure our customer community retains a high degree of autonomy over their activities and programs.	
Total	
Average Score (total divided by 7 less any N/A ratings)	

TABLE A.5

Design Strategy 5 Best Practices – Invite Rituals	Rating
29. We have designed artifacts (unique language or physical elements) enabling customers to create rituals.	
30. Our customers often create their own rituals by personalizing different elements of the experience.	
31. We design processes that free up frontline employees to engage more fully with customers.	
32. We train frontline employees on the interpersonal skills required for handling challenging customer situations.	
33. Our managers coach frontline employees to reinforce a sense of community with our customers.	
34. We provide digital artifacts to extend customer rituals to the metaverse.	
Total	
Average Score (total divided by 6 less any N/A ratings)	

TABLE A.6

Design Strategy 6 Best Practices – Provide Immersive Experiences	Rating
35. We experiment with different technologies when designing immersive experiences.	
36. We promote the exclusivity associated with certain products or services.	
37. We develop 'smart products' that enable connectivity and data sharing.	
38. We often combine human, physical, and digital touchpoints in the design of immersive experiences.	
39. We apply several integrated technologies (big data, mobile apps, etc.) to personalize immersive experiences.	
40. We provide technology enabling customers to create their own personalized products or services.	
41. We ensure our brand values are amplified in the immersive experiences we design for customers.	
Total	
Average Score (total divided by 7 less any N/A ratings)	

TABLE A.7

Strategy 7—Link digital assets	Rating
42. We link digital technologies to amplify their collective value to customers over costs.	
43. We file patents on technologies that strengthen our position in our digital ecosystem.	
44. We apply rapid experimentation in our product development process.	
45. We collect multiple sources of product-in-use information.	
46. We derive incremental value from product-in-use information.	
47. We use application programming interfaces (APIs) to improve our position in our digital ecosystem.	
Total	
Average score (total divided by 6 less any N/A ratings)	

TABLE A.8

Average score (total divided by 6 less any N/A ratings)	
Outcomes	Rating
48. Our company achieves a significant share of its revenue through digital channels.	
49. Our company leads our industry in providing digital-first solutions to our customers.	
50. Our company is seen as an employer of choice.	

Highest Scoring Design Strategy:

Lowest Scoring Design Strategy:

Insights:

APPENDIX 2

The CX/Digital design accelerator

Overview

CX/Digital's consulting practice works with our clients in applying the steps described in previous chapters using AI and journey management tools to deploy improved, digital-first experiences faster and sustained through continuous optimization. Once an organization begins delivering immersive, personalized experiences, the tools you need to keep exceeding customer expectations change. Here is a brief overview of our approach.

0 Create a Data Hub

We begin by integrating all your sources of customer data (digital, web and mobile analytics, CRM, call center, point of sale, voice of the customer, and others). Once your customer data is unified, then the separate pieces of data that have been collected on each individual customer must be associated through identity matching, a process that recognizes which data refers to the same customer.

1 Journey discovery

Journey discovery is a quantitative approach to customer journey analytics where customer behavior data is analyzed across touchpoints and over time to uncover meaningful behavioral segments and the paths taken to achieve a specific goal.

2 Experience mapping

This is research and visualization of the current employee and customer experience. It includes:

- enrolling the core team, key stakeholders, and a guiding coalition;
- mapping the AS IS customer and employee journeys;

- summarizing and sharing qualitative insights;
- mystery shopping competitors and benchmarking best practice companies.

3 Validate insights and business case

Quantitative validation links customer behaviors to financial impact and other business measures. This data forms the basis for the business case.

4 Digital-first design

A design process as described previously produces an ideal customer experience storyboard and other artifacts to improve the current customer experience that will deliver on the financial targets and business measures estimated in the business case.

5 Rapid experimentation

Agile methods are applied to design, test, improve, and validate the design elements proposed during the digital-first design step.

6 Journey orchestration

Journey orchestration is the part of customer journey analytics that uses predictive and/or rules-based approaches to automate real-time interactions in order to improve journey flow and drive desirable outcomes.

7 Journey optimization

Journey optimization is achieved by employing a test-and-learn approach that explores all of the contributing factors: touchpoints, people, training, process, communication, metrics, and technology—which can lead to opportunities to improve the journey.

There are several unique features to our approach that include:

- Quantitative focus groups: Conducting large-scale live virtual focus groups with hundreds of participants over a 30-minute to 60-minute focus group to validate qualitative findings and invite real-time suggestions from customers to generate rank-order improvement opportunities to the experience.

- Customer identification and behavioral segmentation: The ability to accurately build customer profiles based on a variety of customer interactions and data points and apply these data to develop behavioral segments that complement and extend a client's established customer segmentation.

- Automated events: Design of automated responses to customers based on their needs in the moment. For example, a customer that searched for a product that was out of stock could be directed to a similar product with the required size they need, or a customer that had a positive interaction with a call center agent might be invited to join a quantitative focus group to brainstorm new product ideas with a product management team.

Summary

CX/Digital's professional services bring both research and client experience to apply the latest thought leadership to advance our clients' digital-first ambitions. Combining this capability with state-of-the-art technology delivers the best of both worlds. Visit us at cxdigital.ai for more information.

REFERENCES

Introduction

1 Kelso, A. (2018) Robotic pizza maker Zume says automation is the key to food's labor problem. www.forbes.com/sites/aliciakelso/2018/08/08/startup-ceo-restaurant-automation-will-create-more-jobs/?sh=6a4ccb4efb50 (archived at https://perma.cc/SP2N-SSHA).

2 Hynum, R. (2023) Whatever happened to Zume's pizza-making robots?, *PMQ Pizza* Magazine, 26 February. www.pmq.com/zume-sustainable-packaging (archived at https://perma.cc/DY65-YBBZ).

3 Sawhney, M. (2020) Reinventing the customer experience: Lessons from Jio. www.forbes.com/sites/mohanbirsawhney/2020/08/17/reinventing-the-customer-experience-lessons-from-jio/?sh=48c5a7d9632e (archived at https://perma.cc/H66T-LGBN).

4 Pymnts (2020) Nike CEO: Digital is the new normal, PYMNTS.com, 23 September. www.pymnts.com/news/retail/2020/nike-ceo-digital-is-the-new-normal (archived at https://perma.cc/ZDY6-E4SG).

5 Porter, M. E. and Heppelmann, J. E (2015) How smart, connected products are transforming companies, October, *Harvard Business Review*.

Chapter 1

1 https://lifepod.com/ (archived at https://perma.cc/96DT-CA52) corporate video.

2 Metcalf, D. *et al.* (2020) *Voice Technology in Healthcare: Leveraging voice to enhance patient and provider experiences* (HIMSS Book Series). 1st edn. Productivity Press.

3 https://lifepod.com/ (archived at https://perma.cc/96DT-CA52) corporate video.

4 ibid.

5 Metcalf, D., Fisher, T., Pruthi, S., and Pappas, H. P. (2021) *Voice Technology in Healthcare: Leveraging voice to enhance patient and provider experiences.* Taylor & Francis.

6 Vliet, V. van. (2022, January 24). Strategic triangle (3Cs). Toolshero. www.toolshero.com/strategy/strategic-triangle (archived at https://perma.cc/Y5QX-P86G).

7 Wilhelm, H. and Kellner, T. (2022) Amazon is making your life easier through ambient intelligence. www.aboutamazon.com/news/devices/amazon-is-making-your-life-easier-through-ambient-intelligence (archived at https://perma.cc/HP2Z-K37H).

8 Anders, G. (2017) Alexa, understand me, *MIT Technology Review*, August 9.

9 What is generative AI? McKinsey & Company. www.mckinsey.com/featured-insights/mckinsey-explainers/what-is-generative-ai (archived at https://perma.cc/8G6W-6BZV)

10 https://chat.openai.com/chat (archived at https://perma.cc/2M5K-NU4T).

11 Adapted from: Shaw, J. and Gold, K. (2022) What is edge computing and why does it matter? www.networkworld.com/article/3224893/what-is-edge-computing-and-how-it-s-changing-the-network.html (archived at https://perma.cc/2VFC-6RXE).

12 ibid.

13 Stackpole, T (2022) What is Web3?, *Harvard Business Review*, 8 November. https://hbr.org/2022/05/what-is-web3?ab=hero-main-text (archived at https://perma.cc/3ULD-JA6Z).

14 Adapted from Bhattacharya, J. (2022) What is Web 3.0? The future of the internet. www.singlegrain.com/web3/web-3-0 (archived at https://perma.cc/8TFT-25ZE).

15 ibid.

16 la Capra, E. (2022) What is the role of a decentralized autonomous organization in Web3? https://cointelegraph.com/explained/what-is-the-role-of-a-decentralized-autonomous-organization-in-web3 (archived at https://perma.cc/BS88-XSYC).

17 What is Web3? (2022) https://hbr.org/2022/05/what-is-web3?ab=hero-main-text (archived at https://perma.cc/39E4-KNBR).

18 ibid.

19 https://reports.globant.com/reports/2022/2022-Globant-Metaverse-Report-ENG.pdf (archived at https://perma.cc/FF6D-ZKAN).

20 ibid.

21 Orban, S. (2017) *Ahead in the Cloud: Best practices for navigating the future of enterprise IT*, CreateSpace Independent Publishing Platform.

22 Long term evolution for machines: LTE-M (2022) www.gsma.com/iot/long-term-evolution-machine-type-communication-lte-mtc-cat-m1 (archived at https://perma.cc/UXK3-EL47).

23 Holslin, P. (2022b) What is 6G internet and what will it look like? www.highspeedinternet.com/resources/6g-internet (archived at https://perma.cc/D8Y6-7VDV).

24 ibid.

25 Think with Google (2020) Omnichannel journey 02. www.thinkwithgoogle.com/consumer-insights/consumer-trends/store-visit-after-online-research-data (archived at https://perma.cc/M44V-PTGA).

26 Form 10-K. www.sec.gov/Archives/edgar/data/1085734/000119312510058339/d10k.htm (archived at https://perma.cc/DU74-6MW2).

27 Christensen, C. (2016) *The Innovator's Dilemma*, Harvard Business Review Press.

28 Rogers, D. L. (2016) in *The Digital Transformation Playbook: Rethink your business for the digital age*, New York: Columbia University Press, pp. 202–208.

29 ibid, pp. 210–211.

30 *The Guardian*. (2022) Disney edges past Netflix in streaming subscribers as it raises ad-free prices. www.theguardian.com/film/2022/aug/10/disney-plus-netflix-streaming-subscribers (archived at https://perma.cc/ZG93-AT5Y).

31 CBS News (2022) LinkedIn chief economist on "The Great Resignation," employment trends. www.cbsnews.com/video/linkedin-chief-economist-great-resignation-employment-trends (archived at https://perma.cc/U446-XHDK).

32 Mitra, S. (2021) What's the new social contract between employees and employers. www.hrkatha.com/features/whats-the-new-social-contract-between-employees-and-employers (archived at https://perma.cc/8JQV-W36D).

33 Weise, K. (2021) Amazon's profit soars 220 percent as pandemic drives shopping online, 29 April. www.nytimes.com/2021/04/29/technology/amazons-profits-triple.html (archived at https://perma.cc/2WET-2GWV).

34 Shih, W. (2022) Global supply chains in a post-pandemic world, *Harvard Business Review*, 17 October. https://hbr.org/2020/09/global-supply-chains-in-a-post-pandemic-world (archived at https://perma.cc/4TAX-5WK4).

35 WGII summary for policymakers headline statements. www.ipcc.ch/report/ar6/wg2/resources/spm-headline-statements (archived at https://perma.cc/2YPU-TYSH).

36 The climate pledge—Amazon sustainability (2021) https://sustainability.aboutamazon.com/environment/the-climate-pledge (archived at https://perma.cc/S3JR-WMQJ).

37 www.xerox.com/downloads/usa/en/x/Xerox_CSR_Report.pdf (archived at https://perma.cc/CPV6-WFSY)

38 Breaking barriers: FY21 Nike, Inc. impact report (2022) nike.com. https://about.nike.com/en/newsroom/reports/fy21-nike-inc-impact-report-2 (archived at https://perma.cc/KN5B-5896).

39 Sorkin, A. (2021) BlackRock chief pushes a big new climate goal for the corporate world, nytimes.com, 26 January. www.nytimes.com/2021/01/26/business/dealbook/larry-fink-letter-blackrock-climate.html (archived at https://perma.cc/QD8Y-WKAG).

40 Wei, S., Ang, T., and Jancenelle, V. E. (2018) Willingness to pay more for green products: The interplay of consumer characteristics and customer participation, *Journal of Retailing and Consumer Services*, 45, 230–238. https://doi.org/10.1016/j.jretconser.2018.08.015 (archived at https://perma.cc/G9H8-EYZN).

41   Satran, R. (2022) Shein's rise was nearly overnight. The backlash came just as fast, WSJ, 29 June. www.wsj.com/articles/shein-haul-backlash-11656504321?mod=e2tw (archived at https://perma.cc/8YUV-R5SV).

42   ibid.

43   ibid.

Chapter 2

1   Lemonade.com corporate website.

2   CEMEX USA (2018) What MLB Roofing and Decks is saying about CEMEX Go, YouTube. www.youtube.com/watch?v=_APyUpeyQzY (archived at https://perma.cc/9D35-CTLY).

3   (2022) Amazon Go—San Francisco, CA. www.yelp.ca/biz/amazon-go-san-francisco-11?sort_by=rating_desc. www.yelp.ca/biz/amazon-go-san-francisco-11?sort_by=rating_desc (archived at https://perma.cc/2L4W-YJ3W).

4   Keiningham, T. and Vavra, T. (2001) *The Customer Delight Principle: Exceeding customers' expectations for bottom-line success.* New York: McGraw-Hill Education.

5   Chase, R. and Dasu, S. (2001) Want to perfect your company service? Use behavioral science, *Harvard Business Review*, June.

6   BehavioralEconomics.com (2019) Choice architecture. www.behavioraleconomics.com/resources/mini-encyclopedia-of-be/choice-architecture (archived at https://perma.cc/WC48-C6TT).

Chapter 3

1   Levi, D and Ariely, D (2021) What makes people do what they do? *Judicature*, 29 December. https://judicature.duke.edu/articles/what-makes-people-do-what-they-do (archived at https://perma.cc/DU6F-NCC5).

2   BRANDTRUST. Building a trusted brand. https://brandtrust.com/wp-content/uploads/2021/05/Building-A-Trusted-Brand-Brandtrust.pdf (archived at https://perma.cc/555H-V4CB).

3   Stackla survey reveals disconnect between the content consumers want & what marketers deliver (2022) www.nosto.com/blog/report-consumer-marketing-perspectives-on-content-in-the-digital-age (archived at https://perma.cc/3AER-DD5G).

4   HawkPartners (2022) Home. https://hawkpartners.com (archived at https://perma.cc/9WUD-CHK5).

5 Hernandez-Fernandez, A. and Lewis, M. C. (2019) Brand authenticity leads to perceived value and brand trust, *European Journal of Management and Business Economics*, 28(3), 222–238. https://doi.org/10.1108/ejmbe-10-2017-0027 (archived at https://perma.cc/N7YM-8DW7).

6 ibid.

7 Georgiou, M. (2021) How and why to build brand authenticity, Forbes.com, 15 March. www.forbes.com/sites/forbescommunicationscouncil/2021/03/15/how-and-why-to-build-brand-authenticity/?sh=5f26dc9c55b5 (archived at https://perma.cc/J45A-MXYM).

8 Synchronoss.com corporate website.

9 Statista (2022) Level of trust in insurance companies among consumers in the United States as of July 2017. www.statista.com/statistics/727446/level-of-consumer-trust-in-insurance-companies-usa (archived at https://perma.cc/5DAA-RK5P).

10 Why is public trust in insurance still so low? *Insurance Business New Zealand*. www.insurancebusinessmag.com/nz/news/breaking-news/why-is-public-trust-in-insurance-still-so-low-171630.aspx (archived at https://perma.cc/G3NU-E3LA).

11 Trust in insurance. International Insurance Society. www.internationalinsurance.org/sites/default/files/2018-04/Trust%20in%20Insurance%20Final.pdf (archived at https://perma.cc/86KE-6BFB).

12 Levi, D. and Ariely, D. (2021) What makes people do what they do? *Judicature*, 29 December. https://judicature.duke.edu/articles/what-makes-people-do-what-they-do (archived at https://perma.cc/V7ZY-2RSM).

13 Azhar, A. (2019) Disrupting the insurance industry with AI, exponential view with Azeem Azhar, 22 August. www.exponentialview.co/p/-disrupting-the-insurance-industry (archived at https://perma.cc/82WA-V8X7).

14 Fromm, J. (2017) How startup Lemonade is redefining insurance for millennials. www.forbes.com/sites/jefffromm/2017/07/12/how-startup-lemonade-is-redefining-insurance-for-millennials (archived at https://perma.cc/YW9L-FCJC).

15 Definition of edge computing—Gartner information technology glossary. www.gartner.com/en/information-technology/glossary/edge-computing (archived at https://perma.cc/VV6T-JR6H).

16 Faridi, O. (2022) Insurtech Lemonade's 2022 giveback celebrates 6th year donating to organizations in need, *Crowdfund Insider*, 15 July. www.crowdfundinsider.com/2022/07/193671-insurtech-lemonades-2022-giveback-celebrates-6th-year-donating-to-organizations-in-need (archived at https://perma.cc/MLJ8-3KST).

17   Wininger, S. Introducing the Lemonade Crypto Climate Coalition. www. lemonade.com/blog/crypto-climate-coalition (archived at https://perma.cc/ P2WU-ZFLJ).

18   ibid.

19   Schreiber, D. (2021) Lemonade sets new world record. www.linkedin.com/ pulse/lemonade-sets-new-world-record-daniel-schreiber (archived at https:// perma.cc/DPK2-7P5R).

20   La Capra, E. (2022) What is the role of a decentralized autonomous organization in Web3? https://cointelegraph.com/explained/what-is-the-role-of-a-decentralized-autonomous-organization-in-web3 (archived at https://perma. cc/U7KA-SDYH).

21   Marous, J. How fintech unicorn Lemonade is disrupting insurance. https:// thefinancialbrand.com/banking-podcasts/fintech-unicorn-lemonade-disruption-insurance-insurtech-banking-transformed-podcast-daniel-schreiber (archived at https://perma.cc/FH96-FXHW).

22   What is Web3? AAPL Publication (2022) www.physicianleaders.org/articles/ what-is-web3 (archived at https://perma.cc/4F59-NQ28).

23   ibid.

24   Motley Fool Transcribing (2022) Lemonade, Inc. (LMND) Q1 2022 earnings call transcript. www.fool.com/earnings/call-transcripts/2022/05/10/lemonade-inc-lmnd-q1-2022-earnings-call-transcript (archived at https://perma.cc/ PHG8-2CZG).

25   Lemonade (2022) Listening to LTV6. www.lemonade.com/blog/lemonade-ltv6 (archived at https://perma.cc/K7F8-XLBQ).

26   ibid.

27   Eckstein, A. Building Lemonade for the future. www.lemonade.com/blog/ lemonade-company-model (archived at https://perma.cc/E9NM-DJYG).

28   Lemonade (2021) Lemonade to acquire Metromile. https://investor.lemonade. com/news-and-events/news/news-details/2021/Lemonade-To-Acquire-Metromile/default.aspx (archived at https://perma.cc/U5QG-E2MT).

29   Berg, J., Dickhaut, J., and McCabe, K. (1995) Trust, reciprocity, and social history, *Games and Economic Behavior*, 10(1), 122–142.

30   BehavioralEconomics.com (2020) Chunking. www.behavioraleconomics.com/ resources/mini-encyclopedia-of-be/chunking (archived at https://perma.cc/ QA9R-WBRP).

31   BehavioralEconomics.com (2019b) Peak-end rule. www.behavioraleconomics. com/resources/mini-encyclopedia-of-be/peak-end-rule (archived at https:// perma.cc/C7FF-DXZH).

32   Motley Fool Transcribing (2022) Lemonade, Inc. (LMND) Q1 2022 earnings call transcript. www.fool.com/earnings/call-transcripts/2022/05/10/lemonade-inc-lmnd-q1-2022-earnings-call-transcript (archived at https://perma.cc/ JL7U-G9FY).

Chapter 4

1 Spotify 2022 Investor Day transcript (2022, June 8) https://investors.spotify.com/investor-day-2022 (archived at https://perma.cc/5NLF-GALJ).

2 DeNora, T. (2000) *Music in Everyday Life*. Cambridge University Press.

3 Lee, J. M. and Rha, J. Y. (2016) Personalization—privacy paradox and consumer conflict with the use of location-based mobile commerce, *Computers in Human Behavior*, 63, 453–462.

4 Bleier, A. and Eisenbeiss, M. (2015) The importance of trust for personalized online advertising, *Journal of Retailing*, 91(3), 390–409. https://doi.org/10.1016/j.jretai.2015.04.001 (archived at https://perma.cc/MP53-JVK2).

5 Goswami, S. (2020) The rising concern around consumer data and privacy, *Forbes*, 14 December. www.forbes.com/sites/forbestechcouncil/2020/12/14/the-rising-concern-around-consumer-data-and-privacy/?sh=288c2c4487e8 (archived at https://perma.cc/6YGX-WETM).

6 ibid.

7 ibid.

8 Think with Google (2020b) Personalized brand experience statistics, Think With Google, 3 September. www.thinkwithgoogle.com/future-of-marketing/creativity/personalized-brand-experience-statistics (archived at https://perma.cc/3SK6-DP4D).

9 ibid.

10 Kozyreva, A., Lorenz-Spreen, P., Hertwig, R. *et al.* (2021) Public attitudes towards algorithmic personalization and use of personal data online: Evidence from Germany, Great Britain, and the United States, *Humanities and Social Sciences Communications* 8, 117. https://doi.org/10.1057/s41599-021-00787-w (archived at https://perma.cc/58AK-K5KL)

11 Shahid, S. and Ayaz, R. A. (2018) Practicing market orientation for customer engagement: The mediating effect of personalization and multi-channel marketing, *Lahore Journal of Business*, 7(Autumn), 1–32.

12 Vroom, G., Boquet, I., and Deshmane, A. (2021) Spotify: Face the music (update 2021), IESE Business School, IES869.

13 Spotify, About Us. www.spotify.com/au/about-us/contact (archived at https://perma.cc/99P2-GJDJ).

14 Spotify R&D (2021) VP of Personalization Oskar Stål talks the future of ML at TransformX, YouTube. www.youtube.com/watch?v=n16LOyba-SE (archived at https://perma.cc/WKR6-A3W4).

15 Marketing to millennials on Spotify: Key streaming moments, Spotify Advertising. https://ads.spotify.com/en-NL/millennials-on-spotify (archived at https://perma.cc/RWY2-EQLT).

16 Fassler, A. F. (2020) Soundtrack your life with Spotify: Music as a technology of the self in the age of affective algorithms. Senior Thesis. Vassar College.

17   ibid.

18   Hickey, W. (2014) Spotify knows me better than I know myself. FiveThirtyEight, September 16. fivethirtyeight.com/features/spotify-knows-me-better-than-i-know-myself (archived at https://perma.cc/B4LF-LJWB).

19   Fassler, A. F. (2020) Soundtrack your life with Spotify: Music as a technology of the self in the age of affective algorithms. Senior Thesis. Vassar College.

20   Spotify R&D (2021) VP of Personalization Oskar Stål talks the future of ML at TransformX', YouTube. www.youtube.com/watch?v=n16LOyba-SE (archived at https://perma.cc/R6AE-2HHT).

21   ibid.

22   Fassler, A. F. (2020) Soundtrack your life with Spotify: Music as a technology of the self in the age of affective algorithms. Senior Thesis. Vassar College.

23   American Psychological Association. APA Dictionary of Psychology. https://dictionary.apa.org/affect-theory (archived at https://perma.cc/9SWZ-SV5J). https://dictionary.apa.org/affect-theory (archived at https://perma.cc/2WDK-U7LQ).

24   Siles, I. *et al.* (2019) Genres as social affect: Cultivating moods and emotions through playlists on Spotify, *Social Media + Society*, 5(2), 205630511984751. https://doi.org/10.1177/2056305119847514 (archived at https://perma.cc/LA2G-DUPA).

25   ibid.

26   DeNora, T. (2000) *Music in Everyday Life*. Cambridge University Press.

27   Siles, I. *et al.* (2019) Genres as social affect: Cultivating moods and emotions through playlists on Spotify, *Social Media + Society*, 5(2), 205630511984751. https://doi.org/10.1177/2056305119847514 (archived at https://perma.cc/SF8F-QS2V).

28   ibid.

29   Fassler, A. F. (2020) Soundtrack your life with Spotify: Music as a technology of the self in the age of affective algorithms. Senior Thesis. Vassar College.

30   Spotify platform rules (2022-01-30) www.spotify.com/us/platform-rules (archived at https://perma.cc/9JQK-DQVD).

31   Fan Study (September 2022) https://fanstudy.byspotify.com/ (archived at https://perma.cc/N8DA-NVL8)

32   Kim, S. Playlisting—Spotify for Artists. https://artists.spotify.com/en/playlisting (archived at https://perma.cc/DR22-JMK3).

33   Spotify reports first quarter 2022 earnings (2022) https://newsroom.spotify.com/2022-04-27/spotify-reports-first-quarter-2022-earnings (archived at https://perma.cc/TB46-FDDQ).

34   US podcast advertising revenue study (2022) iab.com. IAB and PwC. www.iab.com/wp-content/uploads/2022/05/IAB-FY-2021-Podcast-Ad-Revenue-and-2022-2024-Growth-Projections_FINAL.pdf (archived at https://perma.cc/N2Q9-GDW7).

35 Pizza Hut serves up game-day hype with immersive audio, Spotify advertising. https://ads.spotify.com/en-US/inspiration/pizza-hut-ad-studio-case-study (archived at https://perma.cc/EMZ5-GJPF).

36 Spotify 2022 Investor Day transcript (2022, June 8) https://investors.spotify.com/investor-day-2022 (archived at https://perma.cc/JMM8-ZBLT).

37 Spotify R&D (2021) VP of Personalization Oskar Stål talks the future of ML at TransformX, YouTube. www.youtube.com/watch?v=n16LOyba-SE (archived at https://perma.cc/9YFL-YGD5).

38 ibid.

39 Yang, Z. (2019) Better bandit building: Advanced personalization the easy way with AutoML Tables. https://cloud.google.com/blog/products/ai-machine-learning/how-to-build-better-contextual-bandits-machine-learning-models (archived at https://perma.cc/SC4E-H3VQ).

40 Spotify R&D (2021) VP of Personalization Oskar Stål talks the future of ML at TransformX, YouTube. www.youtube.com/watch?v=n16LOyba-SE (archived at https://perma.cc/HFR3-WWYC).

41 ibid.

42 ibid.

43 Dragone, P., Mehrotra, R. and Lalmas, M. (2019) Deriving user- and content-specific rewards for contextual bandits, WWW '19: The World Wide Web Conference. https://doi.org/10.1145/3308558.3313592 (archived at https://perma.cc/VFA5-AEGP).

44 Ajao, E. (2022) Spotify personalizes audio experiences with machine learning, Enterprise AI, 4 April. www.techtarget.com/searchenterpriseai/feature/Spotify-personalizes-audio-experiences-with-machine-learning (archived at https://perma.cc/K8CV-DJC7).

45 Luo, H. and Lin, C. (2022, April 8) Spotify's audio-first strategy: Leading the podcasting market. 9-721–439. Harvard Business School.

46 CNBC (2022) Spotify CEO Daniel Ek addresses Joe Rogan podcast controversy. www.cnbc.com/video/2022/02/03/spotify-ceo-daniel-ek-addresses-joe-rogan-podcast-controversy.html (archived at https://perma.cc/N9LX-5XWF).

47 Spotify founder and CEO Daniel Ek's Investor Day 2022 remarks (2022) https://newsroom.spotify.com/2022-06-08/spotify-founder-and-ceo-daniel-eks-investor-day-2022-remarks (archived at https://perma.cc/G9FQ-ZTPP).

48 The latest Spotify audience network innovations for advertisers and anchor creators (2021) https://newsroom.spotify.com/2021-10-06/the-latest-spotify-audience-network-innovations-for-advertisers-and-anchor-creators (archived at https://perma.cc/444Y-QWAT).

49 Taking podcast ads to the next level, Spotify advertising. https://ads.spotify.com/en-CA/news-and-insights/2021-podcast-ads-announcements (archived at https://perma.cc/DU7K-CE9B).

50 "Spotify 2022 Investor Day Transcript" (June 8, 2022) https://investors.spotify.com/investor-day-2022 (archived at https://perma.cc/S49T-7ERV).

51 ibid.

52 ibid.

53 ibid.

54 ibid.

55 ibid.

56 ibid.

57 ibid.

58 ibid.

59 ibid.

60 ibid.

61 ibid.

62 ibid.

63 ibid.

64 Top 223 Spotify reviews (2022). www.consumeraffairs.com/online/spotify.html (archived at https://perma.cc/MHC5-BHMH).

Chapter 5

1 Author interview with Jesus Caviedes Mondragon, August 2, 2022.

2 Ashtiani, A. Z. (2022) Ikea Effect. www.behavioraleconomics.com/tag/ikea-effect (archived at https://perma.cc/2GQJ-72SX).

3 Kreps, D. M. (1979) A representation theorem for "preference for flexibility," *Econometrica*, 47(3), 565. https://doi.org/10.2307/1910406 (archived at https://perma.cc/9BLA-NSRQ).

4 Zhang, M. *et al.* (2018) The impact of channel integration on consumer responses in omni-channel retailing: The mediating effect of consumer empowerment, *Electronic Commerce Research and Applications*, 28, 181–193. https://doi.org/10.1016/j.elerap.2018.02.002.e (archived at https://perma.cc/H6SG-P4JY).

5 OpenBuilt (2021) OpenBuilt—the wings of transformation, YouTube. www.youtube.com/watch?v=b-pk7UVAaQU (archived at https://perma.cc/3CN9-SB4G).

6 CEMEX (2022) https://alteia.com/customer/cemex/#results (archived at https://perma.cc/K2U6-NG6Z).

7 Our 2030 targets—CEMEX. www.cemex.com/sustainability/esg-reporting-center/our-2030-targets (archived at https://perma.cc/8B42-WUSN).

8 Author interview with Jesus Caviedes Mondragon, August 2, 2022.

9 Greciano, A. (2022) About us. www.cemexventures.com/about-us (archived at https://perma.cc/J823-JA7K).

10 Samson, A. (Ed.) (2022) The Behavioral Economics Guide 2022. www.
behavioraleconomics.com/be-guide (archived at https://perma.cc/4F34-JTVS).

11 ibid.

12 ibid.

13 Wathieu, L. *et al*. (2002) Consumer control and empowerment: A primer,
Marketing Letters, 13(3), 297–305. https://doi.org/10.1023/a:1020311914022
(archived at https://perma.cc/6SC2-KW7N).

14 Samson, A. (Ed.) (2022) The Behavioral Economics Guide 2022. www.
behavioraleconomics.com/be-guide (archived at https://perma.cc/P9M6-
RYTN).

15 Opportimes, R. (2021) Cemex Go increases users to 42,000, but lowers order
orders. www.opportimes.com/cemex-go-increases-users-to-42000-but-lowers-
order-orders (archived at https://perma.cc/6WSX-XMC6).

16 Romero, D. *et al*. (2019) Five management pillars for digital transformation
integrating the lean thinking philosophy, 2019 IEEE International Conference
on Engineering, Technology and Innovation (ICE/ITMC) [Preprint]. https://doi.
org/10.1109/ice.2019.8792650 (archived at https://perma.cc/43PY-E6SD).

Chapter 6

1 vBrownBag (2018) Lindy Collier-Grady @indylindy22—My journey as a
VMUG leader, YouTube. www.youtube.com/watch?v=YjYgPTWDX84
(archived at https://perma.cc/WDU2-U6LB).

2 Heskett, J., Sasser, E., and Wheeler, J. (2008) *Ownership Quotient: Putting the
service profit chain to work for unbeatable competitive advantage*. Harvard
Business Review Press.

3 Pathak, B., Ashok, M., and Leng Tan, Y. (2021) Value co-creation in the B2B
context: A conceptual framework and its implications, *The Service Industries
Journal*, 42(3–4), 178–205. https://doi.org/10.1080/02642069.2021.1989414
(archived at https://perma.cc/XY3X-GZPP).

4 Fernandes, T. and Remelhe, P. (2015) How to engage customers in co-creation:
customers' motivations for collaborative innovation, *Journal of Strategic
Marketing*, 24(3–4), 311–326. https://doi.org/10.1080/0965254x.2015.1095220
(archived at https://perma.cc/3SCW-LH44).

5 VMware, About us. www.vmware.com/company.html (archived at https://
perma.cc/9EB9-VVWD).

6 McManus, B. (2021) A new chapter for VMware: Spin-off from Dell
Technologies completed. https://news.vmware.com/releases/vmware-announces-
completion-of-spin-off-from-dell-technologies (archived at https://perma.cc/
AE2G-YRTQ).

7   Tan, H. (2022, December 6). Open letter to the VMUG community. VMUG. com. www.vmug.com/wp-content/uploads/2022/12/FINAL-AVGO-VMUG-Open-Letter-from-Hock.pdf (archived at https://perma.cc/YP4D-V5TR)

8   Haranas, M. (2022) Goodbye VMworld, Hello VMware Explore "Multi-Cloud Universe" event. www.crn.com/news/cloud/goodbye-vmworld-hello-vmware-explore-multi-cloud-universe-event (archived at https://perma.cc/CXQ9-N6ZB).

9   Leavy, B. (2013) Venkat Ramaswamy—a ten-year perspective on how the value co-creation revolution is transforming competition, *Strategy & Leadership*, 41, No. 6, 11–17. https://doi.org/10.1108/SL-07-2013-0058 (archived at https://perma.cc/ZN2H-9VQ3).

10 Ramaswamy, V. and Ozcan, K. (2014) *The Co-Creation Paradigm*. Amsterdam University Press.

11 O' Connell, A (2009) Lego CEO Jørgen Vig Knudstorp on leading through survival and growth, *Harvard Business Review*, 1 August. https://hbr.org/2009/01/lego-ceo-jorgen-vig-knudstorp-on-leading-through-survival-and-growth (archived at https://perma.cc/C22R-W2VR).

12 VMware reports fourth quarter and fiscal year 2022 results (2022) https://ir.vmware.com/download/companies/vmware/Quarterly%20Reports/VMW%20Q4FY22%20Earnings%20Press%20Release.pdf (archived at https://perma.cc/H4RY-ZKLD).

13 How VMware partners with customers to design products (2019) www.alida.com/the-alida-journal/how-vmware-partners-with-customers-to-design-products (archived at https://perma.cc/8J2Z-LX9Y).

14 ibid.

15 Leavy, B. (2013) Venkat Ramaswamy—a ten-year perspective on how the value co-creation revolution is transforming competition, *Strategy & Leadership*, 41, No. 6, 11–17. https://doi.org/10.1108/SL-07-2013-0058 (archived at https://perma.cc/5C5N-X453).

Chapter 7

1   Starbucks 2022 Investor Day Conference (2022) https://investor.starbucks.com (archived at https://perma.cc/8C6Z-672L). https://investor.starbucks.com/events-and-presentations/current-and-past-events/event-details/2022/Starbucks-2022-Investor-Day/default.aspx (archived at https://perma.cc/4FHX-46SB).

2   Habitat for Humanity. Habitat Humanitarians: The Carters. www.habitat.org/stories/habitat-humanitarians-carters (archived at https://perma.cc/Q4P6-K2PE).

3   Time to build, time to weep, time to laugh. www.habitat.org/stories/time-build-weep-laugh (archived at https://perma.cc/G6FH-BHNK).

4 Duhigg, C. (2014) *The Power of Habit: Why we do what we do in life and business*. Random House.

5 ibid.

6 Hobson, N. M. *et al.* (2017) The psychology of rituals: An integrative review and process-based framework, *Personality and Social Psychology Review*, 22(3), 260–284. https://doi.org/10.1177/1088868317734944 (archived at https://perma.cc/7ZXZ-KSZF).

7 Ozlek, J. (2015) Starbucks' Consumption Rituals and Brand Loyalty in Relation to its Consumers Experience, Product Consistency, and Terminology. Senior Thesis. Malmo University.

8 Kim, K., Sezer, O., Schroeder, J., Risen, J., Gino, F., and Norton, M. I. (2021) Work group rituals enhance the meaning of work, *Organizational Behavior and Human Decision Processes*, 165 (197–212), ISSN 0749-5978.

9 Clark, M. and Joyner, A. (2006) *The Bear Necessities of Business: Building a company with heart*. Hoboken, NJ: Wiley.

10 Howard Schultz quote: https://quotefancy.com/quote/2294373/Howard-Schultz-I-ve-never-thought-of-the-third-place-just-as-a-physical-environment (archived at https://perma.cc/HY39-LBT8).

11 Rocky Mountain Starbucks (2015) YouTube Rocky Mountain Starbucks. https://youtu.be/nER0eWGDxCs (archived at https://perma.cc/QEN9-JJ5L).

12 ibid.

13 Starbucks reports Q2 fiscal 2022 results. https://investor.starbucks.com/press-releases/financial-releases/press-release-details/2022/Starbucks-Reports-Q2-Fiscal-2022-Results/default.aspx (archived at https://perma.cc/7AZS-TRHM).

14 Rainey, C. (2022) What happened to Starbucks? How a progressive company lost its way, fastcompany.com, March 13. www.fastcompany.com/90732166/what-happened-to-starbucks-how-a-progressive-company-lost-its-way (archived at https://perma.cc/J5GW-8HUM).

15 Ko, M. (2022) Starbucks awards stock options annually to partners; here's how some have used Bean Stock. https://stories.starbucks.com/stories/2022/week-in-review-starbucks-partners-share-ideas-on-restoring-trust (archived at https://perma.cc/QCV6-DRVK).

16 Jamieson, D. (2022) Starbucks workers have unionized more than 50 stores in the US, yahoo.com, May 3. https://finance.yahoo.com/news/starbucks-workers-unionized-more-50-203127624.html (archived at https://perma.cc/Z6JU-WTCB).

17 Danziger, P. (2022) First Starbucks, now REI: The movement to unionize retail workers picks up', Forbes, March 3. www.forbes.com/sites/pamdanziger/2022/03/03/first-starbucks-now-rei-next-amazon-and-apple-the-movement-to-unionize-retail-workers-picks-up/?sh=26f3de6710ad (archived at https://perma.cc/9B57-EUT3).

18 ibid.

19 ibid.

20 Week in review: Starbucks partners share ideas on restoring trust (2022) starbucks.com. https://stories.starbucks.com/stories/2022/week-in-review-starbucks-partners-share-ideas-on-restoring-trust (archived at https://perma.cc/B78P-E75E).

21 Motley Fool Transcribers (2021) Starbucks Corp (SBUX) Q2 2021 earnings call transcript. www.fool.com/earnings/call-transcripts/2021/04/27/starbucks-corp-sbux-q2-2021-earnings-call-transcri (archived at https://perma.cc/25BZ-DM4D).

22 Motley Fool Transcribing (2022) Starbucks (SBUX) Q2 2022 earnings call transcript. www.fool.com/earnings/call-transcripts/2022/05/04/starbucks-sbux-q2-2022-earnings-call-transcript (archived at https://perma.cc/K2T4-3SV2).

23 Behar, H. (2009) *It's Not about the Coffee: Leadership principles from a life at Starbucks*. Penguin.

24 Chickowski, E. (2019) Starbucks' digital flywheel strategy continues to pay off, Digirupt.io, 8 April. https://digirupt.io/starbucks-digital-flyweel-strategy-continues-to-pay-off (archived at https://perma.cc/S9JK-HQ5N).

25 ibid.

26 ibid.

27 ibid.

28 ibid.

29 Meisenzahl, M (2022) Starbucks customers have more than $1 billion sitting on gift cards, *Business Insider*, 4 May. www.businessinsider.com/starbucks-says-over-1-billion-is-sitting-on-cards-2022-5?international=true&r=US&IR=T (archived at https://perma.cc/EGC5-4RZN).

30 ibid.

31 Garcia, T. (2021) Starbucks and Amazon Go collaborate for the launch of a New York City store, MarketWatch, 18 November. www.marketwatch.com/story/starbucks-and-amazon-go-collaborate-for-the-launch-of-a-new-york-city-store-11637246768 (archived at https://perma.cc/R9LK-ZEWJ).

32 ibid.

33 Starbucks 2022 Investor Day Conference (2022) https://investor.starbucks.com (archived at https://perma.cc/S4SL-CY4H). https://investor.starbucks.com/events-and-presentations/current-and-past-events/event-details/2022/Starbucks-2022-Investor-Day/default.aspx (archived at https://perma.cc/3GTE-GNP3).

34 ibid.

35 ibid.

36 Starbucks Corporation (2022) Starbucks reports Q4 and full year fiscal 2022 results, Starbucks Stories, 4 May. https://stories.starbucks.com/press/2022/starbucks-commits-one-billion-in-fy2022-investments-to-uplift-partners-employees-and-the-store-experience (archived at https://perma.cc/W99R-BPHU).

37 Starbucks 2022 Investor Day Conference (2022) https://investor.starbucks.com (archived at https://perma.cc/Y75M-JT4R). https://investor.starbucks.com/events-and-presentations/current-and-past-events/event-details/2022/Starbucks-2022-Investor-Day/default.aspx (archived at https://perma.cc/B4YV-MUMB).

38 ibid.

39 ibid.

40 Kastrenakes, J. (2021) Beeple sold an NFT for $69 million, *The Verge*, 11 March. www.theverge.com/2021/3/11/22325054/beeple-christies-nft-sale-cost-everydays-69-million (archived at https://perma.cc/XL79-6D7Y).

41 Clark, M. (2022) NFTs, explained: What they are and why they're suddenly worth millions, *The Verge*, 6 June. www.theverge.com/22310188/nft-explainer-what-is-blockchain-crypto-art-faq (archived at https://perma.cc/SSL8-BCPM).

42 Starbucks 2022 Investor Day Conference (2022) https://investor.starbucks.com (archived at https://perma.cc/A5HM-XU5F). https://investor.starbucks.com/events-and-presentations/current-and-past-events/event-details/2022/Starbucks-2022-Investor-Day/default.aspx (archived at https://perma.cc/FTF4-CRRA).

43 Michelli, J. (2013) *Leading the Starbucks Way: 5 principles for connecting with your customers, your products and your people*. McGraw-Hill.

44 Duhigg, C. (2012) *The Power of Habit*. Random House Publishing Group.

45 Behar, H. and Goldstein, J. (2007) *It's Not About the Coffee*. Penguin Publishing Group.

46 Ko, M. (2022) Starbucks awards stock options annually to partners; here's how some have used Bean Stock. https://stories.starbucks.com/stories/2022/a-message-from-howard-schultz-the-next-chapter-of-starbucks-reinvention (archived at https://perma.cc/F8Z7-8A52).

47 Starbucks 2022 Investor Day Conference (2022) https://investor.starbucks.com (archived at https://perma.cc/Q9HF-K8TQ). https://investor.starbucks.com/events-and-presentations/current-and-past-events/event-details/2022/Starbucks-2022-Investor-Day/default.aspx (archived at https://perma.cc/T8GN-ULNK).

48 Motley Fool Transcribing (2022) Starbucks (SBUX) Q2 2022 earnings call transcript. www.fool.com/earnings/call-transcripts/2022/05/04/starbucks-sbux-q2-2022-earnings-call-transcript (archived at https://perma.cc/K59L-H8M2).

49 ibid.

50 Week in review: Starbucks partners share ideas on restoring trust (2022) starbucks.com. https://stories.starbucks.com/stories/2022/week-in-review-starbucks-partners-share-ideas-on-restoring-trust (archived at https://perma.cc/LRN6-ADCA).

Chapter 8

1   Thomas, L. (2020) Nike's online business is booming—"digital is here to stay," CEO says, CNBC, 23 September. www.cnbc.com/2020/09/23/nikes-ceo-says-digital-is-here-to-stay-e-com-business-fuels-sales.html (archived at https://perma.cc/WL5H-VRNY).

2   Zhang, C. (2020) The why, what, and how of immersive experience, IEEE Access, 8, 90878–90888. https://doi.org/10.1109/access.2020.2993646 (archived at https://perma.cc/W5HH-HAJK). Department of Electronic Systems, Norwegian University of Science and Technology (NTNU), 7491 Trondheim, Norway.

3   What is augmented reality? www.interaction-design.org/literature/topics/augmented-reality (archived at https://perma.cc/H8EX-B9V9).

4   Chmielewski, D. (2017) Apple's Tim Cook says augmented reality will "change everything," Deadline.com, 2 November. https://deadline.com/2017/11/apple-tim-cook-augmented-reality-fourth-quarter-2017-earnings-1202200710 (archived at https://perma.cc/GH4Z-NTW9).

5   Mishra, S., Malhotra, G., Chatterjee, R., and Shukla, Y. (2021) Consumer retention through phygital experience in omnichannel retailing: Role of consumer empowerment and satisfaction, *Journal of Strategic Marketing*, 1–18. 10.1080/0965254X.2021.1985594.

6   Oberoi, M. C. (2020b) Nike's target markets: Everything you need to know. https://marketrealist.com/2019/10/nikes-target-markets-everything-you-need-to-know (archived at https://perma.cc/JJS8-VZLG).

7   Abel, K. (2022) Exclusive: How Heidi O'Neill rose to become Nike's most powerful woman overseeing $40b in annual revenues, Footwearnews.com, 16 May. https://footwearnews.com/2022/business/power-players/nike-heidi-oneill-female-executive-company-revenue-1203287000 (archived at https://perma.cc/9DM9-UDT8).

8   Marr, B. (2022) The amazing ways Nike is using the metaverse, Web3 and NFTs, Forbes, 1 June. www.forbes.com/sites/bernardmarr/2022/06/01/the-amazing-ways-nike-is-using-the-metaverse-web3-and-nfts/?sh=1969edde56e9 (archived at https://perma.cc/QQ2H-PWRD).

9   ibid.

10 Motley Fool Transcribing (2022) Nike (NKE) Q3 2022 earnings call transcript, The Motley Fool, 22 March. www.fool.com/earnings/call-transcripts/2022/03/21/nike-nke-q3-2022-earnings-call-transcript (archived at https://perma.cc/4LUR-367Y).

11 How the metaverse is transcending digital limits and reinventing our place in the physical world: Sentinel report (2022) globant.com. Globant. https://reports.globant.com/reports/2022/2022-Globant-Metaverse-Report-ENG.pdf (archived at https://perma.cc/6X2L-5VWE).

12 Nike (2022) Nike launches .SWOOSH, a new digital community and experience. https://about.nike.com/en/newsroom/releases/nike-launches-swoosh-a-new-digital-community-and-experience (archived at https://perma.cc/RGF8-UXS3).

13 Nike By You custom shoes. www.nike.com/nike-by-you (archived at https://perma.cc/9EVN-FU2W).

14 Nike (2022) Investor news details. https://investors.nike.com/investors/news-events-and-reports/investor-news/investor-news-details/2022/Nike-Inc.-Reports-Fiscal-2022-Fourth-Quarter-and-Full-Year-Results/default.aspx (archived at https://perma.cc/E4GY-E4PB)

15 Padua, D. and Cicerchia, S. (2021) The digital transformation in the sneaker market: Nike's in-store customer experience, Anno Accademico [Preprint], (Dipartimento di Impresa e Management). http://tesi.luiss.it/30691/1/233621_CICERCHIA_STEFANO.pdf. (archived at https://perma.cc/ST4U-VEJ5)

16 ibid.

17 Fast Company (2022) Inside Nike's LeBron James Innovation center, Fast Company. www.youtube.com/watch?v=VCRXfGtwX9Y (archived at https://perma.cc/72BH-8WV3).

18 Newcomb, T. (2021) Nike opens LeBron James Innovation Center, new home of Nike Sport Research Lab, Forbes, 4 October. www.forbes.com/sites/timnewcomb/2021/10/04/nike-opens-lebron-james-innovation-center-new-home-of-nike-sport-research-lab/?sh=d9103f7e0569 (archived at https://perma.cc/9S2Y-EHQE).

19 Business Wire (2018) Nike, Inc. acquires data analytics leader Zodiac, 22 March. www.businesswire.com/news/home/20180322006343/en/Nike-Inc.-Acquires-Data-Analytics-Leader-Zodiac (archived at https://perma.cc/V9RV-ZWF6).

20 Business Wire (2018b) Nike, Inc. acquires computer vision leader Invertex, 9 April. www.businesswire.com/news/home/20180409006395/en/Nike-Inc.-Acquires-Computer-Vision-Leader-Invertex (archived at https://perma.cc/44E5-XEDH).

21 Ogus, S. (2019) Nike looks to use technology to help prevent ill-fitting shoes with Nike Fit app, Forbes, 28 May. www.forbes.com/sites/simonogus/2019/05/28/nike-looks-to-use-technology-to-help-prevent-ill-fitting-shoes-with-nike-fit-app/?sh=6fc4384c3427 (archived at https://perma.cc/B3XS-ZBPL).

22 Motley Fool Transcribing (2020) Nike Inc (NKE) Q1 2021 earnings call transcript, The Motley Fool, 23 September. www.fool.com/earnings/call-transcripts/2020/09/22/nike-inc-nke-q1-2021-earnings-call-transcript (archived at https://perma.cc/DT7U-ZSUA).

23 What to know about Nike's stance on tackling climate change (2019). https://about.nike.com/en/newsroom/releases/nike-move-to-zero-climate-change-initiative (archived at https://perma.cc/CRB9-CFXU).

24 Breaking barriers: FY21 Nike, Inc. Impact Report (2022) nike.com. https://about.nike.com/en/newsroom/reports/fy21-nike-inc-impact-report-2 (archived at https://perma.cc/SS6T-3D9T).

25 Padla, R. (2022) Nike sustainable apparel and footwear take center stage in 2022 Move to Zero Collection. www.yankodesign.com/2022/03/08/nike-sustainable-apparel-and-footwear-take-center-stage-in-2022-move-to-zero-collection (archived at https://perma.cc/949E-AYBA).

26 BehavioralEconomics.com (2019) Scarcity (heuristic). www.behavioraleconomics.com/resources/mini-encyclopedia-of-be/scarcity-heuristic (archived at https://perma.cc/WZ7B-67YA).

27 Aggarwal, P., Jun, S., and Huh, J. (2011) Scarcity messages: A consumer competition perspective, *Journal of Advertising*, 40, 19–30.

28 BehavioralEconomics.com (2019a) Peak-end rule. www.behavioraleconomics.com/resources/mini-encyclopedia-of-be/peak-end-rule (archived at https://perma.cc/VAJ7-LQVW).

29 Top 546 Nike reviews (2022). www.consumeraffairs.com/sporting_goods/nike.html (archived at https://perma.cc/GP7Y-W6E5).

Chapter 9

1 Author interview with Mr. Dilip Kumar, September 14, 2022.

2 Kaplunou, P. (2021) What we can learn from Lemonade: An InsurTech case study, Smart IT, 19 March. https://smart-it.io/blog/what-we-learn-from-lemonade-insurtech-case-study (archived at https://perma.cc/JQD9-BFX7).

3 A machine first approach to digital transformation (2019) Volume 12, *Perspectives*. https://issuu.com/vishankjagtap/docs/volume-12-perspectives-machine-first (archived at https://perma.cc/WS8Y-2VHX).

4 Talin, B. (2022) What is a digital ecosystem?—Understanding the most profitable business model, morethandigital.info, 4 July. https://morethandigital.info/en/what-is-a-digital-ecosystem-understanding-the-most-profitable-business-model (archived at https://perma.cc/MUZ8-BRM8).

5 Subramaniam, M., Iyer, B., and Venkatraman, V. (2019) Competing in digital ecosystems, *Business Horizons*, 62(1), 83–94. https://doi.org/10.1016/j.bushor.2018.08.013 (archived at https://perma.cc/3S5H-6BLZ).

6 Palmer, A. (2022) Amazon's sprawling grocery business has become an "expensive hobby" with a cloudy future, cnbc.com, 22 February. www.cnbc.com/2022/02/19/amazons-sprawling-grocery-business-has-become-an-expensive-hobby.html (archived at https://perma.cc/2FVT-KFXR).

7   Author interview with Mr. Dilip Kumar, September 14, 2022.

8   Fernandes, T. and Pedroso, R. (2017) The effect of self-checkout quality on customer satisfaction and repatronage in a retail context. *Service Business*, 11. 10.1007/s11628-016-0302-9.

9   Stone, B. (2012) *Amazon Unbound: Jeff Bezos and the invention of a global empire*. Simon & Schuster.

10 Author interview with Mr. Dilip Kumar, September 14, 2022.

11 GlobeNewswireVideo (2019) Retail Business Services frictionless store technology, YouTube. www.youtube.com/watch?v=8QvWljCZXsc (archived at https://perma.cc/W6AF-CVQN).

12 Levy, A. (2019) Amazon Go stores could be incredibly profitable. www.fool.com/investing/2019/01/07/amazon-go-stores-could-be-incredibly-profitable.aspx (archived at https://perma.cc/V2VE-92WA).

13 Stone, B. (2012) *Amazon unbound: Jeff Bezos and the invention of a global empire*. Simon & Schuster.

14 Lalley, H. (2022) Inside the newest Amazon Fresh store, *Winsight Grocery Business*, 15 July. www.winsightgrocerybusiness.com/amazon/inside-newest-amazon-fresh-store (archived at https://perma.cc/7EU4-3C57).

15 England, R. (2020) Amazon's first big "Go" grocery store opens in Seattle with 5,000 products. www.yahoo.com/now/2020-02-25-amazon-big-go-grocery-store-seattle-cashless.html (archived at https://perma.cc/Y4EJ-SK2V).

16 Amazon Fresh groceries. www.amazon.com/fmc/m/30003175?almBrandId=Q W1hem9uIEZyZXNo (archived at https://perma.cc/2EQR-2TC8).

17 Author interview with Mr. Dilip Kumar, September 14, 2022.

18 GRA (2022) The next evolution of the Dash Cart: New features and expansion to first Whole Foods Market store, 13 July. www.gra.world/the-next-evolution-of-the-dash-cart-new-features-and-expansion-to-first-whole-foods-market-store (archived at https://perma.cc/8A6A-5ND7).

19 Walton, C. (2022) 5 reasons why Amazon Go is already the greatest retail innovation of the next 30 years, forbes.com, 1 March. www.forbes.com/sites/christopherwalton/2022/03/01/5-reasons-why-amazon-go-is-already-the-greatest-retail-innovation-of-the-next-30-years/?sh=35c2fcf11abc (archived at https://perma.cc/66J2-PVTS).

20 GlobeNewswireVideo. Retail Business Services frictionless store technology. www.youtube.com/watch?v=8QvWljCZXsc&list=PPSV (archived at https://perma.cc/X3PF-L28N).

21 Dastin, J. (2020) Amazon launches business selling automated checkout to retailers, US, 10 March. www.reuters.com/article/us-amazon-com-store-technology/amazon-launches-business-selling-automated-checkout-to-retailers-idUSKBN20W0OD (archived at https://perma.cc/L2F3-T3NM).

22 "Just Walk Out" bringing just walk out shopping to your stores. https://justwalkout.com (archived at https://perma.cc/MQX4-ZVG7).

23 Iddenden, G. (2021) Amazon slashes cost of Just Walk Out tech by 96% paving the way for wider roll out, 1 December. www.chargedretail.co.uk/2021/11/18/amazon-slashes-cost-of-just-walk-out-tech-by-96-paving-the-way-for-wider-roll-out (archived at https://perma.cc/66EP-J2TB).

24 ibid.

25 CB Insights (2022) The 12 industries Amazon could disrupt next. www.cbinsights.com/research/report/amazon-disruption-industries (archived at https://perma.cc/J9G7-2QKE).

26 Patent: Aerial vehicle delivery on items available through an e-commerce shopping site. https://patents.google.com/patent/US20170110017A1/en (archived at https://perma.cc/Y43U-BBYX).

27 Palmer, A. (2020) Amazon wins FAA approval for Prime Air drone delivery fleet, CNBC, 31 August. www.cnbc.com/2020/08/31/amazon-prime-now-drone-delivery-fleet-gets-faa-approval.html (archived at https://perma.cc/T6FU-HFLJ).

28 Subin, S. (2021) Alphabet's drones delivered 10,000 cups of coffee and 1,200 roast chickens in the last year, CNBC, 26 August. www.cnbc.com/2021/08/25/alphabet-wing-drones-delivered-10000-cups-of-coffee-in-the-last-year.html (archived at https://perma.cc/G3LB-Q6X7).

29 Kellner, T. (2022) Amazon's new head of Alexa shares his vision for the future, including new shopping and entertainment features. www.aboutamazon.com/news/devices/amazons-new-head-of-alexa-rohit-prasad (archived at https://perma.cc/BHV9-NA7Z).

30 Tritschler, C. (2021) Meet Astro, a home robot unlike any other, US About Amazon, 28 September. www.aboutamazon.com/news/devices/meet-astro-a-home-robot-unlike-any-other (archived at https://perma.cc/NYY2-34MR).

31 ibid.

32 The best way to invent the future is to predict it (2022) www.parc.com/blog/the-best-way-to-invent-the-future-is-to-predict-it-2 (archived at https://perma.cc/PQ52-UM5A).

33 CB Insights (2022) The 12 industries Amazon could disrupt next. www.cbinsights.com/research/report/amazon-disruption-industries (archived at https://perma.cc/7US4-TGCP).

34 ibid.

35 Amazon launches new physical retail store analytics service (2022) www.aboutamazon.com/news/retail/amazon-launches-new-physical-retail-store-analytics-service (archived at https://perma.cc/5GD3-H2Q2).

36 ibid.

37 Vasen, S. M. D. (2022) Amazon reimagines in-store shopping with Amazon Style. www.aboutamazon.com/news/retail/amazon-reimagines-in-store-shopping-with-amazon-style (archived at https://perma.cc/ZQA3-HAYW).

38 "Just Walk Out' bringing just walk out shopping to your stores. https://justwalkout.com (archived at https://perma.cc/4LS3-ZY5F).

39 ibid.

40 Yuanyuan (G.) C., van Esch, P., and Jain, S. P. (2021) Just walk out: The effect of AI-enabled checkouts, *European Journal of Marketing* [Preprint]. www.emerald.com/insight/content/doi/10.1108/EJM-02-2020-0122/full/html (archived at https://perma.cc/5FBS-DF5T).

41 Albrecht, C.-M., Hattula, S., and Lehmann, D. R. (2017) The relationship between consumer shopping stress and purchase abandonment in task-oriented and recreation-oriented consumers, *Journal of the Academy of Marketing Science*, 45(5), 720–740. https://doi.org/10.1007/s11747-016-0514-5 (archived at https://perma.cc/9M6S-BCAS).

42 Ghazwani, S. (2021) The impact of AI-enabled checkouts on shoppers' attitudes and purchase intent in Saudi Arabia. Degree of Master of Business. Auckland University of Technology.

43 Amazon (2021) Amazon 2021 Annual Report. https://s2.q4cdn.com/299287126/files/doc_financials/2022/ar/Amazon-2021-Annual-Report.pdf (archived at https://perma.cc/QG9K-ANG6).

44 nytimes.com (2021) Amazon's profits triple, 29 April. www.nytimes.com/2021/04/29/technology/amazons-profits-triple.html (archived at https://perma.cc/2CCT-X2JQ).

45 Interesting concept—review of Amazon Go, Seattle, WA, Tripadvisor. www.tripadvisor.com/ShowUserReviews-g60878-d14775008-r694242971-Amazon_Go-Seattle_Washington.html (archived at https://perma.cc/YAT5-JSM3).

46 Amazon Go reviews 2022, JustUseApp Reviews. https://justuseapp.com/en/app/1183036929/amazon-go/reviews (archived at https://perma.cc/VWS9-H3V8).

47 Nordmark, J. (2021) Amazon's ecosystem map—Jon Nordmark, *Medium*, 14 December. https://medium.com/@jonnordmark/amazons-ecosystem-map-d25abcac9613 (archived at https://perma.cc/HK85-9F6F).

48 ibid.

Chapter 10

1 Schlesinger, L. (2002) TACO Bell case presentation, 12 August, Boston MA.

2 Heskett, J. L., Sasser, E. W., and Wheeler, J. (2008) *The Ownership Quotient: Putting the service profit chain to work for unbeatable competitive advantage.* Harvard Business School Press.

Chapter 11

1 Geiger, E. (2020) Why leaders should run toward pressure, not away. www.namb.net/church-replanting/resource/why-leaders-should-run-toward-pressure-not-away (archived at https://perma.cc/ZR2N-YHNX).
2 Smith, S. and Wheeler, J. (2002) *Managing the Customer Experience: Turning customers into advocates*. Pearson Education.
3 Chase, R. and Dasu, S. (2001) Want to perfect your company service? use behavioral science, *Harvard Business Review*, June.
4 Lee, S. (2014) *PIG Strategy: Make customer centricity obsolete and start a resource revolution*. iMatchPoint.

Chapter 12

1 Romero, D. *et al.* (2019) Five management pillars for digital transformation integrating the lean thinking philosophy, 2019 IEEE International Conference on Engineering, Technology and Innovation (ICE/ITMC) [Preprint]. https://doi.org/10.1109/ice.2019.8792650 (archived at https://perma.cc/MT8R-3ND3).
2 Zaltman, G. (2003) *How Customers Think: Essential insights into the mind of the market*. Harvard Business Press.
3 Good, I. J. (1972) Statistics and today's problems, *The American Statistician*, 26(3) (Invited lecture at the 129th meeting of the Institute of Mathematical Statistics on April 22, 1971), June, Taylor & Francis, Abingdon, Oxfordshire (JSTOR). www.jstor.org/stable/2682859 (archived at https://perma.cc/PD4E-AA8T).
4 Parasuraman, A., Zeithaml, V. A. and Berry, L. L. (1985) A conceptual model of service quality and its implications for future research, *Journal of Marketing*, 49(4), 41. https://doi.org/10.2307/1251430 (archived at https://perma.cc/PK2T-NY8N).
5 Campos, D. F. and Nóbrega, K. C. (2009) Importance and the zone of tolerance of customer expectations of fast food services, *Journal of Operations and Supply Chain Management*, 2(2), 56. https://doi.org/10.12660/joscmv2n2p56-71 (archived at https://perma.cc/Y29W-SVCN).

Chapter 13

1 Bliss, J. (2016) Customers as assets: Getting there quickly. www.customerbliss.com/customers-as-assets (archived at https://perma.cc/QJA3-GWXY).

2 Ofek, E., Libai, B., Muller, E., and Harvard Business School Publishing (2018) Customer lifetime social value (CLSV). *Harvard Business Review*. https://store. hbr.org/product/customer-lifetime-social-value-clsv/518077 (archived at https:// perma.cc/R2KL-6Y5R)

Chapter 14

1 Berry, L. L. (2000) Cultivating service brand equity, *Journal of the Academy of Marketing Science*, 28(1), 128–137. https://doi.org/10.1177/0092070300281012 (archived at https://perma.cc/B5B8-VJPK).

2 Smith, S. and Wheeler, J. (2002) *Managing the Customer Experience: Turning customers into advocates*. Pearson FT Press

3 ibid.

4 What is human-centered design? (2022) www.interaction-design.org/literature/ topics/human-centered-design (archived at https://perma.cc/4B28-5MD7).

5 What is human-centered design? (2022) www.interaction-design.org/literature/ topics/human-centered-design (archived at https://perma.cc/E5F6-TNN4).

6 Dam, R. F. and Siang, T. Y. (2023) Personas—a simple introduction. www. interaction-design.org/literature/article/personas-why-and-how-you-should- use-them (archived at https://perma.cc/8U4V-YMX5).

7 Adobe (2021) 10 tips to develop better empathy maps, Adobe XD. https:// xd.adobe.com/ideas/process/user-research/10-tips-develop-better-empathy- maps (archived at https://perma.cc/PBQ8-D7YT).

8 Bliss, J. (2021) Experience TV episode 6: How to leave your CX legacy featuring Jeanne Bliss, Customer experience blog the latest in CX strategy, technology, and innovation, 29 January. https://blogs.oracle.com/cx/post/ experience-tv-episode-6-how-to-leave-your-cx-legacy-featuring-jeanne-bliss (archived at https://perma.cc/Z552-83F7).

9 Thaler, R. H. and Sunstein, C. R. (2008) Nudge: Improving decisions about health, wealth, and happiness, Choice Reviews Online, 46(02), 46–0977. https://doi.org/10.5860/choice.46-0977 (archived at https://perma.cc/VZ67- TB7G).

10 Prichard, S. (2018) 10 examples of nudge theory. www.skipprichard.com/10- examples-of-nudge-theory (archived at https://perma.cc/JXY7-62E5).

11 ThinkwithGoogle (2022) Winning the moments that matter: Right person, right message, right time, every time. www.thinkwithgoogle.com/intl/en-gb/ consumer-insights/consumer-trends/winning-the-moments-that-matter-right- person (archived at https://perma.cc/F763-FJ32).

12 ibid.

13 Rogers, D. L. (2016) *The Digital Transformation Playbook: Rethink Your business for the digital age*. New York: Columbia University Press.

14 ibid, pp. 106–117.

15 Parker, G. G., Van Alstyne, M. W., and Choudary, S. P. (2016) *Platform Revolution: How networked markets are transforming the economy and how to make them work for you*. W. W. Norton.

16 ibid, pp. 125–128.

17 Rogers, D. L. (2016) *The Digital Transformation Playbook: Rethink your business for the digital age*. New York: Columbia Business School Publishing.

Chapter 15

1 Branson, R. (2010) *Screw It, Let's Do It: 14 lessons on making it to the* top while having fun and staying *green*. Virgin.

2 Alves, L. (2021) The details are not the details. They make the design. www.creativefabrica.com/the-artistry/inspiration/the-details-are-not-the-details-they-make-the-design (archived at https://perma.cc/N3NG-RVPR).

3 Turing, A. M. (1950) Computing machinery and intelligence, *Mind*, LIX(236), October, 433–460. https://doi.org/10.1093/mind/LIX.236.433 (archived at https://perma.cc/M6K3-H5C9).

INDEX